America Moved

America Moved

Booth Tarkington's Memoirs of Time and Place, 1869–1928

EDITED BY
Jeremy Beer

Front Porch Republic *Books*

AMERICA MOVED
Booth Tarkington's Memoirs of Time and Place, 1869–1928

Frontmatter and notes Copyright © 2015 Jeremy Beer. All rights reserved. Except for brief quotations in critical publications or reviews, no part of this book may be reproduced in any manner without prior written permission from the publisher. Write: Permissions, Wipf and Stock Publishers, 199 W. 8th Ave., Suite 3, Eugene, OR 97401.

Front Porch Republic Books
An Imprint of Wipf and Stock Publishers
199 W. 8th Ave., Suite 3
Eugene, OR 97401

www.wipfandstock.com

ISBN: 978-1-62564-843-3

Cataloging-in-Publication data:

Tarkington, Booth, 1869–1946

    America moved : Booth Tarkington's memoirs of time and place, 1869–1928 / Booth Tarkington ; edited by Jeremy Beer.

    xiv + 270 p.; 23 cm

    ISBN: 978-1-62564-843-3

    1. Tarkington, Booth, 1869–1946—Biography. 2. United States—Social life and customs. I. Beer, Jeremy. II. Title.

PS2972 A45 2015

Manufactured in the USA

"*As I Seem To Me*" articles © 1941 SEPS licensed by Curtis Licensing, Indianapolis, IN. All rights reserved. "*The World Does Move*" is reprinted here by permission of the Newton Booth Tarkington Trust, which retains all right, title, and interest therein.

Contents

Editor's Introduction   vii
Acknowledgments   xiii

PART ONE: *As I Seem to Me*   1

I. Vain Child   3
II. Beaten Boy   19
III. Snips and Snails and Puppy Dogs' Tails   35
IV. Trousers Transition   50
V. Where Do We Go from Here?   65
VI. Turning Out to Be an Idiot   80
VII. The End of Those Days   95

PART TWO: *The World Does Move*   113

Editor's Introduction

THE TEMPLATE IS FAMILIAR. Writer is widely praised and universally loved during his lifetime. Same writer is widely scorned and all but entirely forgotten less than a generation later—usually, one hastens to add, for good reason.

Newton Booth Tarkington—author of *The Magnificent Ambersons, Alice Adams, Seventeen*, and the Penrod stories, and at one time perhaps America's most beloved and popular author—certainly seems to fit the mold. By the time Tarkington died in 1946, the critics had already consigned him to irrelevance, and they have not yet seen fit to substantively alter that opinion.

As early as 1921, Carl Van Doren savaged him (mostly) in *The Nation* ("rarely has so persistent a reputation been so insecurely founded"; "whenever he comes to a crisis in the building of a plot or in the truthful representation of a character he sags down to the level of Indiana sentimentality").[1] More than eighty years later, in a Tarkington retrospective published in *The Atlantic*, Thomas Mallon confirmed the establishment view: Tarkington wrote "in the throes of nostalgia"; he was (contra Paul Fussell) not just of his time but positively "oafish" on matters of race; and he was "finally . . . intent on offering his readers a pleasant Sunday drive—along with the sociological reassurance that they weren't really the Babbitts and boobs that Sinclair Lewis and H. L. Mencken kept taking them for."[2]

But when it comes to whom is worth remembering and whom we ought to let molder away, unloved and unwanted, in one-dollar used-bookstore bins, the critics don't always get it right. That's why we have revivals. These memoirs make abundantly clear why Tarkington is someone with whom it is still very much worth spending time. More so, perhaps, than some of his celebrated contemporaries.

---

1. Carl Van Doren, "Contemporary American Novelists: Booth Tarkington," *The Nation*, February 9, 1921, 233–35.

2. Thomas Mallon, *The Atlantic Monthly*, May 2004.

EDITOR'S INTRODUCTION

It is interesting to compare Tarkington to a fellow Hoosier author more highly thought of by the arbiters of literary greatness. The lives of Newton Booth Tarkington and Theodore Dreiser overlapped almost exactly. Tarkington was born in 1869 and died in 1946. Dreiser's dates are 1871 and 1945.

And that, more or less, is where the similarities end. The differences are instructive. Start with their backgrounds.

Tarkington came from a happy, bourgeois home. His uncle Newton Booth, for whom he was named, served as California's governor from 1871 to 1875. Tarkington's father was a lawyer and judge, his mother proud of her old-American lineage. Although the Tarkington family—there were just four of them—was not always financially well off, they were never truly poor, and they were always respectable.

The Dreiser brood was decidedly not. They *were* poor, they were peripatetic, and, to be blunt, they were considered white trash. Two of Dreiser's sisters may have at least occasionally engaged in prostitution. Dreiser's father, John Paul, was a harsh and unforgiving man who rationalized his character flaws by grounding them in a twisted version of his Roman Catholic faith.

Dreiser left Indiana University after one year, having detested the experience, and eventually found his way onward and upward in the cutthroat world of turn-of-the-century journalism. Tarkington prepped at Exeter before matriculating first at Indiana's rival state university, Purdue, then transferring to Princeton. Like Dreiser, he failed to leave with a degree, but he recalled his time on both campuses fondly, and at Princeton he was one of the leading figures in his class.

Tarkington was a Republican, a man of moderately conservative political opinions, which he did not try to conceal, and a surprisingly good-humored and tolerant cultural reactionary; he wrote war propaganda and stumped for Wendell Wilkie while maintaining profound respect for Eugene Debs. Raised a mainline Protestant, he eventually drifted toward a genial Unitarianism. Dreiser was a man of fashionably progressive views. Indeed, he was a fellow traveler who with stout intrepidity joined the Communist Party in 1945—six years after the Nazi-Soviet pact, when for most American progressives the bloom had rather come off the Red rose. He was an aggressive atheist.

Tarkington loved his home state without minimizing its Midwestern foibles, crudeness, and ridiculous bombast (his critics on this point read Tarkington with a marked lack of charity). He never decamped permanently from Indiana, instead living in Indianapolis for at least six months a year virtually his entire life. Dreiser left Indiana, for good, as soon as possible. His report of his automobile tour back to Indiana is recorded with the eye of a bemused and caustic anthropologist, not a loving son, in *A Hoosier Holiday* (1916).

Near the end of *America Moved*, Tarkington frets about what he sees as the avant-garde's obsession with sex. Dreiser, of course, famously challenged contemporary sex mores. *Sister Carrie* had the good luck effectively to be banned for seven years after its initial publication—and thereby obtained the imprimatur of H. L. Mencken, among many others.

Tarkington was championed by such as Hamlin Garland and Barrett Wendell and James Whitcomb Riley, all of them today even more forgotten than he. Besides Mencken, Dreiser's admirers have included Alfred Kazin, Irving Howe, Joseph Epstein, and Harvey Pekar, among myriad others.

Take it all in, and is it any wonder that where Tarkington found many more readers, Dreiser has been far more popular with the literary establishment?

In the major biographies competition, it's 3–1 Dreiser (the most recent was published in 2005). Number of entries under "criticism and interpretation" in the Library of Congress catalog? 39–1, Dreiser. Number of books with a separate entry in that catalog? 4–0, Dreiser. Dreiser has two Library of America volumes. Tarkington, amazingly, has none. A journal titled *Dreiser Studies* was published from 1970 to 2006. Dreiser is recognized as a leading exponent, perhaps *the* leading exponent, of American naturalism.

No biography of Tarkington has been published since 1955. Tarkington is almost never anthologized or read in the schools, unlike Dreiser and others of his contemporaries, including Sinclair Lewis, Willa Cather, Edith Wharton, even Upton Sinclair. Tarkington is not remembered as the progenitor or exemplar of an influential genre or school, nor as the literary conscience of an important social movement. No Tarkington panels are organized at academic conferences. No journal is dedicated to Tarkingtoniana.

During Tarkington's lifetime, the critical contest wasn't so lopsided. Both *The Magnificent Ambersons* (1918) and *Alice Adams* (1921) won Pulitzer Prizes (in 1919 and 1922, respectively), and Tarkington is the only writer to have two novels win Pulitzers. In a 1921 *Publisher's Weekly* poll of booksellers, Tarkington was named the most "significant" contemporary author (Wharton came in second, Dreiser fourteenth). In 1922, *Literary Digest* named him the greatest living American author, and in the same year he was the only native writer to appear on the *New York Times*'s list of the ten greatest living Americans. In 1933 he became just the third person to receive a gold medal from the National Institute of Arts and Letters. Twelve years later he received from the American Academy of Arts and Letters the William Dean Howells award, given just once every five years.

On top of all that, Tarkington moved product. From 1902 to 1932, nine Tarkington titles appeared in the top ten of *Publisher's Weekly*'s year-end bestseller lists. Dreiser never had a bestseller.

It certainly isn't Dreiser's superior prose style that has endeared him to literary gatekeepers. Tarkington's prose—still rewarding and enjoyable, as *America Moved* demonstrates—has aged as gracefully as Sophia Loren; Dreiser's—clunky, verbose—more like Bea Arthur.

So what happened? The pages of these memoirs go a long way, I think, in explaining why Tarkington's star faded so quickly after the end of his major period—let us say, circa 1930. In a word, Tarkington was uneasy with the literary, social, cultural, and political changes that transformed American life during the late 1800s and early 1900s. In terms of style, he wrote in the tradition of Howellsian realism, rejecting naturalism (a decision he defends in these pages) and remaining completely untouched by the advent of literary modernism. Politically, he might pass as an old-fashioned liberal, and he certainly manifested and even promoted the virtue of liberality in his life and writing, but he was not a Progressive and certainly no leftist. Culturally, he believed that there were real goods worth defending in the older, slower America of small towns, human-scale cities, and closely knit communities, whatever that America's defects.

He was out of step, in other words, even with the *au courant* writers and critics of his own day, and laughably so with those of succeeding generations. Yet interestingly enough, many readers in the twenty-first century might find in him a remarkably kindred spirit. For those who have rediscovered the values of place, rootedness, and community; who have grown wary of the technologies and aspirations of giantism; and who are keenly alive to the environmental costs of mass transportation and industrialization,[3] Tarkington looks wiser than he did to previous generations, for whom the narrative of individual liberation, even when drenched in Dreiser's deterministic irony, trumped all else.

Thus, in the second part of *America Moved*, "The World Does Move," Tarkington ponders the price of a frenetic commercial-industrial society, of the rise of mass culture, and of the ideology of American Progress. In this part, especially, his theme is the radical alteration in society's mores since the *fin de siècle*. His reflections are often prophetic. Take Tarkington's reportage on the changes wrought by the arrival of the "horseless carriage." Recalling a dinner in Paris in 1903, he puts into the mouth of an

3. Thomas Mallon claims that "only general ignorance of his work has kept [Tarkington] from being pressed into contemporary service as a literary environmentalist—not just a 'conservationist,' in the TR mode, but an emerald-Green decrier of internal combustion."

unidentified companion a remarkable prophecy. The automobile, said this "elderly American,"

> will obliterate the accepted distances that are part of our daily lives. It will alter our daily relations to time, and that is to say it will alter our lives. Perhaps everybody doesn't comprehend how profoundly we are affected by such a change; but what alters our lives alters our thoughts; what alters our thoughts alters our characters; what alters our characters alters our ideals; and what alters our ideals alters our morals. . . . We are just entering the period when most of what we have regarded as permanently crystalline will become shockingly fluid—that is to say, we are already in the transition period between two epochs. . . . Restfulness will have entirely disappeared from your lives; the quiet of the world is ending forever.

The historian John Lukacs's judgment that there was more profound social and technological change in the period between the Civil War and World War I than there has been since is amply attested to by Tarkington in these pages. In an era of such vertiginous change, some reflection on what it all means would seem warranted. Among the major American writers of his day, Tarkington undertakes this reflection with more care and nuance—whether we finally agree with his assessments or not—than nearly anyone else. The tone he takes is that of a hopeful lover—a lover of the world, of the good that has been lost, but also of the good that remains, and of the good that he is confident will yet be wrought.

There is a humanity in Tarkington that is absent in the all too self-consciously pitiless Dreiser. Dreiser was concerned with social justice, abstractly conceived, yet refused to offer any grounds for hope to his socially marginalized characters, for whom he simultaneously had both pity and contempt. He reduced men and women to little more than beasts and presented the universe as intrinsically meaningless. Free will, human dignity, and any immaterial reality were shams. Power relations were all that mattered. Tarkington probably had Dreiser in mind when he recalled, approvingly, his friend James Whitcomb Riley's hatred of "the ponderous humorlessness of the French realism with which Zola was then beginning to stimulate the long succession of followers who still urge upon us the dismal dirtiest of life as the most of it."[4]

Considered in conjunction with Tarkington's great "Growth" trilogy—which consists of *The Turmoil* (1915), *The Magnificent Ambersons*, and *The Midlander* (1924)—and *Alice Adams*, these memoirs, long out of print and

---

4. See pages 61 and 159 for this quote and the block quote above, respectively.

unread, make the case that Booth Tarkington matters. They show that he stands, if not among the first rank of American writers, squarely and securely among the second.

There have been those who believed that all along. John Lukacs, David Frum, Peggy Noonan, and Roger Ebert have shared appreciations of Tarkington's achievement, Ebert going so far as to say that Tarkington's Penrod volumes "earn full comparison with the somewhat later P. G. Wodehouse, whose style and word mastery resembles him."[5] And Tarkington's fellow Indianapolis native, Kurt Vonnegut, in a 2007 lecture, could hardly contain himself, crediting "the example of the life and works of Booth Tarkington" for inspiring him to pursue a writing career. "His nickname in the literary world, one I would give anything to have, was 'The Gentleman from Indiana.' When I was a kid, I wanted to be like him. We never met. I wouldn't have known what to say. I would have been gaga with hero worship."[6]

Let Vonnegut have the last word. Read *America Moved*, and decide for yourself whether Booth Tarkington is worth reading—and his America worth remembering.

---

5. The chapter "1939" in Lukacs's *A Thread of Years* (New Haven, CT: Yale University Press, 1998) was inspired by Tarkington, according to Lukacs. For Frum, see http://frum.nationalreview.com/post/?q=YjhkMjMyYTgxMjI1MmEzMzM4NWFkMWY2ODNmNzE4OGE=. For Noonan, see http://frum.nationalreview.com/post/?q=ZDQ5YTU3ZTZiMWQyYTg4NmM1OTE0NzExMzhmYzhlYTM=. For Ebert, see http://dramatic-insights.org/tarkington/index.php/2010/roger-ebert-penrod-fan. All accessed June 10, 2011.

6. Lecture at Clowes Hall, Indianapolis, April 27, 2007. See http://dointhegrownup.com/2011/02/24/3483887290/. Accessed January 9, 2014.

Acknowledgments

THE TEXT OF *AMERICA Moved* consists of two works of memoir by Booth Tarkington that have never before appeared together in book form. Part One was never collected in book form at all. Under the title "As I Seem to Me," it was serialized in seven issues of the *Saturday Evening Post* in July and August 1941, in the order presented here. Here Tarkington covers the period of his life from his birth in 1869 until 1899 (more or less), when his novel *The Gentleman from Indiana* was published. The titles of the individual chapters, as well as the subheads, appear here as they did in the *Post*.

Part Two of this volume, "The World Does Move," was published in 1928 under the same title by Doubleday, Doran and Company, and is reproduced here by permission of the Booth Tarkington estate. Less conventionally autobiographical than "As I Seem to Me," it covers the years from 1895, when Tarkington moved to New York to try to forge a career as a writer, until near the time of its publication, when Tarkington was well established in the literary world. Even more than in Part One, Tarkington in these pages often frustratingly declines to specify the men and women whom he discusses. I have provided identifications of as many of them as possible.

Nearly every chapter in "The World Does Move" was first run in the *Saturday Evening Post* between April 7 and July 7, 1928. The exceptions are chapter XX (first published in *Red Book Magazine* in May 1921, and later in *The Fascinating Stranger and Other Stories* [1923], as "Jeannette"); chapter XXII (*Collier's*, May 14, 1927, as "When Is It Dirt?"); and part of chapter XXV (*The Forum*, March 1926, as "The Veiled Feminists of Atlantis").

The only editorial change I have made to the text, besides correcting occasional typographical errors, is to add the Oxford comma. All ellipses are in the original, and all footnotes are mine, not Tarkington's.

This book has been some years in the making, and I am deeply grateful to a number of people for their assistance and encouragement. An earlier version of the editor's introduction ran in the *University Bookman* (vol. 46,

ACKNOWLEDGMENTS

no. 3). I am grateful to editor Gerald Russello for permission to reuse some of that material here. Along the way, Cory Andrews, Keith Bice, Richard Brake, Montgomery Brown, Jeff Cain, Kate Dalton, Matt Dellinger, Joseph Epstein, Andrew Ferguson, Matthew Gerken, Darryl Hart, Mark Henrie, Bill Kauffman, Dennis Lager, John Lukacs, Mark Mitchell, Anne Neal, Peggy Noonan, Amie Peele-Carter, Jason Peters, Cris Piquinela, Jeff Polet, Scott Russell Sanders, Lee Slade, Whit Stillman, Howard Trivers, and the staff of the Indiana Historical Society, among many others not mentioned here, offered useful advice, assistance, and encouragement. I offer all of them my sincere gratitude.

Near the end of this project, I was thrilled to make contact with one of Booth Tarkington's great-great-nephews, Booth Jameson, his wife Jennifer, and his parents, John and Elizabeth Jameson. They not only expressed enthusiasm for this project, but they freely shared information, stories, and memories about Tarkington, his family, and his literary estate. I was inspired by their loyalty to Tarkington's legacy, and I hope to learn more from them in the years to come.

My wife, Kara, is always encouraging no matter how dimwitted my ideas. Every husband should be so lucky.

PART ONE

As I Seem to Me

I. Vain Child

COUNTING BY REALISTIC TIME, astronomical time, I was born a very short while ago—less than a few minutes ago—and yet my mother's father, Beebe Booth, who lived until I was a grown man, did some soldiering in the War of 1812. In his infancy, if he'd happened to be in France instead of Connecticut, he could have seen Marie Antoinette and Robespierre; and when Wellington died both of my grandfathers were past middle age. When I was born,[1] in a small but active Indianapolis, there was no German Empire, Napoleon Bonaparte's nephew was Emperor of the French, Queen Victoria had more than thirty years to reign over Britain, there weren't any telephones or electric lights in the world; and our Union's supreme war hero, General Grant, was President of the United States.

This is the long and the short of it; but just after my birth I was so busy getting used to having a body that for a while I wasn't aware of even General Grant. I didn't at once perceive that I'd come among beings of my own kind; I saw people as assistants only; though later, when I was a full year old, I took their principal function to be that of applause.

I'm explaining that at the age of one year I was a celebrity and regarded myself as such. Babies are like anybody else; they accept the wildest and most ill-founded adulation as deserved tribute; naturally, their self-conceit is egregious. Their minds are already busy and, though they can't use distinct words as symbols of their thoughts, they draw conclusions. Long before they can add two to two they can put two and two together.

First Words

I was seldom approached without a kind of servility and professions of utter admiration. For almost half of my life I'd been entreated daily, and sometimes hourly, to enchant audiences with repetitions of the vocal performances that had made me famous. The outcries evoked by my talent were

1. On July 29, 1869.

so inevitable that sometimes, bored, I declined to give a show. One year old, I knew as well as did the boastfulest of my kinsfolk that I was the star of the age because I'd begun to talk when I was only seven months old.

I knew the whole of this triumph, especially how I'd scored on two competitors—Marjorie Harrison, next door, who was a month older than I, and Victor Hendricks, up at the next corner, almost precisely my own age. It was thought singularly creditable that my first comprehended utterance wasn't "Mamma" or "Papa" but "Hyuh, Jock!" Out of a clear sky I had called the dog. By the time I was a year old I was almost sated with the story: how my father, within the hour of my startling first performance—probably within the half hour—had gone next door to tell Marjorie Harrison's parents all about it and how Mr. Harrison had angrily denied its plausibility; how he had been brought to me and the dog let in, and how I had not failed in this crisis, but had distinctly said "Hyuh, Jock!"—twice—in Mr. Harrison's presence; and how he had then stalked out of the house without a single word, returning in fury to his extinguished Marjorie.

Having thus begun, at seven months, by calling the dog, I talked on, never saying a thing that wasn't quotable. Behind the Infant Prodigy there still remain in memory—for background of my second year—a few faint pictures like pale old water colors: that pleasant bit of Meridian Street—sunshine on green lawns—our ample brick house and its brick stable in the shade of trees illimitably high; two lovely big ladies dancing about me in ballooning white dresses and indistinguishable from adults, though they were my sister Hautie and a friend of hers, both twelve years old.

How far back into childhood can we remember? I remember the first snow of my second winter, when probably I hadn't reached the age of eighteen months; I remember how that snow disappointed me. I know it was the first snow of the winter because I'd been looking forward to it.

There's much argument about rememberings. One of the younger members of a family claims to recall something; the others tell him he couldn't; they say he only thinks he does because he's heard it described by his elders, and of course it's true that we not seldom find it difficult to discriminate between what we ourselves recollect and what's been put into our minds by frequent hearsay. Nevertheless, having been born at the end of July, 1869, I remember the first snow of the winter of 1870–1871. If that snow fell in December of 1870 I was between sixteen and seventeen months old.

A novelist must make the exercising of his memory—as well as other self-searchings—a constant practice, or he will not understand and make real the creatures he puts into his books; but if other people did the inward delving that he professionally does, they would no doubt turn up as much from their own obscured infancies. My earliest recollection isn't here recorded as a feat; it leads to a suggestion.

A Very Young Man Goes West

When, at probably less then eighteen months, I looked out of a window at the first snowflakes of that year, I was disappointed because of their smallness. I was disappointed because I then remembered snowflakes that had been as large as the palm of my hand, and these now weren't half that size. Thus, though I don't remember the larger snowflakes that fell when I was less than a year old, I remember that when I was less than eighteen months old I did remember them, and that at less than a year old I had observed their size as compared to the size of the palm of my then hand.

I didn't tell anybody about this, hence nobody told me about it later; I remember it. The suggestion is that the youngest baby has more than what are called "prenatal memories"; that he's not only thinking, he's already recollecting, and that conscious memory is an activity within us at birth.

Two years old, I was complacently aware that I owed some of my importance to the achievements of another person, for whom I'd been named. Our family possessed, besides worthy ancestors, a living Great Man; and, like all other families that have this privilege, we borrowed greatness from our hero. He was my mother's brother, Newton Booth. Physically delicate, just out of college, and beginning the practice of law in that agreeable town, Terre Haute, he'd suddenly swung his placid young life to Western roads of adventurous and sometimes tragic hardship. Now—generous, rich, still young, and still a bachelor—he'd become the governor of California. My mother and my sister and I went to spend a year with him in Sacramento.[2]

Uncle Newton made much of me; so did the circle of gay early Californians surrounding him. Toys almost glutted me; I heard tales loudly told of me, saw groups of expectant faces about me awaiting the delights of my wisdom; and bearded men, as well as hourglass-shaped ladies, professed themselves ravished by photographs of me in kilts and velvet jacket. The flatteries I received might easily have convinced me that I was a philosopher, or a wit, or a great beauty. They did. I thought I was all three.

Much was made, too, of some imagined companions of mine, a family I'd found in the air. Where I got the name of these ghostly people, the "Hunchbergs," and the name of their dog, "Simpledoria," nobody knew,

---

2. Newton Booth—brother of Tarkington's mother Elizabeth—assumed the governorship of California on December 8, 1871. He served until February 1875, when, having been elected to the U.S. Senate, he resigned.

nor did I; but Mr. and Mrs. Hunchberg, and their son and daughter, almost grown up, and Simpledoria, appear to have had reality for me. I talked with them at great length, when actual people were present as well as when I was alone. I quoted the Hunchbergs incessantly, played with Simpledoria on the carpet, spoke to him from my bed at night. Uncle Newton gave a dinner for the Hunchbergs, with chairs placed for the four of them and a plate on the floor for Simpledoria. Through me, the translator as it were, my uncle talked seriously with Mr. Hunchberg, had cigars passed to him and was regretful that he didn't smoke. To my three-year-old eyes those empty chairs weren't vacant; I saw the dear Hunchbergs there, and my uncle understood because in his own childhood he'd had an unseen companion—a boy braver and more dashing than himself and known to him as "Bill Hammersly."[3]

The Way of a Transgressor

In that whole year in the golden land, my happiness was as unclouded as my self-esteem—except for two slight setbacks. These were caused by social errors on my part that evanescently dimmed me; and both are now known to me mostly through hearsay, though memory brings flickerings. The first of the two episodes reflects even less credit upon my innate character than does the second—which was, morally speaking, disgraceful—for the first seems to show that I deliberately tried to be funny. Humor isn't accomplished in that way.

A lady, a stranger to me, was making an admiring to-do over me; and we two were the center of a group after lunch at my uncle's. Conspicuous to me were her nose and a beautiful gold tassel at the end of a chain about her neck. In response to her courtesies, I asked, "What do you wear that pretty gold tassel for? To dust your big ugly nose with?"

Out of a startled hush my uncle for the first time spoke to me sharply. He said, dumfoundingly, "Tut! Tut!"

In a panic, I spoke hastily, "I mean, do you wear that tassel to dust your little pretty nose with?"

---

3. The Hunchbergs, Simpledoria, and Bill Hammersly all appear in Tarkington's *Beasley's Christmas Party* (1909). In that novella, Uncle Newton serves as the model for Congressman David Beasley, who entertains his handicapped young cousin Hamilton Swift, Jr., by playing games with Simpledoria and the imaginary Bill Hammersley (spelled this way) and by having the Hunchbergs for dinner. *Beasley's Christmas Party* itself is a reworking of Tarkington's story "Beasley and the Hunchbergs," published in *Cosmopolitan* in 1905. The names Beasley and Hunchberg show up, too, in unpublished Tarkington juvenilia.

I was hustled away, crestfallen; but later in the day my vanity was again inflated. What I'd said to the lady I overheard repeated by several people—and not as a reproach to me. From all I could learn I had behaved excellently.

The second instance, somewhat grotesque, sheds out of the long ago a faint light upon the California of that period. Uncle Newton gave a great dinner for gentlemen important in the affairs of the state, and probably few tables in the country could have been surrounded by owners of more picturesque pasts; most of the banqueters, like my uncle, must have been men of the early gold rush.[4] It had been arranged that the governor's nephew and namesake should be presented to them, and, in evening clothes—white dress and blue satin sash—I was brought in, toasted noisily, and urged to remain.

Accustomed to tributes, I was anything but embarrassed, and readily occupied a chair—or the top of a dictionary upon a chair—among flushed new friends. Far away at the other end of the beflowered long table, my uncle didn't observe what happened to me. Someone offered me a glass of champagne. I drank it, and seemed to perceive that in affording me this pleasure life was promising to consist entirely of exaltation. In fact, it's all too significant that even so early I took to champagne, asked for more, got it, and became uninterruptedly talkative.[5] The hardy forty-niners about me made merry; I may be said to have been plied with wine, and it was afterward hushedly related that I astonished the pliers by a precocious talent for absorption. Thus, in one particular line of accomplishment, I am now probably without a living colleague. I doubt that any other inhabitant of the year 1941 has the right, so to put it, of recording that he got howling drunk in the state of California in 1872.

There comes to me faintly, faintly a picture of results: wholly unexpected dreadful illness, expressions of indignant solicitude uttered by those who put me to bed. I suffered; and yet—and yet, as days passed, there stole into me from without—perhaps from heard whisperings—more than a suspicion that again I had done something remarkable; that once more, in a manner of speaking, I had distinguished myself.

The gilded year in California ended; my mother and my sister and I came back to my father and to Indianapolis—and to something near penury. Calamity was upon the country, for that was the first year of a great depression. The word "depression" wasn't used; everyone talked of the "panic," and the period became, historically, the Panic of '73.

4. Newton Booth first arrived in California in 1850.

5. Tarkington alludes here to his alcoholism. He swore off alcohol for good in early 1912, soon after he had suffered a heart attack—and after his first wife, Louisa, divorced him.

We didn't return to our fine brick house on Meridian Street; it was lost to us—taken away by the panic. My father, whose commencement address at college had made him secretary to the governor of Indiana, was a "rising young lawyer," when, unfortunately, he accepted a judgeship. Though for the rest of his long life his fellow citizens never spoke to him or of him except as Judge Tarkington, in our Hoosier way, the title was inadequate compensation for the clients he lost through his term on the bench. When he returned to the bar he'd begun to get some of them back; but the Panic of '73 banished legal fees to the realm of illusion.

The Frown of Fortune

Suddenly we were poor, lived in a small wooden house; then moved to a side street, where we occupied only a lower floor, with another depleted lawyer and his family over our heads. We still owned our two loved horses, Gray and Fly—my father could never bear to sell a horse—but they were economically in the country, at pasture, and we were no longer carriage folk.

Present-day little children, born into this depression, the day of the New Deal, unemployment, and terrible wars, will have their memories of the bad period even if they live long enough to emerge into another Golden Age, as we did after the long pressure of the Panic of '73. For these present-day children, too, there may come a time when the world again seems settled, responsible, and solid, when politicians and dictators will not be upsetting everything, threatening every hearthstone and every earned dollar; and when from that emergence into placidity—if it comes—they look back upon the pinched times of their childhood, I hope that their recollections may be as cheerful as are mine now of the days of the Great Panic.

Possibly I shouldn't remember that disaster at all if we hadn't lost our house and the sunny green yard where I'd played. No recollections of protests or wailings from my father, my plucky mother, and my sparklingly pretty fifteen-year-old sister recall it to me; their endurance of the change hadn't a flinch, though the blows must have been heavy and many for all three of them. About me there seemed always the sound of laughter, and my father's indomitable gaiety kept my world in place, made living in it an experience safely all of gusto and merriment.

An addition to my evening prayers, however, indicates that my mother had special hopes. After the customary conclusion, "I pray the Lord my soul to take," I was instructed to append, and did: "Please bless papa and mamma and Hautie and Boothie, and make Uncle Newton senator and papa county clerk." The governor's term of office in California drew near its close, and the county clerkship, at home, was rewarded by fees that sometimes, I believe, approached thirty thousand dollars a year—probably about thirty times the income my father was then somehow wringing out of his legal practice.

It was at this period, when I was four and five and six, that my complacent view of myself began to be damaged. Explanation mayn't be needed that the shocking vanity of children shocks nobody; mine was inside me and I have been told that I was regarded as a rather solemn little boy, quiet and given to ruminations. Nevertheless, my life, so far, had brought me no cause to look upon myself as imperfect in any detail. My conduct was sometimes directed, but never criticized, and I hadn't yet begun to wonder what sort of person I was—or what sort of looking person I was. A complete content with myself and a subservient world prevailed—until I encountered the boy called Brick-top.

There was no lawn about the frame house where we lived in dusty New York Street—in summer all the streets not cobbled were mostly dust—but the sidewalk, close to the front door, was shady and became my playground. Children of the neighborhood joined me there, played with my toys, held converse with me, and thus I became acquainted with Brick-top, who was a head taller than I was and the son, as he often mentioned, of a professional fireman.

Whenever I had to wear my little light blue velvet breeches and Brick-top saw me in them, he would tell me again that his father was a fireman.

On a promising afternoon I had a dime and was on my way to the corner drugstore to buy candy. Aged five, I had no conception of any other sensible use of money; this infrequent dime brought heaven close, for my palate was what I most dearly cared about. I held it to be the high seat of pleasure, and was indifferent to objects with which it had already dealt and passed on to the alimentary canal. When such objects roused an enemy within me, so long as the urge of taste lasted I would go on eating—sometimes even moaning a little—what my stomach fought to tell me it could not include. Real money was high in 1874, commodities were low, and my shining dime foretold a longish debauch.

Low Finance

Outside the drugstore Brick-top stopped me and made inquiries. I opened my hand, showed the dime, and announced my purpose, naturally not adding any hospitable offer.

"I got a good deal more money than that," Brick-top said; and took from his pocket a large copper two-cent piece and an even larger one-cent piece, coinage of that epoch. Beside them the small dime looked inconsequent. "This money o' mine's lots more money than that dime o' yours," said Brick-top.

"Is it?" I asked. "Would it buy more candy than my dime would, Brick-top?"

'Lots more," he told me, and frowned, seeming to ponder. "I'll tell you what I'll do, though," he said. "I'll trade you all this money for your dime. Mine's more; but I like you and I'll trade. All this money I got is too heavy to carry around. It kind of weighs me down."

"It kind of weighs me down" were his long-remembered words precisely. I was not wholly senseless; I needed a real argument to persuade me to the exchange, and there it was. "It kind of weighs me down." Brick-top didn't want to get tired. I traded my dime for three cents, not without a troubled kind of gratitude.

Brick-top was not to be seen when I came out of the drugstore after a startling talk with a derisive clerk. I walked home laggingly, pausing often, and becoming on the way a slightly different sort of person.

An Enemy Raid

The psychologists tell us that these childish jolts affect our whole lives. Deeply puzzled as I returned from the enlightening drugstore, I had a vague realization, for the first time in my life, that a fellow being had made a fool of me. Dazingly it began to appear to me that some people did such things and that I wasn't all-wise. This seems to have been my first self-doubt.

Brick-top, ere long, gave me another. I had the most magnificent hobby-horse in the world, a maned and tailed and caparisoned bright creature, the gift of Uncle Newton, and brought to me all the way from California. One day I left it on the sidewalk during the noon meal; and when I came back to it, to ride again, I was sickened. A horrible decapitation had taken place. My horse stood headless, with raw wood showing plaintively where the neck had joined the sculptured and painted shoulders.

"Brick-top did it!" said the little girl who had remained near by to inform me. "Brick-top threw a brickbat at it and knocked its head off and grabbed it and ran away with it!"

I stood and stood. I began to suspect that I was not universally loved—even that I could be disliked. My impression now is that although Brick-top's father's pay as a fireman probably exceeded what my father was making in his law office, Brick-top felt that he was right to despoil me and be my enemy, because I was a Little Rich Boy who sometimes wore blue velvet breeches.

Subsequently, Brick-top did other things to me. I don't recall what they were, but one of them brought me another mystification about myself. All alone, I was whispering, and at intervals speaking aloud, my topic being the most recent of Brick-top's inflictions upon me.

"What do you stand it for?" I asked. "What makes you let him treat you like that?"

"Well, I'm not going to much longer," I responded. "Brick-top better look out! If you were me you wouldn't let him act like that, would you?"

"No, I wouldn't," I said. "But all you do's talk. Why don't you show him?"

"You make me sick!" I said truculently. "Didn't you just hear me say I'm going to——"

I stopped muttering, having realized that I was almost quarreling with somebody. With whom?

I stood in wonder, becoming aware that it was a habit of mine to hold debate with this unknown; and there seemed to be, also, a third person present—somebody who listened coldly to both of us—but of him I could make nothing at all except that it was uncomfortable to think about him. The second person, my talkative opponent, tried to goad me into actions that I couldn't take; yet at heart seemed really sympathetic. What puzzled me most was the way we said "You" to each other, since both of us must, after all, be me. I hadn't solved the puzzle when, at about this time, I became—almost officially with some people—the Worst Boy in Town.

My mother's piano had been salvaged from the financial wreck; evenings on New York Street were gay with the singing of the three older members of my family—ballads, songs old and new, melodies from *The Bohemian Girl* and the Verdi operas—and once a week a shattered friend of my mother's taught a small dancing class of children in our parlor, with an assistant at the piano. The children were accompanied by their mothers, and one of these ladies had an emotional aversion to cats. Therefore, our cat, though lovable, was kept in a back room during the dancing hour, but one day an older boy secretly talked me into becoming a comedian. He convinced me that if I'd fetch the cat privately, approach little Eva Townley's mother from behind as she sat watching the lesson, and drop pussy over her shoulder to alight upon her lap, Mrs. Townley'd be surprised and all would be joy and nice harmless merriment. I needn't tell anybody that the idea was his; I could take all credit for it.

Expecting to delight the world, I tried for the credit and got it. More uproar, confusion, and fury can seldom have been so simply created; and it was I who had the real surprise. When Mrs. Townley stopped screaming her opinion of me, she ran from the house, dragging her daughter with her, nevermore to return; the dancing class dispersed, and I was placed in a sequestration lasting longer than pussy's. Released from this first actual punishment, I had it made clear to me, verbally, that even my father couldn't look upon me as a funny dog. Neither he nor my mother could bear to think of the reputation I'd made for myself.

They were right. For the following fifteen years Mrs. Townley never mentioned me, or heard anyone speak of me, without supplying her unvaried synonym for me; and reiteration so sincere carries weight. I had many an acquaintance who at times became temporarily known as the Worst Boy in Town; but they were only runners-up. I held the title longest.

Conviction of Sin

When I was six, my father had begun to get a little the better of the Panic of '73. We moved into a commodious house in the new North Side, had a yard and big trees again, had a cook again, had a horse and vehicles. We rented this house, extravagantly, for fifty dollars a month, which was high for those days in Indianapolis; and now I didn't play with street children. Beyond an iron fence, on the day of our installation, I saw two clean-faced, dressed-up children, a brother and sister near my own age. They looked at me; and immediately I began to display my New York Street accomplishments.

In New York Street were current various knowing phrases too shady to be used in the presence of grown people; I'd acquired them from Brick-top and others. Upon the clean little boy and his sister I tried one of these mots after another. I looked at them derisively and called out, "Wipe off your chins!"

I was sat upon, not admired; they took a moral tone with me. "That's bad. You're bad! You mustn't say that."

I went further. "Wipe off your chins and pull down your vests!"

The brother and sister, grave and instructive, said. "That's bad. You mustn't say that. You're bad!"

They invited me to come into their yard and play with them. I again tried to be clever in the New York Street manner. "I don't haf to!" I said. "Doctor says it ain't healthy!"

"That's bad," the brother and sister told me. "You mustn't say that. You're bad!"

Dispirited, I gave up the effort to impress them and just talked naturally.

"That's bad. You're bad," they said, as before, and began to reform my vocabulary.

They became my playmates, but I never felt quite on a level with them—even when they were most genial they were still helpfully critical, always right and two to one. The little girl, six, one day informed me—in the manner of a notification—that I was her sweetheart, and I said, "Am I? Well—all right"; but neither she nor her brother, who was unblushingly present, seemed to feel that my new position placed me upon an equality with them—nor did I.

Of course I hadn't thus precociously lost my high opinion of myself; but the mirrorlike surface of self-conceit was showing a few dents. I'd begun to find difficulties in proving myself as important as I felt. In all gatherings of my kind I of course strove incessantly to be the central figure. Desiring applause, I would squeal, bellow, try to sing, try to whistle, would leap, run, hop, and fling myself about, screeching, "Look at me! Look at me, everybody! Look at me—me—me!"

They wouldn't. They, too, were screaming, "Look at me!" What they did seemed to me of no merit and uninteresting; and, when those who could stand on their heads did so, and I couldn't, I squealed, "Look at me," announced that I would turn somersaults, tried, and but flopped soggily upon the grass.

I was approaching defeat by something profound, years beyond my comprehension. Every one of these other children had been as brilliantly an infant prodigy in his own family as had I in mine. In one way or another, all of them had been applauded celebrities; hence every one of them now believed himself the beloved sole star of the age. This was hard on me, but good for the human species; we're told that babies and little children, not made much of, thrive ill. A deep instinct in the race makes the fuss over little children that enlarges their vanity. Egoism, fertilized early from without, is one of humanity's necessities; fertilized only from within, it can become as monstrous as Hitler.

When our country was just a hundred years old, the year of the great Philadelphia Centennial Exposition, I was seven, had a little "campaign uniform" with a lard-oil lamp fastened to my blue-and-white-oilcloth cap, and discovered that I was a Republican. The children of our neighborhood were all Republicans, loved Hayes and Wheeler, hated Tilden and Hendricks, and learned to squeal fiercely at known or suspected opponents:

"Stewed rats and dead cats

Are good enough for Democrats!"

I hadn't yet been sent to school, and couldn't write; but for a year or two I'd been able to read, though I've no recollection of learning this art. The only child in the house, and enticed by suggestive talk in the small family circle, I'd rather prematurely read *Uncle Tom's Cabin*, *Don Quixote*, *Robinson Crusoe*, and *The Old Curiosity Shop*; and my first literary attempt was made at about this time. As I couldn't write, my indulgent sister, chivalrously concealing her amusement, became my amanuensis. I dictated to her the opening of a story, and, though the manuscript disappeared, I remember that it concerned a full-grown young man who rode forth from a castle on a bright morning and would have had a startling adventure if I'd been able to construct one for him. I seem to have encountered the obstacle of complete vacuity after the first paragraph or two; nevertheless, I had great praise for this effort, as well as for the now modernistic drawings and water colors that I produced on rainy days.

A Place in the Sun

Moreover, without embarrassment or any other symptoms of modesty, I made a public appearance—no novelty to me, as I was already accustomed to confront seas—or at least ponds—of upturned faces. I must here offer the confession that I was a child declaimer. At the Christmas celebration of our Sunday school, when I was four, my father had lifted me to the platform, where I stood before the lighted tree and recited I know not what so loudly and rapidly that I was defined as sensational. Every now and then I was taken to recite somewhere, even to a reunion of Civil War soldiers to whom I shouted Barbara Frietchie in supposedly German dialect—heaven forgive me and my proud and loving parents!

I recited at home, before callers; even without callers I recited at home; there was never a family party when the loyalty of uncles, aunts, and cousins wasn't strained by my gift. In my hearing no one called me a dreaded little show-off; people said, with a benignity I didn't perceive to be the mask of pain, "It's so nice he never needs to be urged."

In 1876 there prevailed a patriotic effort at entertainment called, I think, Martha Washington's Tea Party. Every city, town, and village contained an inhabitant who was believed, at least by himself, to look like George Washington—a little, anyhow. For Martha Washington's Tea Party he got himself insecurely into what was called Revolutionary costume, but wasn't; and he and a lady thought to resemble Martha walked out before audiences in the local theater, or Odd Fellows' Hall, or perhaps in a tent on the lawn of the courthouse yard. Except Benedict Arnold, all the great

Revolutionary personages, also in Revolutionary costume, had their names shouted, came in, and bowed to George and Martha. Then music sounded, George and Martha led a grand march, and the marchers performed a minuet. That was all. The audience was then supposed to go home, patriotic and satisfied that it had seen something.

In Indianapolis we had not only this spectacle enacted by grown people but also a children's Martha Washington's Tea Party, coached by my sister, not quite eighteen and just out of the convent school at Georgetown. In curly white wig, black velvet tailed coat, satin waistcoat, and little black velvet breeches—with lace frills at the knee in the fashion of Louis XIII—I was thought remarkable in the role of Aaron Burr. I thought so myself and so did the nearest of my relatives. After the performance the prettiest little girl in town, in Revolutionary costume, and I, as Aaron Burr, were taken by our mothers to the photographer's—and after that I always listened attentively when our family album was brought forth and somebody'd say, "This is Boothie as Aaron Burr."

I didn't care much for the visitors when they just responded, "Is it?"

My superintended evening prayer had changed in a detail because that part of my earlier petition had met a favorable response from Above. The great California uncle had been elected to the United States Senate, and here and there over the country he was "spoken of for higher office." I now said nightly, by my bedside, "Please bless papa and mamma and Hautie and Boothie, and make Uncle Newton President and papa county clerk."

Our hero came from California, that summer of 1876, to make speeches up and down his native state of Indiana for Hayes and Wheeler, and there were grand nights when shouting and glittering long processions tramped down the street with bands blaring, and, through the flare and smoke of torches, we saw Uncle Newton exalted but tranquil as he was borne by in an open carriage on his way to stir the multitude. For all of his relatives he brought splendid presents as usual, and his gift to my mother was so magnificent that now she and my father saw their way to build a house, one that should surpass the lamented edifice in which I had been born.

Pride Before a Fall

The new house was a year in building, and to us the ponderous stone foundations seemed cathedral-like; we were sure that never would there rise a nobler house. Such a one today there could not be for a dozen times the cost. A foreman said to my father, "I'm getting a dollar a day and glad to grab it. Why, after the war and up to the panic, I used to make as high as five dollars a day sometimes and could afford to wear a silk hat! Do you think times are ever going to get any better?"

Times did get better. Thrift and endurance made them better. Men toiled at jobs they didn't like, did anything until the day should come when they'd once more have the kind of work they desired. They worked for any pay they could get, lived on the little they made, and so won their way back to silk hats again. It wasn't until the present depression had burdened us for a decade that I began to understand what, in less than half the time, "We the People" then accomplished unaided and undeterred by our agents, the Government in Washington. When our house was finished and my mother kept open house on New Year's Day, the bright new rooms were crowded with jolly and optimistic people dressed in their newest best.

An orchestra played, gentlemen flourished skin-tight lemon-colored gloves; and ladies in close satin basques and long-trained skirts laughed and sang to the music. They were all coming out on top of the Panic of '73.

I was in school now, a good little pupil near the top of my class and sometimes appointed—as an honor—to wet the slate-cleaning sponges that dangled from the desks. During my second school year there were moments of sheer smugness when in the schoolyard I heard jealous murmurs of "Teacher's pet!" Something was awaiting me, though—an event that was to reduce—at least for long—the vanity so fondly built up within me by my tenderhearted parents and my ever gallantly devoted sister.

It happened at a children's party. The sunshine of that ancient afternoon is warm and strong in my mind's eye now; I see myself setting forth, newly polished shoes glistening, wide collar white about my slender throat, and in my head and heart nothing but eagerness to take the coming joy. It was a large and, at first, a decorous party. Among the throng of sleeked boys moved exquisite maidens with golden curls, pink or white or pale blue fluffy dresses, and gleaming little slippers—but for me the shiniest pink satin sash was that of little Hattie. In my tremulous perception of her she hadn't any last name and didn't need any; she was just a beautiful pinky blond glow called Hattie.

Children played kissing games in those days. At that party we played post office. All of the little girls withdrew to the hall outside the large room where the boys remained; we stood in a circle, every one of us behind a vacant chair. The grown-up hostess, by the closed door, asked the boy nearest to her to mention the name of one of the little girls. That boy then spoke the name of her who was his heart's first choice; whereupon the lady opened the door and called out: "A lovely letter for little Olive!" Little Olive entered from the hall and the door was closed.

With solemn silence all about her, she looked over the vacant chairs and conscientiously seated herself in one of them. If it was the chair behind which stood the boy who had sent her the letter, he now publicly kissed her; then she demurely returned to the hall. If she took the wrong chair, the boys all clapped their hands derisively, upon which she would rush back to the hall, not so demurely.

My turn came, and, from a quivering throat, I contrived to utter the revered name. Our hostess opened the door and called, "A lovely letter for little Hattie!"

I realized that in a moment a sacred being would appear in the doorway; a terrible agitation shook me. "Shook" is the right word. I trembled excessively, comprehending too late that if Hattie should seat herself in the right chair—mine—I couldn't kiss her. I didn't know how; and I looked upon her as unapproachable, a rosy ethereality rather than a fellow mortal. Stage fright took me; and four feet behind me there was an open window. As the ineffable form of little Hattie appeared in the doorway, with all eyes upon her, I found myself to be descending toward green grass. I was falling through fresh air and late-afternoon sunshine, having uncontrollably jumped out of the window.

I crawled away and sat with my back against a brick wall. Indoors, I thought, all must be in turmoil as unprecedented as the act that caused it: the game broken up, the party ruined, the hostess noisily indignant, everybody shouting to everybody else, "He sent Hattie his letter—and then he wasn't there!" I was disgraced, notorious, a pariah; and I couldn't go home to hide my shame. To leave a party before it was over was an action of itself unthinkable, and my hat was in the "gentlemen's dressing room." Nobody could go home without his best hat; he couldn't.

A Deflated Eight-Year-Old

Furtive, despairing, I lurked in shadows that ominously grew longer. Sunset had come when at last I crept round that large house to slide in by the back door—for if I faced hell itself I had to get my hat. On the rear veranda three large ice-cream freezers stood exhausted; refreshments—insanely forfeited by me—were of the past, and the party must be near its shocked close. I slipped into the kitchen unnoticed, passed quiveringly through a rear hall, opened a door—and was at the party again. Boys and girls in paper caps were whooping, running, charging into one another, falling down, upsetting furniture, and banging all over the house in the liberated exhilaration that is the last stage of a successful children's party.

I'd expected a dreadful outcry; I'd thought to see dozens of accusing fingers pointed at me and to hear a cruel damning chorus, "There he is!" Clutching hands would be upon my shoulders while horrid voices screamed for the hostess to come and do her will upon me: "Mrs. Browning, hurry! We've caught Booth Tarkington! Here he is!"

Nobody even looked at me; I might have been an invisible boy. The late Mr. Dillinger walking into a crowded police station only to find himself utterly ignored might have felt part of what emotion then possessed me.

I caught a friend by the arm as he was dashing by me.

"Page, wait!" I begged. "What did Hattie do?"

"Let go me!" Page said. "What did Hattie do when?"

I gulped. "When I—when I jumped out of the window."

"Did you?" Page said. "Let go me! Sam Miller's after me and I got to run!'"

The truth came upon me strangely, strangely. Nobody knew that I'd jumped out of the window. Hattie didn't know it—nobody in the world knew it. Nobody even knew that during most of that party I hadn't been present. Where I was or what I did didn't mean anything to anybody.

I was freed of guilt, but plunged into a profound meditation.

Through the early twilight I walked home alone, with my head down and my shiny shoes moving slowly. Something had departed out of me and I seemed to consist of a walking vacancy. It was then, at about eight and a half years of age, that I lost a great part of the puffed-uppedness devotedly blown into me for years by loved ones at home. For the first time I seemed to perceive that I was nobody at all. So, during that slow trudge homeward after the party, I ceased to be a little child and became a growing boy.

II. Beaten Boy

As I now examine the flowering of my childhood's vanity—my natural-born egoism cultivated daily by the flatteries of my parents and my sister—I find that in contact with the similar blossoms of contemporaries my own began to wilt rather early. Sometimes, however, grown people helped on the withering, and at the age of six I'd had a hot afternoon in Terre Haute when adults made the cherished rose of my self-conceit shed petals copiously. That afternoon, in semipublic, so to say, I told a lie of the kind typically used by unimportant human beings for the purpose of presenting an impressive appearance. It's true, though, that I didn't myself invent the lie; my Grandmother Booth made me a present of it. She didn't realize that it was a lie; she thought of it as a convenience and gave it to me because that was the only way to get me to do what she wished.

I was visiting her in Terre Haute and she'd asked me to go forth and buy a needle for her at the largest dry-goods store on the principal business street of the town. I had never been in that store; and to my mind it was a vast emporium, formidable and likely to be contemptuous of a customer of my size and age. When she gave me a copper cent and told me that was the price of a needle I was to buy, I made a great to-do, loudly declining to enter so awesome a bazaar for the purpose of spending a mere penny. I might be held up to ridicule, I protested.

A Penny Tragedy

"Not at all," my grandmother said. "When the clerk hands you the needle and you give him the penny, just laugh and say, 'I believe this is the very smallest purchase I ever made in my life!' That'll make it all right."

I thought it would. The ladylike laugh and the little lie seemed plausible. I left the house cheerfully, practicing my contemplated airy laugh as I went. All the way to Main Street I rehearsed, amusedly saying over and over, as I trudged along the hot brick sidewalk, "I believe this is the very smallest purchase I ever made in my life!"

Inside the big store I found my confidence at once enfeebled. The noon hour had just passed; the hotness of the day was that of an Indiana town in a midsummer heat wave, ninety-eight in the shade. I was the only customer in that whole cavern; an interminable avenue stretched before me, bordered by polished wooden counters behind which drooped male and female clerks, languidly waving palm-leaf fans in a daunting silence. I went to the nearest counter, spoke to the whiskered, pallid young man behind it, and faintly told him what I wanted. He stopped fanning himself, yawned, sighed, found the described needle, wrapped it in a wisp of paper, silently handed it to me, and I gave him my copper.

Then, already with a sinking feeling and a voice perhaps somewhat tremulous, I did my practiced laugh for him and said bravely, "I believe this is the very smallest purchase I ever made in my life!"

He leaned across the counter and looked down at me, spoke in a startling voice. "What did you say?"

I was sorry I'd said it and wished not to repeat it, but felt that I had to do so. I omitted the society laugh because I wasn't able to produce it. "I—I believe this is the very smallest purchase I ever made in my life."

I desired to leave the place, but couldn't. This man had a powerful air of not having closed the episode. He looked at the clerks behind the other counters, beckoned, and called their names. "Come here," he said. "Come listen to this. I want you to hear something." They came, some gathering about him, behind his counter, and others before it, but all staring down at me. "Sold him a needle for a cent," he told them. "I want you to hear him talk about it." Then his unbearably cold and protuberant eyes refixed themselves upon me. "Say it again," he said. "Say it again."

The accursed words Grandmother had put into my mouth were by this time loathsome to me; yet I saw no option but to utter them once more. I did, miserably, with my head down and speaking to the floor. "I—I believe this is the very—the very smallest purchase I ever made in my—in my life."

Here my memory blurs. Of the immediately following moments I recall only the perception that something monstrous was happening to me and that I was presently outdoors upon the hot brick sidewalk again, filled with a horror of life and of myself. I felt that I was a shoddy little fellow exposed; my soul had been shown naked to the world and consisted of weaknesses, falsities, and deformity. I'd been forced to strip before an audience that derisively saw me as I was, a wretched insectile impostor trying to pose as a person of large affairs familiar with important currency—five and ten dollar bills and suchlike!

Our memories acquire dreadful but useful habits. As I walked back to my grandmother's, millions of locusts seemed to fill the scorching air of all Terre Haute with sizzling, unending proclamations of my shame, hideously letting the world know that I was a cheap snob who'd been showing off—and had got caught at it! Somewhere on that walk I passed a row of catalpa trees. To this hour, sixty-five years later, catalpa trees and the racketing of locusts on a hot day bring back to me Terre Haute at ninety-eight in the shade—and the cure I had of being one special kind of snob.

Our recollections of mortifying scenes in our lives seem to be of ourselves as we were just after those scenes took place. We recall the actual drama itself with a blurring horror; but our sensations immediately afterward often reproduce themselves later with such vividness that we wonder how we could have endured them and gone on living. What burns itself deepest is not the exposure but the crawl home afterward.

The Bridge of Boyhood

In Indianapolis, far downtown in the smoky old and decayed "best residence section," still stands the house in which I began to discover, at a children's party, that I was a nonentity. On days when I drive down into the city's smoke I never pass the place without a painful glance at the window from which I leaped rather than risk having to kiss a beautiful little girl. Nevertheless, my walk home after the party—meditating upon the fact that nobody'd noticed my jump or missed me—remains the sharpest item of that memory too. It was then, at the age of about eight and a half, that I realized something of my cosmic unimportance: I had no weight whatever with anybody, anywhere, except at home.

Transition periods in government or in the life of an individual are the hard ones, and few are more upsetting than the change between being a little child and being a growing boy. I not only had to resign myself to be a nobody among my kind, but, mystified, baffled, and sometimes sore from unpredictable snubbing, I was made to face the fact that I was no longer thought fascinating—or even interesting—by adults, except those of the close family circle. No more at sight of me did every visitor to the house, and every mere caller, set up a caressive powwow and try to coax me nearer. All their previous adulation was gone. The grown-up people I knew had lost the sweet indulgence from their eyes; those eyes didn't beam at sight of me. Not by wickedness but by the simple process of growing, I had forfeited their love and admiration. For the most part, when their gaze guardedly fell upon me, it expressed a consciousness of being in the presence of something chancy and likely to be objectionable.

A barrier had arisen; I began to feel that almost all grown people were of the opposition; therefore everything had to be concealed from them. Some of them inspired in me a strong uneasiness whenever I saw them.

The General's Shadow

The one of whom I was most afraid was General Chapman. A principal advantage in the location of the new house we'd built was that it made us closer neighbors of the Chapman family—the general, his lovely wife, whom I'd always called "Auntie Chapman," and their five small sons, the oldest of whom was no more than a year my senior. The Chapman boys were my most constant playmates. Their mother had a heart that won all children, but the five brothers were somewhat in awe of their father, and I was more so. He'd been an officer of cavalry in the Civil War, and afterward a judge; his eyes, behind the ice of nose glasses, seemed to me disciplinarian and never encouraging. The noisy Chapman house quieted instantly when the general arrived from his law office in the late afternoons; and we of the neighborhood, extraneous noisemakers, went home in a subdued manner. Even in my own front yard, if I was playing there, perhaps with my little gentle old dog, and General Chapman passed by on the sidewalk, I ceased to gambol, felt reproved, and retired with Fritzie to the rear of the house—sometimes slunk into our protective stable to stand brooding there, feeling that I had little right to live.

General Chapman, a kindly man, an old "friend of the family" who'd been one of my father and mother's wedding party, would have been surprised if he'd known how much I thought about him—"and how"! Grown people, unless they study the matter, have little understanding of the effect they have upon some children. What this patriot, good neighbor, good friend, and able citizen made me feel, merely by the reservedness of his facial expression, was that I ought to be banished from the world. I dreamed about him, dreams of terror, and over and over I planned to make up to myself, someday, for the oppression he put upon me.

This was my plan. The general's oldest son, George, was, as we say, the image of him; and everyone saw at a glance that when Georgie Chapman grew up he would be exactly like his father in looks and in manner. I wasn't afraid of Georgie—far from it! I was familiar with him, liked him; I'd several times seen him weep and had even assisted to make him do so. Over and over in my mind I planned a scene that should take place when Georgie became adult, full-grown—forty or fifty, maybe. Georgie would then present to the world precisely the austere appearance that General Chapman did now; but to me he would still be, inside himself, just Georgie Chapman. Inconsistently, in this scene of recompense, I imagined Georgie in the full-sized shell or facsimile of General Chapman; but myself I saw as I still actually was, a boy of nine. I would walk right up to the adult generalesque Georgie, look him full in his nose glasses, give him a push, laugh in loud scorn of his pretensions, and say, "Pooh, you old thing, you! I know you all right! You're nothing but little old Georgie Chapman. Pooh!"

Thus concretely had I perceived that the child is father to the man, and, meditating upon other boys I knew, saw them in my mind's eye as they would be when they should be full-grown and changed into members of the adult opposition. I would still know them then and be as intimately familiar with the details of their real characters as I was now; and in this prediction I now seem to have been substantially justified. Boys are likely to comprehend one another's fundamental characters with a simple clarity—character being more naïvely exposed at that period than later—and adult men who have been "boys together" have a basic knowledge of one another, no matter how they change. After I had grown to manhood, myself, I found that whenever I met a stranger I had an inclination to seek beneath his adult lineaments for the face he'd had when he was a boy. When I can see the boy's face beneath the man's I'm fairly sure that I know what sort of person he really is. Meeting General Chapman now for the first time, I'd look for Georgie.

Georgie's next brother, Launce, also caused me, when I was nine, to make plans for the future. Launce was a carefree strong little boy of whom older people sometimes benevolently said that it was a pleasure to see his animal spirits in action. Usually when they were in action his brothers and I were unhappy. Outdoors he could do everything better than we could, and he could also throw us all down in a heap and jump on us, not caring upon whose face his stout-shod feet landed. He could run, leap, jocosely pull hair, fight, and hurl missiles better than we could; and, laughing heartily, he proved all of this to us whenever he began to feel bored.

Ignominy

He was one of those boys who make the homeward processions of children, after school, into riots; and in our own daily parade he often singled me out to play the poorer part in a jovial performance of which he was fond. Butted from the pavement, I was slammed horribly face down into the gutter, with

Launce sitting upon my head and bellowing jollily for everyone's attention, "Take a head-load, Boothie! Look at Boothie taking a head-load!"

Prostrate, squirming, eyes and mouth filled with dust or mud, I had ignoble glimpses from under the seated Launce of boys and girls rocking in laughter; but I was as helpless as a day-old calf. Later every afternoon I clumsily practiced the manly art with a punching bag in our stable and discouragedly examined muscles that never enlarged enough to fulfill my bitter hope some day to "lick Launce Chapman."

I couldn't lick anybody. For one reason, I couldn't get "mad" enough. Other boys, in conflict, could reach a berserk pitch at which they did actual damage, but I couldn't get that way. Even when they threw stones at my dog I couldn't fight for him; could only crouch over him, receiving helplessly the missiles upon my own body. One day I did somehow find myself in a stand-up fight with a rich little German boy of our neighborhood. He may have known how it came about, I didn't; but there we were, punching each other, with a ring of delighted friends about us, urging us to hit harder and in designated localities, especially the nose. I didn't wish to hit harder; I forcelessly pounded Louis about the chest and shoulders and was wholly incapable, morally, of directing my fist against any part of his face. Louis had no such delicate compunction. He smashed me on the nose, bloodied it, and evoked from me, unfortunately, the shrill reproachful inquiry, "Louis, did you mean that?"

The happy, boyish countenances about us pressed close upon me; all voices shouted in ecstasy, "Did he mean it? Did he? Look at your nose!"

The Clicks

The most elementary self-defense was beyond me. People of today, accustomed to think youthful felonies a product of strictly modern life, may be surprised to learn that well-dressed little boys in such a town as Indianapolis sixty years ago were often held up and robbed by small gangsters of their own age. We victims didn't speak of them as gangsters; we knew them as members of what we called "clicks," deriving the word, I suppose, from "clique." Skating upon frozen little waters about the fringes of the inland town, or swimming in such fluids in summer, boys from our neighborhood would raise the cry, "Look out! Look out! Here comes Mike Donegan and his click!" Those of us who didn't or couldn't flee were surrounded, cursed, overawed, and robbed of penknives, nickels, marbles, tops.

One afternoon Georgie Chapman and I, returning from a matinee, were relieved of belongings almost in the business center of the city. Five or six shabbily dressed boys, none over eleven, an unknown click, surrounded us, pushed us back against a wall; and their chieftain, blaspheming horribly, threatened our throats with the blade of a jackknife.

I said feebly, "My father's a policeman," but Georgie, with a silver quarter in his pocket, had the courage to call for help. He shouted at the top of his lungs, "Help! Help! Help!"

Adult passers-by glanced at us absently and went their ways. The thieves took Georgie's quarter, his necktie and my own, and our handkerchiefs; then walked away—and so did we, in the opposite direction, very resentful, but not inclined to pursue the matter further.

I'd looked forward to being ten years old. In youth the ages of man, expressed in round numbers, loom ahead of him as desirable and impressive—until he attains them. I'd thought that when I reached ten I should automatically be a person of greater consequence than previously, that I should by virtue of years be treated universally with more respect. Nothing like this happened. Outdoors with my fellows, except that I could make as much noise as anybody, I was rather worse than negligible. In every sport I was least among the little. I couldn't hold a thrown or batted ball, not even when I got my hands on it. I couldn't bat; I was a duffer with marbles or at kite flying, and I couldn't wind a string about a top so that the top would spin. I could sit upon a horse and continue to guide him if he was in a tractable mood, but that was about all.

By heredity I should have been able to do all these things well, and I suppose that my chosen environment was what hampered me. I was an indoor boy by inclination and lacked the practice in sports that outdoor boys develop together. Moreover, being less and less equal to them when I went outdoors and among them, I naturally reverted increasingly to the library at home, and my associates were more and more my father and my mother and my twenty-year-old sister.

In the evenings my father had always read much to me—*Tales of a Grandfather* and like books—and during the summer when I was eight I'd gladly come in from play every afternoon to read Guizot's *History of France* with my mother, who had the art of making historical personages dramatically real. I lived in a warming glamour with Guizot's people, from Vercingetorix to Clovis, from Clovis to Louis XI, and from Louis XI to Voltaire and to Louis XVI. At nine and ten I was much occupied with Shakespeare, Dickens, histories of England and the United States, and a scattering run of novels: John Halifax, *Gentleman*; *Ivanhoe*; *Zanoni*; *Beulah*; *The Woman in White*; *Les Misérables*; *Love Me Little, Love Me Long*; *The Vicar of Wakefield*; *Ten Thousand a Year*; *The Spy*—memory fails upon the rest of this potpourri.

A Fourth-Grade Feud

In those days, one or two small private schools for children struggled rather feebly to keep alive in Indianapolis; but our public schools were incomparably better and we who attended them felt superior to the few weaklings at the tenderer institutions. My first three years at school were wholly agreeable. I was a good little boy, loved my teachers, was praised and smiled upon; and then, with a strange abruptness, I reversed all this and my life was changed. We had a new teacher, a brilliantly pretty young woman who produced for me my decisive turning point—and from the first I did not love her.

I had expected to love her and to be beloved in return. I had thought that she would recognize me instantly as her best pupil, but she didn't. I had the manner of being her best pupil, privileged, near the throne, and virtually an official, but she didn't seem to see me in that light. That she didn't was visible to me in her expression. Within the hour when she took charge of us, her lovely bright eyes several times fixed themselves upon my officious young face uncaressingly, and I perceived in them an estimating disfavor. For the first time since my first day in school, I broke a rule; I whispered to the boy across the aisle—and had my first punishment. The boy across the aisle and I were both kept after school.

We were supposed to sit in silence for twenty minutes, but, when perhaps a third of the time had passed, the new teacher, as bored as we were, left the room to chat with somebody in the corridor. I hopped up brightly and began to entertain the other boy by drawing "funny pictures" on the blackboard. This was a great sin and perhaps it was the excitement in him roused by my daring that made him laugh aloud, a sound that brought Miss Jeffson suddenly back into the room. She looked at me and I looked at her, and something fundamentally inimical seemed to be exchanged in the glance.

"Is this what you usually do when you're kept after school?" she asked.

My impulse was to tell her that I'd never before been kept after school; I wasn't that sort of person. Instead, I tried something I thought rather impressive. I'd display before her a more important word than she'd used.

"Usually?" I said. "No; not generally. No, generally I don't."

Upon this a slight change in her face betokened her assurance that, though inexperienced, she knew how to deal with fresh little squirts. "Oh, you don't?" she said. "Not 'generally'!"

She spoke in a tone that then and there ended my career as a best pupil. We were enemies—virtually open ones—from that moment.

Within a month I'd slumped to the bottom of the class. Instructive adults must be both sympathetic and adroit to hold a small boy's attention, and a child's ear closes out the words of a person who dislikes him. I felt not the slightest interest in my new studies; I made no effort to comprehend them or anything the new teacher said to us. I was agin the government, a rebel, and daily, almost hourly, recognized as such.

Schoolhouse Ishmael

It seems evident that being a praised pupil, a "teacher's pet" sort of little boy, had been one of the compensations I'd given myself for my ineptness in sports and for social blows I'd received. Vanity dies hard. It's a cat of more than nine lives: kill it in the front yard and you find it purring in the cellar. My cellar had been the schoolhouse; but Miss Jeffson had stopped the purring there, and the effect was a long disaster.

Probably it's dangerously injurious to any human being to brush away, even temporarily, his last shreds of self-conceit—revolutions can rise from it—and the result upon me was an impairment of that still mysterious equipment sometimes called "the nervous system."

I wasn't aware of any impairment; I knew only that I felt dull and twitchy and itchy and that batting my eyes, moving the greater part of my nose rapidly in various directions, wobbling my head on its slender neck, and making uncouth sounds afforded brief relief. The trouble was that the more outrageously I did these things, the more extensively I seemed compelled to continue and develop them.

They annoyed Miss Jeffson excessively—she said I was deliberately making faces—and they worried my mother so much that she called in the family physician to look at me. I didn't see why I was subjected to his scrutiny. Twitchiness had begun to seem to me my natural condition; but after I'd jerked my nose and clucked and glunked at the friendly doctor for a quarter of an hour he withdrew with my mother; and I, listening covertly, heard some murmurings about St. Vitus's dance that sounded rather attractive.

On the contrary, the doctor prescribed a remedy—"one tablespoonful after each meal"—and when the first of these tablespoonfuls had been inserted, the next day, I could have cursed the hour that I was born, if I'd known how. The medicine was in a quart-sized bottle; poisonous-looking weeds were suspended in a brown liquid, and the ingenuity of a great brain seemed to have exhausted itself in its search for a flavor that should be, of all combinations possible in the universal laboratory, the utmost in repugnance to the human palate. The sense of taste is incomparably more vivacious in children than in adults; my mother, to encourage me by example, was able to swallow a soupçon of this medicine with only a slight leap of her shoulders, while with superb self-control she maintained the strained semblance of a smile upon her face. Three times a day arguments so passionate on my part took place that I wonder she didn't wholly weary of me.

I had now the medicine at home in addition to ignominies in school and on the playground; so I clucked and glunked, twisted, scratched, jerked, and made more horrible faces than ever. I found that I could flutter my nostrils almost like a rabbit's and could wiggle my ears so well that their motion could be seen at quite a distance. Miss Jeffson could see it, for instance, the whole length of the schoolroom, and she sometimes grew red rather than ask me again what I meant by it. My troubles approached a climax, and so did Miss Jeffson.

I can't remember precisely what she said to me one day when, upon her own request, I gave her my honest opinion of a picture; but I know that she used hard words. In the reading class we'd just finished a celebrated poem by James T. Fields—one bit of which is still popularly extant:

> "We are lost!" the captain shouted,
> As he staggered down the stairs.

Artistic Heresy

Many will remember with pleasure that the captain's little daughter was present and calmed everybody—and apparently the tempest also—by uttering a few admonitory words; but I didn't like the poem or the captain or anybody. Under Miss Jeffson I'd become modern before my time, a skeptical analyst, and, above all, an antisentimentalist. The poem said: "Then we kissed the little maiden"; but I was against her; to me she was repellent. I even disliked the illustration in our reader—a woodcut that showed the little maiden taking the captain's icy hand after he'd staggered down the stairs. It wasn't a good woodcut. Miss Jeffson called upon me.

"Describe the picture of the captain's little daughter in the reader."

"She looks cross-eyed," I said with dogged accuracy.

The shock to the class was profound. A multitudinously long-drawn whispered "Oh!" filled the room; and then Miss Jeffson summed up and told everybody, and me, the whole of what she really felt about me. I stood, with burning cheeks, rapidly vibrant features, ears working and all. I hated Miss Jeffson, the school, all the pupils, and the captain. Insanely, I hated the little maiden worst of all. Miss Jeffson's speech about me accomplished nothing of good; I even failed to comprehend that art criticism at the wrong time or in the wrong place is never useful.

I think it was only a few days afterward when in return I gave Miss Jeffson a lesson especially gratifying to myself because it left her with no possible repartee. This was upon a morning when my medicine had agreed with my breakfast rather less than it usually did, and, more and more aware that something was very, very wrong inside me, I sat uneasily at my desk, looking at the two tight pigtails and neatly checked gingham back of the little girl in the seat before me. Sometimes the pigtails seemed to sway and the gingham checks to swirl displeasingly. I put up my hand, and Miss Jeffson frowned at it.

Retort Discourteous

"May I be excused?" I asked thickly.

"You may not."

I sat for some moments; then put up my hand again. "I'm sick. May I go home?"

"No, you may not."

"I'd better," I said, more thickly. "I'm getting sicker."

"That will do!"

Miss Jeffson spoke with such sternness that what had all along been inevitable took place immediately: the genuineness of my illness was proved to her and to everybody. When the convulsion was over I rose, walked up the aisle to the cloakroom door; but paused there—though I could have reached the cloakroom—and had another. All that remained was placed in evidence. Then, over the turned and interested heads of my colleagues, I wanly gave Miss Jeffson a look that said, "There! How about that? You believe it now, don't you?"

Not a little pleased with myself, I floundered home and was put to bed.

It's not easy to say just when children reach the age of class reticence; but it's certain that sometimes the most sympathetic parents in the world can't overcome a child's withholdings. A small boy in particular usually wishes to avoid evoking an interfering sympathy and is embarrassed by tender condolences. I didn't tell my parents about my troubles with Miss Jeffson. I didn't myself understand that she was really what was the matter with me or, of course, that I was just a bit of machinery and she the wrong mechanic to operate it. I didn't and couldn't explain; and so my mother and my father and the doctor, after medicating me and achieving no results except anguish three times a day, were seriously puzzled. They came to one of the strangest conclusions I've ever known intelligent people to reach: they decided that I was studying too much, working too hard in school. I was sent to visit my grandmother.

On a shelf of the whatnot in Grandmother Booth's front parlor, in Terre Haute, there was a dried brown plant from the South Seas. On the whatnot it looked a little like a wooden spider the size of a small tomato; but if you put it in a soup bowl full of water it swelled out until it filled the bowl. At the age of ten, after you'd done that at Grandmother Booth's, there wasn't anything else to do except to go out and watch the ants on the front walk. However, for the higher type of recreation, there was a library; and in the evenings my grandmother talked interestingly upon the four subjects that absorbed her: Carlyle, Emerson, Robert G. Ingersoll, and the French Revolution. Grandfather Booth, eighty-seven and almost always deep in gentle reverie, seldom spoke.

I was supposed to be leading a very quiet life and not to think about school; I led the quiet life all right, and didn't think about school. After several weeks my grandmother decided that I needed to be brightened up; she invited the daughter of an old friend of hers to come and spend a day at play with me.

Little Isabel was a fat, friendly little girl, briskly talkative, and I didn't dislike her. On the other hand, I didn't like her either. We were given a room upstairs to sit down and play in, but Isabel didn't know any games for two and neither did I. Isabel, polite, chatted and chatted, while a longing came over me to go away from her; but I was sure that wherever I went she'd feel it her duty as my guest to go with me. Older people find such problems complicated, requiring delicate handling, but a boy of ten can't be trusted not to solve them with a primordial and atrocious simplicity. I went to an open window, pointed out of it, and said eagerly, "Look, Isabel!"

Isabel came to the window and asked, "Where?"

I pointed to the grass below. "Right down there!"

Isabel leaned out of the window. I retired into the hall, locked the one door of the room that contained good little Isabel, who still looked out of the window. Then I put the key in my pocket, descended the stairs, and strolled out to the street. There, experiencing a sense of relief and freedom, I decided upon a real excursion. I went all the way to the Wabash River at the edge of town, threw pebbles into the water, and enjoyed the landscape. There wasn't a cloud in the sky.

Finally, though, I thought of Isabel again. Maybe she was getting tired of that room by this time and she might be hungry too. It struck me that she ought to be let out. It was a long walk back and I was tired, myself, when I reached grandmother's house, but I found the place more excited than restful.

Whining Schoolboy

Good little Isabel's manners were so excellent that she hadn't made a really important uproar until more than an hour of her seclusion had passed. When I arrived, her mother had been sent for, and she and my grandmother and my grandfather and my Uncle Lucius were trying to comfort Isabel through the door, upon which a noisy and inefficient locksmith was working bafflingly. Isabel's mother was very kind: she just said I seemed to be a strange sort of boy, and took the precaution of leading Isabel home at once. Grandmother Booth was kind, too, but often looked at me speculatively after that. I couldn't tell what she was thinking, but her expression made it plain that she was thinking.

I came home to Indianapolis still bullfrogging in my throat, exercising my nose, and doing talented things with my scalp and my ears; so I was kept on vacation. In the autumn, being now eleven, I went back to school; but I'd of course dropped behind. My former class was a full year ahead of me and I found myself to be again without any interest whatever in education. I had another teacher, a pleasant one; but felt no ambition to shine before her or before anybody. School had become drudgery and confinement; I held a low opinion of it and of myself. Then, one day of that September, I had a flash of aggrandizement and once more, as in my infancy, was able to look upon Master Newton Booth Tarkington as a great person.

The revelation of beauties within me took place at the Indiana State Fair. One of the younger Chapman boys and I had saved up for the fair, and were permitted by our mothers to set forth early in the morning to spend the whole day together among agricultural machines, prize hogs, poultry, cattle, vegetables, fruit, side shows, balloon ascensions, dangerous edibles, trotting races, and dusty crowds. Page and I felt opulent, for, in addition to the lunch our mothers had provided for us, I think we each possessed about sixty-five cents, pure spending money.

Encounter with Life

We spent it more hurriedly than we intended. By noon we'd seen everything, contained candy, peanuts, popcorn, gingerbread, cider, lemonade, were broke, and ate our lunches languidly. After that we listened to barkers, saw two balloons rise from crowds we couldn't penetrate; and then for a long time believed we were watching the races because we were looking at the backs of people over whose shoulders we caught infrequent glimpses of horses' ears and drivers' gaudy caps flitting by.

When we'd conscientiously stayed through the last race, Page and I were separated in the departing throngs, and didn't find each other again. The afternoon was waning, dim autumnal sunset came on; but I wandered through the thinning crowd, scuffing the littered ground, dog-tired, yet not content to be upon my homeward way. There must be something more to see, I thought, something that Page and I had overlooked; and after a while, in a remote part of the fairgrounds, I found it.

It was a strange vehicle, four-wheeled but smallish. Upon the underpinning there was a sort of little house with glass windows, and the windows had neat little lace curtains. Between the curtains was seen a bed—a bed with a clean white coverlet, white bolster, and pillows—and the bed and the lace curtains were all that the little house contained. Moreover, the contraption was not intended to be drawn by a horse. A peculiar man, the owner of the little house, stood between the narrow shafts and, with straps over his shoulders and across his chest, was showing a small crowd of loiterers how he traveled, pulling the vehicle, his home, with him from fair to fair and town to town, he said.

He was a wild-looking man, I thought. His black clothes were tattery; the brim of his old black slouch hat blew back from his unkempt long black hair; he had a ragged black beard; and the whites of his eyes could be seen from an unusual distance. He spoke with an appealing earnestness; though I couldn't hear what he said, because, after I'd looked into his house between the little curtains, something about the owner and his manner embarrassed me, not for myself but for him; and I withdrew to a slight knoll perhaps a hundred feet away. I stood and watched, fascinated yet unwilling to be closer.

The man stepped out of his harness, stood forth, and I comprehended that he was lecturing, so to call it, to the people about him. With great rapidity and that serious eagerness he seemed to be talking about himself, his travels, and his odd little house. I got the impression that he wasn't quite right in his head, and I saw that his closer listeners thought this, too, and it amused them. They were increased in number until there were perhaps fifty or sixty of them, men and boys, all laughing; and the more earnest he became, the more they laughed.

He addressed them with a greater and greater vehemence; his gestures became fantastic, and the crowd about him shouted with mirth. He wasn't angry with them; what he said, so far as I could know, was in the nature of passionate appeal, as if he begged for justice. Then he passed his hat among the crowd, while the laughter grew, and, when he examined what had been put into the hat, I saw that he was in great pain and disappointment; for he turned the hat upside down and sadly emptied it of its contents—peanut shells, tobacco quids, and apple cores. The jokers howled, and he began all over again, trying to prove that he and his house were worth his tormentors' patronage and support.

They constantly interrupted him with cheering. The more he urged his case upon them, the louder they mocked him. Young louts among them flicked pebbles at him, tossed gobs of earth upon him, and, when he paused to wipe the dirt from his face, were in ecstasy. They knocked off his hat, and, when he patiently returned it to his head, daring ones rushed in, shoved him about, and manhandled him. He went on with his speech.

Standing on my knoll in the growing dusk, I watched and thought that my heart must break for that poor man. If I hadn't spent all my money I would have given it to him; I would have given him everything I had. I couldn't lift my voice against the cruel crowd that persecuted him; I didn't know how. It seemed to me that I would give my life to aid this bullied poor creature, but I was as helpless as he. All I could do was to stand there, wrung through my vitals with an agony of pity and tenderness for anyone so oppressed. I felt that of all those who participated in the dreadful spectacle only the victim himself and I were good and would go to heaven—and with this thought, though then I knew it not, the devil tempted me and I fell.

My whole small person filled with self-esteem. I felt that the all-seeing Deity was personally looking down upon me with a sublime approval and that, although I couldn't be of any use to the badgered creature before me, heaven would bless me for being the only person present with a noble heart. It seemed to me that God and the poor wild man and I were brought close together spiritually by my own goodness and that the three of us made a lonely light upon this earth.

Darkness was coming on deeper, and I walked away. When I left, the crowd still harried the unfortunate man; but I trudged homeward exalted. Never before—and I pray heaven never since—did I so praise myself. The supremacy of my virtue wrought a pathos about me; my holiness touched me to the quick. Lamplighters trotted whistling up the long streets, setting their slim ladders against the iron poles, then touching the glass boxes at the top into yellow illumination; and I passed beneath the lights with my hands in my pockets and my head down, my eyes wet with self-appreciation. I still felt excruciatingly sorry for the poor wild man; but the sorrier I was for him, the more credit I gave myself for it. I wept for him, and my tears were tribute to the just-discovered angelic quality of my own character. I was so good I just couldn't bear it.

At home, when they asked me what I'd seen at the fair, I couldn't tell them about my unhappy friend—or about me. I murmured of a Spotted

Wild Boy in a side show, and went to my room to be alone with my sorrow and my perfection.

I was pretty much over it next day and just a dub again, but for grandeur of soul I'd made a great reputation with myself.

III. Snips and Snails and Puppy Dogs' Tails

AGED ELEVEN, I WAS sometimes vaguely disturbed by hearing older people speak of what the world might be like in faraway times to come; though I'd accepted a prophecy that my own future was limited to the next nine years. I was to die that young.

At the beginning of the 1880s long fly brushes, sometimes beautifully of peacocks' feathers, were waved over dining-room tables at mealtimes in warm weather; doors and windows had no fly screens then; and on a summer morning a swallow flew into our kitchen. Finding all doors open to encourage the breeze, the confused bird flew out of the kitchen and across a rear hallway into the library, darted aside through the drawing room, shot leftward into the front parlor, then dipped through the hall and out to the sunshine again by way of the open front doorway. Immediately there was great commotion within the house; my mother and sister couldn't quiet our convulsively noisy fat colored cook.

"Sign o' death!" she shouted. "Bird fly threw house true sign o' death!" She pointed at me. "It's him! Sign o' death fer that chile. He ain' go' live to grow up. That chile never go' live see twenty-one years ole! Bird done say so!"

My mother and sister of course laughed and reassured me; but the cook and the swallow made an impression upon me—I thought that most likely they knew. However, years were so long—in those days—that a possible nine of them, stretching ahead, offered a virtually interminable lifetime. I wasn't much more bothered than if the cook had said I wouldn't live to be a hundred; and I felt rather important because the swallow's performance, and hers, were all about me.

Convinced that I'd never see twenty-one, I was, nevertheless, attentive when older people spoke of what I might see if I lived to be an old man. My grown-up relatives talked of times even farther ahead than that—especially when Uncle Newton stopped to visit us on his journeys between Washington and California. He laughed at himself for being a visionary, but insisted that someday carriages would move without horses to pull them, and he was even fantastic enough to believe that within the next hundred years or so men would fly. People would see them—actual human beings like ourselves—way up there in the sky and not just helplessly floating in balloons, but with made wings, dodging the clouds and as sure of themselves as birds are. He thought, too, that someday there'd be light from electricity, and hotels would no longer have to put up bedroom signs for country people, "Don't blow out the gas."

Few of his kinsfolk could seriously agree with him about men flying; though they all accepted the theoretical possibility that carriages and phaetons and buggies could be made to move, lacking horses. The thing might be done by means of steam engines stoked with coal, they thought; but the machines would always have to be kept off the public highways, of course, because they'd frighten the horses.

Such inventions, it was felt, wouldn't be practical until the millennium, that Utopian era to arrive when everybody had become well-to-do, all-wise, and wholly good. By then all problems, including that of swift transportation, would have been solved, so we'd all live in a leisure devoted to literature, the fine arts, and religious observances. There would of course be no more war—but my mother was positive that already mankind had learned at least that one dreadful lesson. As a girl she'd lived through the Mexican War and as a young matron through the incomparably more heart-rending Civil War; she was sure that nothing so horrible as war could ever happen again. Perhaps this was why my father's sword and a great-grandfather's Revolutionary musket were kept in the attic, where I used them fiercely in many solitary wars against invisibles.

Thus I may have been in myself a demonstration that war wasn't extinct; for doesn't a child's life repeat the history of his species, and aren't most nations still controlled by child instincts? My father, gentlest of men, didn't think the world old enough to be free of war. In fact, he thought it possible that life on this planet might become so torn with fighting that a man would be safest as a trained soldier; so his plan for me was West Point—an idea always quietly but emotionally opposed by my mother.

My father's thought that war would come again he founded upon observation of the world and upon reason, of course; but he had also developed a queer idea. It was a fancifully speculative one, he admitted, and he didn't believe in it—he was always discriminating in his use of the word "believe"—yet he thought the thing could be possible. In the unbounded range of his reading he'd included many books upon the esoteric philosophies; he corresponded with an English expert upon the Law of Karma, and he thought the doctrine of reincarnation so plausible that a quarter of a century later, after an Italian sojourn, he wrote his piquant book upon the question, *The Hermit of Capri*. In that work, however, he didn't mention the odd bit of looking forward militarily that made me shiver once or twice in my boyhood.

The thought was that terrific hordes of the disembodied entities of ancient fighting men—Carthaginian mercenaries, Roman legionaries, turbulent Alamanni, and what not—had perhaps already been reincarnated, some of them killing their way across Asia and into Europe with Genghis Khan maybe, and that the Law of Karma seemed to indicate that they were just about due in quantity upon this earth again. Great numbers of them, he thought, might be born into various nations during the next fifty years—many might already be alive—and, as they were in very essence savage warriors, their presence among mankind would so tend to create prodigious wars that the efforts of civilized peacemakers would be of little avail. The disturbances would not be calculable nor could the world go peacefully forward again until the truculent had been destroyed and the wave of this incarnation of theirs had passed.

The Golden Age

Thus, to me, the far future seemed uncomfortable to think about—with its shadowy crowds of terrible warrior souls fighting, and its skies meteored with winged people flying, and its tooting steamy vehicles frightening horses and ponies into runaways—but, naturally, I didn't think about it often or for long. The younger we are, the more vivaciously we're engaged with every present instant, and, for that matter, we were then all living in the Golden Age, though we didn't know it. We never know such things till afterward, and, as my father pointed out, we seldom say, "I am happy!" though we often look back and say, "I was happy then."

The happy world I lived in as a boy enjoyed the earlier years of a long period of peace for our country, and an enlightened civilization was advancing without having yet become elaborately mechanized. We could have got along pretty well, indeed, without any machinery at all, unless such things as a pump handle, a water-turned mill wheel, or the blade of a plow are to be called machinery. So far as machinery was concerned, my four grandparents, heartily alive throughout my boyhood, had grown up in a world that was almost the same as that of Julius Caesar. In their youth, ships could better sail into the wind than Roman ships could, and of course there was gunpowder; but virtually they lived in machineless country and were the sturdier and happier for the self-reliance and consequent independence of life and thought thus granted them.

I was not quite so fortunate. In my childhood, telegraph poles increasingly defaced the landscape, and on the new railroads we could go to almost any part of the country without changing cars at every junction. When I was eleven, the telephone here and there began to be in use—most likely between a mill in the country and its office in town—but abject dependence upon machinery hadn't arrived, nor, all in all, had the complete change from the youthful life of my grandparents. How dizzied we'd all have been could we have looked forward accurately into this age of then unbelievable machines and incredible speeds—and, despite my father's queer idea, with how crazy an optimism we'd have guessed what the effect of the machines and the speeds would be!

Crisis at Greencastle

At eleven, however, my real concern with the future being for the immediate one, I was little more altruistic about it than I'd been in my infancy; the self-centeredness of a boy is almost equal to a baby's. Yet at this period I had two sharp anxieties about the health of two grown-up persons, one of whom I'd never seen. The other one was my Uncle George Ames.

I didn't know Uncle George very well—he was my mother's sister's husband—and I was aware of him only as a handsome, gray-bearded, religious-looking man whom I didn't see often, as he lived forty miles away at Greencastle. Nevertheless, that summer, when I heard that Uncle George was dangerously ill, I began to worry about him acutely because Adam Forepaugh's Mammoth Circus was approaching Indianapolis and I thought that if anything very bad happened to Uncle George it was almost sure to interfere. I had a nervous week; every day the circus got nearer and Uncle George got worse.

The circus was for Saturday, and on Friday morning a telegram came; Uncle George had died. My father understood what I felt, and on Saturday after lunch, without saying anything about it to my mother, took me to the circus anyhow. I wondered a little if he was doing quite right by Uncle George; but I trusted him to know best and had a glorious afternoon. At the very entrance to the circus my father introduced me to Adam Forepaugh himself—he looked a little like Uncle George, I thought—and I had a full sack of popcorn to look at the animals with. We sat in splendid reserved seats with backs to them and even stayed for the concert after the Grand Performance.

At the concert I was transported when a little girl and a boy in white knee breeches appeared upon the distant platform, singing and dancing in a golden light. I paid no attention to the boy, the little girl so stirred me. I knew that the ballet-skirted bareback riders I'd seen flying through hoops were not little girls—they were specialized and sexless creatures, pretty but not recognizable as human beings exactly—but this little girl with the spangled knee-length pink dress, the jumping amber curls upon her shoulders, and the twinkling slippers that clinked and tinkled as she danced, seemed to me a transfigured sample of what one might actually meet at a children's party—a children's party almost in fairyland perhaps. For me to imagine her as probably nearer thirty than eleven was beyond the range of thought. The sparkling little dress exposed her pink silk legs, and female human legs weren't visible or even known about except when they belonged to little girls.

Grown-up ladies who walked as if they didn't have any were thought the most graceful, and I seldom saw even their whole feet. I'd had what I thought was an argument about legs with a schoolmate, a boy who told me one day that in older circles legs were highly regarded. I scoffed at him, but he maintained his point. "Grown-up men think a whole lot about legs," he insisted. "It's why they get in love and get married."

I laughed at him loudly. "They do not!"

"They do, too!" He was of German parentage and obstinate. "Men like fat legs. They've got to be fat or they won't pay any attention. The bigger women's legs are, the worse the men want to marry 'em. My Cousin Emil got married to Cousin Gertrude because she's got the biggest legs in Indianapolis."

"Then he's crazy," I said. "And so are you. Men marry somebody they think's got a pretty face. They don't get married on account of legs or elbows or knuckles or anything like that; and even if they wanted to, how could they tell what kind of legs they are?"

"That's easy," Albert informed me. "When they're getting in a streetcar or a buggy or something they can see whether they're big or not. Then if they're big enough they get married to them."

I didn't want to get married to the beautiful little girl dancing and singing enchantingly upon the circus concert platform; the exposure of her legs only proved that she truly was a little girl, and the charms that tingled into my heart from her were her flopping curls, her brilliant rose-and-white complexion, her clicky slippers, and the piercing silver voice with which she sang, "Oh, I'm happy, yes, as happy as can be!"

Almost all of the little girls I knew roused in me a feeling of annoyance, particularly those in my sister's Sunday-school class when she had them come to our house for games and cake and lemonade. I was so bitter with them that once when one of them triumphed in argument with me by throwing my new straw hat over the fence, and I could obtain no redress from either my sister or my mother, I decided to run away from home—and did, for as much as two hours. This song-and-dance little girl, transcendently different, sweet, and glittering, was a beautiful revelation. I had dazzling fancies. Sometime, somehow, in a world apart, maybe she would perpetually sing and dance and I would forever look and listen.

Tribal Experience

On the train to Greencastle, next day, with my mother, I heard the car wheels clicking "Oh, I'm happy, yes, as happy as can be!" and amber curls ethereally bounced on spangled pink shoulders in my mind's beglamoured eye; but when we arrived at Uncle George's house and saw the solemn crape upon the front door, I was all interest in the tribal experience for the first time awaiting me. Figures in black moved hushedly about the house; the smell of tuberoses was powerful, and in the parlor there was Uncle George, stately, in his open coffin, waiting for his funeral on the morrow.

My mother was taken upstairs to my widowed aunt and her daughters; I was left alone—and presently, for a few moments, alone with Uncle George. I looked at him earnestly and became aware that he was not there; that the figure in the coffin was not a person at all. Out of curiosity, and with no other feeling whatever, I touched the chill forehead and at once found my investigative forefinger distasteful. Then, as people in black came softly into the room, whispering appropriate lamentations, I stepped out of the side door and into the big sunshiny yard.

There was an orchard behind the house, and, walking slowly with my head bent in imitation of the people I'd seen indoors, I went to stand mournfully beneath the apple trees. I looked as sorrowful as I possibly could, in case anybody should glance from a window; and I was startled when my Cousin George, Uncle George's son, not long out of college, came briskly from the house and called in a cheerful voice, "Hello! How's young Boothie?"

I'd heard that he and his father had never been very congenial; nevertheless, I was shocked by Cousin George's lively manner. I thought his naturalness misplaced—the wrong etiquette for the occasion—and, during the short talk we had about our health and the weather, I didn't let him divert me from what I believed my plain duty as a funeral guest. I kept my face mournful and spoke in a low voice, mainly monosyllables, trying to seem on the verge of breaking down completely with my grief for Uncle George.

This was my manner throughout the day and evening, and during the obsequial ceremonies of the next day. A stranger seeing me might have thought I'd been closer to Uncle George than almost anybody'd been. I was sure this was the effect called for, and, as I came prominently forth from the house, a member of the mourning family, to go to the cemetery, I saw respectful spectators in the yard and on the sidewalk and wished that the transcendent rose-and-gold little circus girl could see me then. In my thoughts she occupied almost as large a place as I did, myself, at Uncle George's funeral.

The other grown person—the one I didn't know—for whom my boyish anxieties became acute was the President of the United States, General Garfield. Every year, with the Chapman family, two branches of the Hendrickses, and half a dozen other neighborly intimates, we had a Fourth of July we dreamed about—the sylvan games, bosky wanderings, and rare foods of an all-day picnic in the woods far out of town —and for the children of this association of old friends the Fourth meant the rose-lighted festival of all the year. On the second of the month that year the President was shot down by an assassin. Trying to act the man, I asked my parents as calmly as I could if the picnic would have to be given up.

Grave, they said, yes, of course; there couldn't be any kind of Fourth of July celebration anywhere unless the surgeons in Washington should decide the next day that General Garfield was going to get well. I wasn't one solitary little monster; every boy I saw on the third of July was as passionately hopeful as I that those doctors in Washington would issue the right kind of bulletins, no matter what. But the eve of the Fourth came, no preliminary rockets hissed up over the housetops, and the nation was in gloom. Late on the morning of the Fourth the news became more encouraging: the President had a chance; and after hesitant consultations it was decided that there were to be no firecrackers, but to the great question—the picnic—the answer at last was yes.

Noon had passed before the family carriages came lurching one by one through the green woods, and immediately the baskets were unpacked and the long white tablecloths laid upon the grass. An hour later, partly gorged, the boys all instinctively withdrew themselves far from the elders and maidens of the tribe; we ran yelping and chasing one another through the woodland until we were securely distant, out of earshot, and had found a stream. Upon its bank we gathered in a chattering clump; a thing forbidden was revealed.

Woodland Casualty

One of us, an adventurous boy, Chase Walker, had it—a pistol. He had blank cartridges, too—he'd not been able to acquire any with bullets, though he'd tried—but he showed us how he could shoot at a mark just the same.

He took small pebbles from the edge of the little creek, pushed them into the muzzle of the pistol, and, with the unsharpened end of a lead pencil, rammed down a wad of paper after them. For a target he fastened a torn bit of newspaper against the rough bark of a tree; then, retiring a few feet, fired and proudly showed two or three holes in the paper made by the pebbles.

He was generous, let all of us shoot pebbles at the mark until he and we found the sport monotonous and tired of it. We waded in the stream, caught crawdads, discovered a deep hole, and went swimming. We sunburned ourselves upon a sandbank, held our heads under water, and clinked stones together to see how much it made our ears hurt; we rioted waterily till the length of our thin shadows on the sandbank made us think of spicy foods again. It would be picnic suppertime soon. Chase Walker, sitting on a large rock at the edge of the sandbank, fired his pistol at a sapling; then reloaded it with pebbles, cocked it to shoot again, but decided that he'd better begin dressing instead.

People sometimes say, "It's a wonder any boy ever lives to grow up!" and, remembering how many times I was near drowning, what weeds, roots, and wild berries I tried to find edible, and how often I just saved myself on roofs, though I was the least daring of my kind, I think there's something in the saying. Chase Walker sat on his rock, dabbling his feet in the water and preparing a pebble-loaded pistol to be carried in his pocket. With the muzzle resting upon his bare leg, as he sat, he held the hammer back with his thumb and pressed the trigger. The hammer should have been restrained by his thumb, but wasn't; the pistol uttered its sharp report—and there was Chase staring, mystified, at a nasty red-and-black spot just above his right knee. Then his face was contorted and he began to whimper a little.

"What can I do?" he said.

We couldn't tell him; he appeared to be ruined and already we were thinking of something else. Nothing was more severely forbidden to every one of us than to have anything to do with a pistol; and, now that Chase had shot himself with one, our alarm—for ourselves—was acute. It gave us, too, a distaste for Chase; but we helped him to tie a wet handkerchief round his leg and to get into his clothes. Then, after several trials and collapses, he found that he could progress hobblingly and we set forth.

For a while some of us lingered scaredly along in the rear with Chase; but when we began to hear distant adult shouts calling us to the picnic supper, the first law of Nature asserted itself. Already the two or three youngest, and therefore most instinctive, were far ahead. Scattering ourselves—every boy for himself—we arrived singly in the glade where our elders and the maidens sat upon the grass, feasting.

We found our places quietly, very quietly; said nothing unless spoken to and carefully didn't look at one another. Seated, we ate slowly—until all of us paused in both eating and breathing when Chase Walker's mother asked a natural question. "Wasn't Chase with the rest of you? Where is he?"

"Where?" I repeated. "Chase? Well—I think he must be coming. I think I saw him walking along behind us somewhere back in the woods. I mean I think I did."

Somebody said, "Yes, there he is, Mrs. Walker," and Chase emerged from a thicket, bravely limping only a little.

"I fell and bumped my knee," he explained, as he contrived to let himself down upon the grass beside the white cloth. "My goodness, mother, don't make a fuss over my just tripping on a root and falling down!"

Mrs. Walker was reassured and the gay chatter of the elders and maidens resumed. Chase ate in a natural manner, and the rest of us preserved the kind of still expressionlessness that always ought to be investigated when boys wear it.

Fool's Paradise

Now the last sunshine had faded from the tops of the trees; the horses were harnessed; and, singing "Good night, ladies, we're going to leave you now," the families all piled themselves into the carriages. The boys contributed little to the song; but, as I jogged sleepily back into the town in the dusty dusk, my anxiety evaporated. Obviously, the episode was closed. General Garfield had been shot, but we'd had our picnic; and Chase Walker had shot himself, but nobody knew it—that is, nobody who'd do anything disagreeable about it. Everything was all right.

The next day at noon, however, I had bad moments. The Pennsylvania Street streetcar, drawn by one mule with a bell hung round its neck, stopped before our house, and my mother got out, looking serious.

"There's sad news for you," she said as I came to the gate to meet her. "A terrible thing happened at the picnic yesterday."

"Did it?" I contrived to ask. "You mean something happened that—that nobody knew about?"

"Yes, to Chase Walker. I've just come from their house. The poor boy had a pistol and he loaded it with some pebbles and accidentally shot them into his knee. Don't you remember when he came to supper he was late and limping, and said he'd fallen down and hurt himself?"

"Did he?" I said. "Well—I think I remember he was limping or something."

"The most dreadful part of it," my mother went on, "was that he didn't tell anybody, and it was almost midnight when his mother and father thought they heard him groaning in his sleep, and went to see and found that he was in a high fever and delirious.

The doctor's afraid Chase has blood poisoning, and he's very, very sick. Isn't it dreadful?"

The Male Animal

I said yes, it was; but felt that it had been dreadful only while I feared she knew I'd been present when Chase shot himself. She seemed gratifyingly innocent not to suspect me; I didn't perceive the inability of a grown person even to imagine that any boy at the picnic—much less all of us—had known the truth about Chase and not instantly sped for adult help to save him. My sensations were of sweet relief; and in this, again, I was not uniquely monstrous. With other boys of the picnic party I joined, that afternoon, in lighthearted sports. Chase had correctly given all adults the impression that he'd been alone when he hurt his knee; and now he was pretty sick, but nobody else was in any trouble at all.

We weren't even grateful to Chase for not incriminating us; we simply dismissed the affair from our minds, and, when Chase palely appeared among us again, some weeks later, neither he nor we more than briefly referred to it. In our whole procedure there appears to be a suggestion that the germs of unwritten and unspoken gangster law reside in the very nature of even the well-brought-up boy. If, however, the episode might seem to show forth human young male animals as lacking all capacity for sympathy, the deduction would be faulty.

With alarmed egoism not in the ascendant, any one of that group of boys could be—though perhaps secretly—as tender as a mother. My own sympathies sometimes kept me busy for hours at a time. I injuriously did my loving best with glue to repair a butterfly with a broken wing; I earnestly dosed and tended sick cats, and adopted, fed, and cherished a blind lost dog. Four newborn she-pups condemned by a neighbor to drown I begged of him and tried faithfully, in spite of jeering criticism, to raise on the bottle. I surreptitiously took large old gray rats from our cook's trap in the cellar, kept them in a straw-filled box in the stable until they made their escape;

then I worried about what would happen to them without my care and the regular three meals a day I'd been giving them. My usually impractical sympathies seem to have extended themselves so unduly, indeed, that I fear I may have been, after all, a sentimental boy.

By the end of July that summer, I was twelve and busy with the imitation of a classic—or at least ancient—dramatic work. I turned to it perhaps because I was a helpless duffer in both the minor and the major sports. I did no better with "mumble-peg" or jackstones or jackstraws than with baseball or marbles or kite flying; but I found that I could, however ineptly, carve and color wood into grotesque faces. Over the country, dime museums were beginning to be the precursors of ten-twenty-and-thirty theatrical entertainments; and at the new Indianapolis Dime Museum I'd been enraptured by a Punch-and-Judy show. I made one, myself, and had a neighborhood success with it; admission, ten pins.

Without difficulty I produced the peculiar vocalizings required by the antique drama; I improvised dialogue, embroidered the story, and provided my wooden-beaded actors with squeaked bits of song and recitative of my own composing. Something of the real showman being within me, I gave as many as three performances in a single afternoon to much the same audience, with mercenary intermissions while its members went home for more pins. To me, the accumulated pins, hoarded in a pasteboard box, mystically represented wealth, and it wasn't until I went upon a vacation visit that my Punch-and-Judy show was offered to the public for genuine money.

Where I went was to a little town that was a boy's sheer heaven. "Loveliest village of the plain," it lay in Illinois just beyond the Indiana border, an emeraldine jewel of a midland county seat in the earliest 8o's: old brick courthouse in the shady green square; stamping and switching farmers' teams hitched all day to the courthouse fence; monosyllabic loafers draped elsewhere upon this fence, whittling a little between reveries; stores sleeping in the sun all round the square; and Main Street stirless dust, except when a dust whirlwind flipped up from it to dance a moment in the sunshine. All the boys in Marshall went barefoot throughout the summer; meadows, woods, creeks, and old covered bridges were within a hop, skip, and jump from anywhere; nobody hurried and everybody seemed to know everybody else amusedly and without severity.

Marshall meant unhampered life and open country to me, a city boy; but also I had there, in my Uncle Lyman's commodious house, the companionship of two boys, my first cousins, the younger of whom, Fenton, was almost precisely my own age. Fenton Booth was a jolly boy given to laughter, mock speechmaking, and an unendurable kind of singing that sometimes upset me into such fits of fury as to delight his soul. On an earlier visit to

Marshall, he'd provided me with the one moment in my life when I was in a condition to attempt the murder of a fellow being, and did attempt it.

For hours indoors I'd been modeling a head out of a great wad of putty and paying no attention to Fenton's many shouted appeals to stop my senseless dabbing and come out and play. Finally he skipped in and, as I happened to turn my back, rushed upon the almost completed work of art that had so long absorbed me, and obliterated it instantaneously; only shapelessness remained. I flew at him, but he sped away, singing tauntingly:

> "Oh, remember while you're young
> That the days to you will come
> When you're old and only in the way!"

He was still singing when he reached the sunshiny village street and I found a brickbat in the dust. Cackling loudly his taunting song, he turned his head to laugh at me over his shoulder and wasn't ten feet from me when with all my force I threw the brickbat straight at his merry face. He hadn't thought me murderous, didn't believe I'd throw, but ducked a little anyhow, and one jagged edge of the brickbat passed swiftly through his hair. If he hadn't moved his head at all it's probable that an exalted judicatory body, the United States Court of Claims, in Washington, would subsequently have operated for many years under a less distinguished Chief Justice. The space of half an inch saved the life of a future personage, and proved to me that an artist, even when interrupted in his full passion of creation, shouldn't be too natural.

Fenton and I both looked at the brickbat where it lay guiltily in the dust, and before long he was able to sing again; but I stayed frightened about myself. I didn't go back to my wad of putty.

Two years later, when we were twelve and I came on this midsummer visit to Marshall, Fenton had become a journalist. His father had given him a printing press and the use of a small vacant warehouse. There, with village-boy subordinates, he had established a newspaper, *The Early Bird*, two cents a copy; and in Indianapolis I had received and admired a sample of every previous week's issue. Fenton wouldn't allow me to unpack my trunk, he was so eager to show me *The Early Bird* newspaper office, and himself and his subeditors, who were also printers, in action. When we got there, though, I was somewhat dashed.

Across the middle of the floor, from one end wall to the other, ran an old wooden balustrade, apparently to exclude the public—and the public, I learned at once, consisted of me. On the other side of the balustrade, Fenton and his assistants immediately busied themselves with the printing press, with their desks, pencils, and paper, shouting crisp orders at one another, setting up an elaborate professional bustle, and leaving me to contemplate a pasteboard sign, keep out, hung over my side of the balustrade! Without knowing it, I was filling the function of audience, and the efforts I made to become something better weren't encouraged. When finally, leaning plaintively over the railing, I asked if I couldn't even be elected or appointed one of the newsboys to deliver the paper to subscribers, nobody seemed to hear me. Then, as I persisted, I was requested not to make so much noise.

"Can't you see we're awful busy here?" Fenton said. "We got to get our paper out day after tomorrow, don't we? You get to look on, don't you? My goodness!"

When suppertime came, six o'clock in Marshall, I was still the public and, as we walked home, responded but feebly to Fenton's bright descriptions of editorial life. The next morning, however, he helped me to finish unpacking my trunk and surprised me by becoming warmly interested when I removed therefrom the dramatis personae of Punch and Judy.

"My goodness, Boothie! You can't make 'em talk, can you?"

I manipulated the puppets—Punch, Judy, their baby, the policeman, the devil, the crocodile—the whole cast—made them all talk.

"Hi!" Fenton shouted. "We'll give a show! We'll give a show the whole town of Marshall'll come to! Three cents admission! Hi!"

"Where?" I asked. "I haven't got any place where I can set up my Punch-and-Judy show."

"We got the best place in the world for our show, Boothie! *The Early Bird* office! First show tonight! Let's go!"

We went, and, with the help of the staff, *The Early Bird* office was energetically made into an auditorium. The balustrade was carried out into the warehouse yard; benches for the audience were improvised; the desks were shoved into corners, and so was the printing press after being used to produce a Punch-and-Judy handbill. Lanterns, candles, and coal-oil lamps were procured and, immediately after supper that night, the courthouse yard and the square were shrill with the voices of ex-editors and printers.

First Night

"Everybody come!" they shouted. "Right this way to *The Early Bird* office, to see the great Punch-and-Judy show! Step fast, laydeez and gentlemun; the great *Early Bird* Punch-and-Judy show's about to begin! Three cents admission for each and every one—only three cents admission for each and all!"

Within the close walls of my theater, a tall box sided with calico, I was busy arranging the puppets in the order of their appearance when I heard a trampling of full-grown feet upon the warehouse floor and the proclamations of Fenton outside: "Kindly step right in, laydeez and gentlemun! There is room for each and all at three cents apiece. Kindly take your places inside, please, without noise and confusion, on account of the Punch-and-Judy show's about to commence!" Then I heard his voice closer, "Kindly each and all sit down, please, without noise and confusion, laydeez and gentlemun. I will now start the show! Punch and Judy, are you ready?"

Responding, I quacked out the demoniac laughter of Punch and made the puppet appear, bowing, in the opening just over my head—to a surprising amount of applause. Punch and Judy can seldom have had a more appreciatively mirthful audience and, flattered, I made the show as long as I could. When I came forth from my enclosure, damp with exertions and the warm summer night, the last of our patrons, almost all adult, were laughing as they clumped away down the wooden sidewalk—and Fenton and his staff had yielded to money madness. We had taken in a dollar and forty-seven cents.

Tragedy in Two Acts

This sum was of course to be shared equally among us, but even so we were all prosperous, and computations already being shouted proved that the future glittered before us with gold as good as in our pockets. We couldn't do Punch and Judy again that night because Marshall went early to bed, but we could give our show every other night from then on unendingly, with a dollar and forty-seven cents as the least possible intake for every performance—the audience had been that enthusiastic! Ten nights would mean fourteen dollars and seventy cents; a hundred nights would bring us a hundred and forty-seven dollars, a sum dumfounding—but there were the figures that proved it was coming to us, and who could deny mathematics? Slightly insane with our certain riches, we went home to bed, babbling of intended purchases.

Again on the following evening thin voices sounded through the dusk of the courthouse yard and the square, "Right this way, laydeez and gentlemun, for the great Punch-and-Judy show! Step fast, laydeez and gentlemun! Only three cents admission for each and all, so hurry; the great Punch-and-Judy show's about to begin!" Tremulous, I stood in my calico enclosure listening for the feet of the undoubted multitude.

These feet didn't arrive, and one by one the heralds, appealing hurtly in the darkness, returned to the small warehouse. Punch and Judy played to an audience of three dumbly gum-chewing little children—nine cents—and the next night business fell off precisely that much. We waited and waited and waited, drooping about outside our lamplighted door, hearing ironical katydids, and looking up and down the dim night of the empty village street for at least a single patron. None appeared—a mystery inexplicable until our sunken minds slowly absorbed the fact: except the three children at our second performance, everybody in Marshall with three cents to spend on a show had been there the first night. There weren't any more.

The Early Bird had died too. In one day the theater had so wrecked the newspaper and printing establishment that even the thought of a restoration was laborious; the poor old balustrade remained among weeds in the warehouse yard, a reproachful relic.

Perhaps if I hadn't brought the Punch-and-Judy show to Marshall, Fenton might later have worn the ink-stains of an editor instead of the frown and gown of a judge. As for me, I think the exploded dazzle of Punch and Judy in Marshall did me, too, a service. Twenty years later, when a play of mine gave me a great warm-hearted audience for my first First Night, I didn't trust it.

IV. Trousers Transition

Turned twelve I had a long mortification, involving sufferings never comprehended by my parents. Sympathetic in all other matters, indulgent beyond what their means afforded, they were, nevertheless, merely amused whenever I strove to make plain to them the special bitterness that was eating me. Among all the weaknesses of my character, as I now examine it, I find my twelve-year-old excitement about what was on my inconsequent legs to be one of the most humiliatingly revelatory. I wasn't mortified by the dunderhead exhibitions I made of myself in the schoolroom; I wasn't mortified by the disgraceful statistics reported by the teachers on damning cards sent to my parents after examinations; I wasn't mortified by the batting of my eyes and fluctuations of my nose and ears in public, or by my throat's clucking and glunking at people when I tried to talk to them. No; custom had dulled me to these inevitabilities—so I regarded them—and what made me so ashamed that I didn't see how I could bear to go on living, unless I could effect a change, was the fact that I still wore knee breeches.

Boys of later generations will not understand this, least of all now when four-year-olds of both sexes are freely betrousered to the instep, but for a long period in American history boys were universally convinced that the first splendid step forward toward manhood was getting into long trousers. Immediately upon that uplifting enclosure we believed ourselves freed of the most poignantly offensive of all adjectives—"little." A boy in long trousers wasn't, ruinously, a little boy any more; he was a boy—in fact, almost a youth. Some of us, pets of destiny in being granted careless parents, accomplished the great change at ten; more were emancipated at eleven; and at twelve only a few were fondly and fashionably still pinioned down in knee-breeched little-boyness. Purgatorially, I was one of these.

Clothes Unmake the Man

With the peculiar aid of a grandfather, I had attempted a great stroke to improve my condition. Grandfather and Grandmother Booth spent the winters with us now; and he, almost ninety, retaining the fashion of the considerable men of his day, never wore outer garments except of dark broadcloth. Without difficulty I talked him into giving me two elderly pairs of his trousers and a dollar, and these I bore to a wearied foreign tailor with whom I'd been privately conducting urgent negotiations. I was small for my age, and my grandfather was of normal size for his; but the tailor was sure that even for a dollar he couldn't get enough good cloth out of one pair of trousers somewhat worn; so there had to be two. The garment he made for me I brought home through the dusk of an eager day, and, examining the work by gaslight in my own room, I believed that I had a pair of trousers equal to any youth's in the world.

After breakfast the next morning I put them on, got out of the house unobserved, and, on my way to school, walked down the street in a man's sunlight. I went most of the way without passing anybody, then at a corner encountered a long shabby male person with auburn thin whiskers—I remember them. He observed me with some attention and burst into a loud, discordant laugh.

He upset me, rather, though I hadn't the faintest idea what was the matter with him. At long last here I was, properly clad for the first time in years! He must be a doggone fool, I thought; something must be wrong with him to just look at a person and laugh like that. It appeared that even in long trousers you could never tell what whisker-growing adults were likely to do.

Making myself right for this life had brought me late to school, and when I reached my seat in the back row the teacher called upon me to come forward to her desk and try to explain my tardiness. I was so used to doing this, and my classmates were so accustomed to seeing me do it, that it was virtually routine; but as I passed down the aisle a titter followed me. It increased, grew louder irrepressibly, and, as I stood enduring it in the open space before the teacher, it attained the full volume of unanimous schoolroom laughter. I turned in plaintive inquiry; the teacher tapped her pencil sharply upon the desk, and then, as I turned back to her, I found that she'd grown red and seemed unable to express herself.

Feeling naked, I looked down at me, and saw only perfection. My mind was lost in mystification as she indistinctly dismissed me to my seat and I returned to it through a spluttering aisle.

At recess, immediately surrounded, I moved helplessly as the center of a ring of mirth lovers who made but one response to all my inquiries: "Look at your britches!"

I did, again and again, but without enlightenment. Not until I was on my homeward way for lunch did a true friend help me to discover what my dreamy grandfather hadn't considered, what I in my happy haste hadn't observed, and what the tailor hadn't worried himself about.

"It's your britches," Henry told me. "They're different colors."

"But they aren't!" I cried. "They're just black! Haven't I looked a thousand times?"

"Yea, but you keep looking down at you in front," he said. "Maybe the nap in back's turned a different way from the nap in front, or maybe they're made out of somebody else's different britches; but you may be black in front, but you're gray behind. Anyhow you're different colors."

I was; and a few seconds after I reached home my agony in Grandfather Booth's mixed trousers was over. The kind old man, lost in reverie, didn't even notice that he never saw me in them. I gave him up as an ally.

Back into knee breeches and little-boyness again, I brooded longingly upon the far future when I'd be twenty-one and legally independent of a mother's care. Especially on Saturdays, on my way to dancing school, I made plans for my twenty-first birthday, when I'd begin never wearing overshoes any more and would decline ever again to have anything whatever fastened on me with pins. I wouldn't wear a white collar outside my jacket collar; I'd have a collar from a men's store and it would be made secure with collar buttons. I wouldn't have a wide silk ribbon under the collar and I wouldn't permit any woman to tie such a ribbon into a bow under my chin; I'd have a ready-made necktie fastened with a buckle. And most of all I wouldn't let any woman brush my hair; I'd have a barber come to the house every morning before breakfast and brush my hair for the day, no matter what he charged.

Dancing school was in the ballroom of the finest and largest house in Indianapolis, a neighbor's; but that didn't brighten my performances and undergoings there. I was no better at dancing than I was at anything else I tried to do with my feet, or hands, or both. Round and round the great room the small couples went, while the piano tinkled and the professor called: "One, two, three! One, two, three! One, two, three!"—and almost every single time any little girl shouted "Ouch!" it was because I'd stepped on her. Whenever I took my place in one of the formations for the quadrille or lancers, all the other participants looked about to see if they couldn't get into another; and in the whole of my dancing-school experience, just one encouraging thing happened. It didn't encourage me long.

At the center of the polished floor the most beautiful of the little girls—the star in all the dancing—stood holding a small round cap in her hand; and all the boys, under instructions from the professor, circled about her, learning a special figure of the dance then called the "german." She was to place the cap upon the head of the boy with whom she wished to dance—and, startlingly, she stepped toward him who least expected to be chosen. Dazed, I felt the cap upon my transfigured head. Intoxicated, blue lights swimming about me, I danced with her, walked upon her little slippers, slid, skidded, staggered, bumped into everybody and floundered in Elysium. When it was over, another true friend of mine whispered to me congratulatingly:

"I'm glad Nellie picked you. It's nice because some of the class think she's stuck-up, but this proves to everybody how kindhearted she is."

So it did—even to me.

Another maiden of the class showed kindness to me, or at least was philosophic and bore pain stoically; for, though her sensitive small face quivered, she never outright screeched when I stepped on her. I ill-requited her goodness. She was the littlest girl, exquisite, but only five years old, and, when her evil star doomed her to be my partner and I went clumping round the ballroom, towing her fairylike lightness and usually damaging it, I had no thought for her, but only pitied myself for looking too much the bigger half of an ill-assorted couple.

Jesse James, a Tragedy in Fourteen Acts

This self-pity was what caused me finally to write a note to her, palliating my absence from the last meeting of the dancing class that year, an occasion upon which the poor child was to have been my partner for the whole session. Fifteen years later, when in full-grown loveliness she burst upon me, so to speak, at another kind of dance and I entreated to be her partner, however briefly, she said yes, if I'd behave better than last time. Then she repeated verbatim the note I'd sent her "last time," for her mother still kept it in a scrapbook. Long after that, when I was writing a story about a boy who was not at all myself, though of course here and there, in scattered spots, a slight reflection of bits of me, I printed the note as his; and this was it:

> *Dear Madam:* Please excuse me from dancing the cotillion with you this afternoon as I have fell off the barn
>
> Sincerely yours,
> Newton Booth Tarkington.[1]

When summer again approached and I was near upon thirteen, still in knee breeches, I'd begun to grow lanky and I completed the manuscripts

---

1. The fictional letter-writer was Penrod Schofield, who really does fall off the stable roof, in *Penrod*.

of two literary works. The first was a play, purest realism and also tragedy unmitigatedly. It dealt with the rise of its hero to great heights of ill fame, detailed not only his deeds of thievery but several accompanying murders; and it reached its climax and last curtain with his assassination—shot in the back as he stood on a chair hanging a picture, his destroyer being inexorably one of his own followers who, like most people, wanted to make some money. This play, I firmly recall, was a very model of austere playwriting; it conveyed no moral, had no bias, petted none of the "characters," and, with the icy Olympian detachment that is the mark of the highest type of authorship, sought only to reveal its people by their own uncompelled acts and utterances. Its title had the esthetic starkness of the rest of it—*Jesse James*.

The cast was all male. In the last act only two appeared, the hero and his assassin; and both the action and the dialogue here stood forth in sharp relief against nothing—a masterpiece of that elimination of nonessentials now so favored in all the arts. Space permits me to quote the entire act. This was it:

ACT 14

Enter JESSE JAMES and BOB FORD.

JESSE: Well it is a nice day so I believe I will get on this chair and hang this picture up on the wall.

BOB: All right do.

JESSE gets up on the chair so BOB shoots him in the back with his revolver. JESSE falls off of the chair and dies down on the floor.

CURTAIN

Our stable being vacant for the time, except of vehicles, I directed, rehearsed, and produced *Jesse James* in the empty hayloft, coming thus into competition with another active theater two blocks up the alley. This other theater, also in a hayloft, was pretentious; and I visited it in a purely critical spirit. Its great boast was that it had a Gallery, a dangerous structure holding four, admission to the Gallery being five cents instead of the three cents charged for a safer and more comfortable seat nearer the stage.

Wearing an intendedly scornful expression, I paid the higher price, sat in the Gallery, and soon became aware of something familiar in the play enacted before me. I seemed to perceive certain resemblances—especially when one of the boys, wrapped in a previously white tablecloth, said to another: "Listen here; you listen now. You're my son and I used to be your father; but now I'm his ghost and you got to do something because, listen, I was lying down somewheres taking a nap, and—well, your uncle came sneaking around and he poured some kind of stuff in my ear, and so—well, so it killed me, so now I'm a ghost, and after that he and your mother got married, so now you got to get after him."

Mingling with the audience, and also with the actors, after the play, I made myself offensive, telling everybody that plagiarism had taken place. What we'd seen was nothing but Hamlet, I declared. However, nobody knew what I was talking about, not even the manager-author-actor, Johnny Geiger, the fattest boy in Indianapolis, who'd played the avenging son of the ghost. It was openly said that I was jealous: and I openly was, not yet having learned to conceal my viler emotions and knowing myself too clumsy a carpenter to attempt a five-cent Gallery for my own theater.

Box-Office Publicity

A few days later, however, while *Jesse James* was still in rehearsal, we had a triumph, one that our whole cast felt scored all over Johnny Geiger's theater. We found ourselves in a newspaper. On the face of it, the item was wholly laudatory. Its writer praised the inspirational seizure upon a recent happy event in the Western border town of St. Jo, Mo., for a drama theme, promised the audience "many a thrill," gave the cast of characters, and declared that just the scenery, let alone the acting, would be worth anybody's three cents. Members of our company of players, seeing their names in print for the first time in their lives, glowed with enthusiasm for themselves; and so did I for me—until I read the last sentence for the third or fourth time: "The author of this dramatic chef-d'oeuvre, himself of course to appear in the title role as Jesse James, is Master Newton Booth Tarkington, whose hairs have been whitened by the snows of some thirteen summers."

Thinking this over, I somehow didn't quite like it. There appeared to be a covert meaning in that bit about my hairs having been whitened by the snows of thirteen summers, and I didn't altogether believe in the newspaper's sincerity. My colleagues, on the contrary, felt that the unexampled publicity assured us a vast audience. Bright boyish souls, they weren't disappointed when the great afternoon of the single performance arrived and our "box office" amounted to twenty-one cents, all paid by little girls, since every boy of the neighborhood not included in the cast proudly stayed away.

After Page Chapman, as Bob Ford, had shot me in the back with a cap pistol and I'd fallen from the chair and died thumpingly on the floor, the audience remained seated, stupidly expectant of something more, and maybe better, until I had to step forth and ask them if they didn't have sense enough to know when a play was over, so why on earth didn't they go home.

First Poem

I had a sense of anticlimax, a feeling that remained with me for some time after the production of this, my first play, which was also my first literary work to be completed. The second, a month or two afterward, had a success that astonished me. I mean a success with other people; I wasn't astonished when what I did was a success with myself.

I wrote and illustrated something I conceived to be a poem. The two illustrations, in subconscious imitation of most illustrators, weren't closely related to the text. One was the drawing of a capped-and-belled jester—a popular theme at the time—and he was depicted on a bare hilltop in a tragic posture, careless of the adjacent lightning of a thunderstorm. The other drawing showed him sitting under a tree, quiet, but looking as sad as I could make him look. I bound the two pictures into a little pamphlet, and between them I placed a page of my rhymed meditation:

THE TREES

When the soul knows but sadness
   No hope and no gladness
Then the soul in its sighing
Finds rest in leaves dying
   And shadows of leaves at play.
When the soul knows but sorrow
   And the birth of tomorrow
Will bring but the death of today
   Turns the soul to the trees
   Moving cool in the breeze
Keeping time to the summer's sigh
   Finds rest and finds sadness
But no hope and no gladness
   For the Trees answer not
     Passion's cry.

I left this output, as if inadvertently, upon the library center table, and withdrew modestly to the yard, where, lingering beneath an open window of the library, I heard 'ere long a favorable commotion within the house—the two ladies of my family in a state of exclamation. Then my mother came rushing forth, calling me loudly. When I appeared unto her, walking slowly and asking with odious affectation, "Now what's all the matter?" she fairly shouted over me, embraced me effusively, and took me into the house to read my "poem" to me, and to my congratulatory sister, over and over.

My mother was convinced that it was a poem and that I was a poet and an artist. Never in her fond life had she made such an enraptured fuss over me; her delight was so exorbitant, indeed, that I had almost the grace to blush and to feel the rightful guilt of a person who knows himself overpraised. Her joy of me didn't end with the moment or the day. She sent copies of my "poem" to kinsfolk near and far, and altogether was so triumphant that now, in retrospect, I wonder! Her sudden and uplifted excitement over "The Trees" seems to indicate a previous lengthy depression during which she must have been fearing that she'd brought something pretty flat into the world.

From that day, I think, she was always a little different with me, and always, even when I brought her grief, treated me as if I contained something precious that must be cherished. I'd just had my thirteenth birthday when I composed the verses that so moved her, and now I had no more opposition to the discarding of knee breeches. Besides long trousers, I was allowed to wear shirts with stiff bosoms, collar buttons, hard cylindrical cuffs, and a ready-made necktie fastened with a buckle, not pins. My collars, from the haberdasher's, pleased me most. Rigid upright white linen bands, they bore on the inner side of them, distinctly printed, a label: Youth's First Base. Size 13. I was a youth. My collars said so.

The Marks of a Dude

A new word had begun to appear in the American vocabulary, supplanting "fop," "swell," and "dandy." This word signified the disappearance of an old type of exquisite gentleman and the emergence of a novel creature among us, called the "dude." The previous sample, the swell, had been given to long Dundreary side whiskers, velvet jackets, loose pantaloons, and wide open collars. The dude was marked particularly by the extreme height of his round white cylinder of a collar, by the spoon-shaped crown of his hard hat, by his razor-pointed shoes, by the flare of the skirts of his Chesterfield black frock coat, by the shortness of his fawn overcoat, and, above all, by such tightness of his trousers that no one could explain how he got his feet through them. It was important, too, that the trousers should show no crease, for a crease disgracefully proved the garment to be a "hand-me-down"—that is, not made by a tailor, but handed down from the shelf of a shop where ready-made clothes were kept folded.

Dudes appeared spontaneously, it seemed, upon the streets of cities all over the country, increasing in numbers just after the commencements of the Eastern colleges. The dudes carried slim, twirly canes and were regarded by the sturdier population as insufferable because of their clothes and because they smoked cigarettes. It was thought permissible for children to prance burlesquingly behind a sample of this new species on the street, squawking, "Yay, come look at the dude! Look at the dude! Look at the dude!"

I didn't wish to be a dude precisely; I only hoped to be well dressed. My new long trousers were moderate, not skintight, and my Youth's First Base collars were only an inch high, whereas a true dude's collar was sometimes thrice that. On the other hand, it's true I may have taken some pride in feeling that a Youth's First Base was perhaps a little bit dude-ish, and no doubt my manner became rather self-consciously youthly. Anyhow, I laid myself open to a criticism I received one day from a volunteer.

I was returning from an errand downtown when the converging perspective of the sidewalk revealed in the distance the figures of three boys coming from the opposite direction. Perceiving these to be strangers to me, I had a nervous flutter in the chest and hoped that they would turn into a cross street instead of coming to a near view of me. Most grown men have forgotten and few women ever know, I suppose, what a boy feels when he sees even one other boy, a stranger, approaching on the same side of the street. No more than a dog who sees a strange dog coming does either boy know what is going to happen; and, both with boys and dogs, anything may. Even at thirteen the passage may become an encounter; at the best it will be an embarrassment.

The three approaching figures, three times worse than one, didn't turn into a side street, and, as they drew nearer, I perceived them to be wholly undude-ish, sturdy fellows and already too much interested in me. Rabbit-minded, I thought of crossing to the opposite sidewalk; but in their look I read that it would be a tactical error, so I came on slowly, frowning as if preoccupied with business computations. When we were almost face to face I courteously made way, gave them the sidewalk, and moved out to the curbstone to pass them; but they impeded me. The smallest of the three placed his distended chest unpleasantly against me.

Of my age, though shorter than I, he was so sternly assured of himself and so iron of morale that even had he lacked the backing of his larger friends he might have been able to impose his will upon me. He had a lumpily modeled face which, as he pressed it upon me, was scarlet with a manly fury. He breathed loudly and his voice loosed the violence of an offended person who knows his right to resent gratuitous injury.

"You listen!" he said. "I can tell all about you by just lookin' at you and it makes me mad! It'd make this whole town mad just to look at you! You try to be a dude, but you ain't. You think that's a dude's collar, but it ain't. I wouldn't even laugh at it! You want to be a dude, but it ain't in you. Go on home and give up!"

I said nothing; he seemed to be unanswerable, and by no means did I realize that I was having a peculiar experience in which I should have been interested not only as a participant but as an observer. Rarely indeed does anybody come in contact with a critical faculty so roused as to demonstrate to a stranger that his mere outward appearance makes people actually angry.

"Go on home!" the stern boy said, with imperious gestures. "Go on and quit tryin' to look like somebody. Go on; you hear me? Go home!"

I went, not looking back. I was impaired, vacant inside, and feared that my face, as well as my clothes, offered a too visible stimulant to such estimates of me. Besides this impulsive critic, maybe a whole lot of other people, when they happened to see me, felt a pressure to relieve themselves similarly. Life, it began to seem, could at any moment become startlingly unfavorable. One went about one's business—which might be no more than to walk absently in the sunshine of a placid day—then suddenly, out of nowhere, there might be in the path something that wanted to bite. The sensations I endured that afternoon were to be many, many times undergone later in my life until what is called "philosophy" should come to the rescue; for, though I then little suspected it, I was to follow one of those callings that of their very nature bring not one but a horde of critics, seemingly out of nowhere, to beset the path indignantly.

"... And one man in his time plays many parts, his acts being seven ages"; but I think seventy would be truer—if the man live so long—and thirteen and fourteen and fifteen and sixteen and seventeen are among the most ignominious of all the ages.

At thirteen, believing myself now proved to be certainly a youth, I was continually rebuffed because I thought my youthness entitled me to privileges. Only to be ignored, I interrupted grown people in their talk. Only to be sat upon, I gave forth my opinions pompously in a voice that had begun to change and went falsetto inopportunely. In company I tried to wear an expression of airy superiority that strained the muscles of my face, especially when I wasn't well received. I was archly humorous at the wrong times and got my feelings hurt for insisting upon being an inappropriate joker. When I tried to be winsomely lively, I was like to damage furniture;

and when at table I illustrated a narrative with dramatic gestures, I upset the coffeepot to an accompaniment of dolorous cries.

An Obnoxious Little Brother

Of all my objectionablenesses the worst were those I put upon my unresentful sister. She was a girl of happy disposition, witty always goodnaturedly; she possessed in high degree what were then called "accomplishments," and she was distinguishedly handsome. Gentlemen various in their ages were charmed by her, came to our house in numbers assiduously, sent copious offerings—bouquets in filigreed paper, long boxes of loose flowers, many boxes of candy—and suffered from me as stoically as they could. I was the most intrusive nuisance of a "little brother" that I have known; I had a powerful curiosity about every one of these gentlemen and must have been almost impossible to be rid of. I corrected mistakes they sometimes made if they spoke of history, proffered a connoisseur's suggestions in all matters, and often took the lead in conversation, no matter how microscopic the encouragement. When suitors were not present, I played the lofty humorist and made fun of them to my sister, not discriminating between those she liked and those she didn't; but there was one among them of whom I never spoke lightly and with whom I was never pushy, for he enchanted me.

He had first come to our house when I was about eleven. I remember the brightness of my mother's face on the morning when she first spoke of him to me. "Someone's coming here this afternoon," she said. "Someone different from anybody you've ever seen. Someone delightful! He's coming to see your sister, but you can meet him, too, if you stay indoors, and I think you'll be pretty glad."

I stayed indoors, met him, and was glad. Never had a grown person unaffectedly treated me so completely as a natural-born equal. In his manner toward me, as toward everybody else, there was neither self-assertion nor indulgence. Moreover, never had I seen anybody at all like him. He didn't look in the least like anybody I'd ever seen; his talk wasn't like anybody else's, and he was gayer than anybody I'd ever met. He didn't try to be different from other people; he tried to be like them. His pale blond hair was trimmed close to his head, brushed sleekly, and his dress was of a dignified elegance; but nothing could make commonplace the inexpressible jauntiness of his carriage, the eloquence of his large nose and comedian's long upper lip, or the glinting blue lights behind his twinkling nose glasses. No description of him in words, however, can more than hint a little of him;

nor, for that matter, does Sargent's portrait of him, nor the bronze statue of him that stands at the center of his native town.

He was not yet out of his twenties, that day when my boyish gaze first fascinatedly rested upon him; and, though his name was already a household word in Indiana, his fame hadn't spread till it reached into every farmhouse in the United States. In his own lifetime it did that, though he never carried the consciousness of fame about him, knew its fluctuant value, and wouldn't be surprised now if in his seat among laureled national poets he could hear a radio-program quiz identifying James Whitcomb Riley principally as the author of Little Orphant Annie!

From the first, his manner with my sister, like hers with him, was of the liveliest mock coquetry; they were having a tremendous affair in which there was nothing—nothing but gaiety. It was a pretty friendship, none the less devoted and long for being pretty, and, having first come to see my sister, he thenceforth came to see the whole family, of which in no time at all he appeared to be virtually a member. When my sister wasn't at home he'd spend hours with my father and mother and me, or with any one of us, if the others were lacking; and for me those many hours never ceased to be of gold.

Hobnobbing with Greatness

He'd linger a whole afternoon, sometimes with me alone; perhaps describing a play he'd seen, and acting it better—even then I knew—than had the actors—or, it might be, telling me the story of a book he'd read, and acting it, too, and so truly that the book's author must have been tearful with self-appreciation if he'd been there. What he loved was the realities of human character and the fine expressions of these by artists with accurate ears and eyes. Romances and romancing, mere hero-and-heroine adventure make-believe, he detested as heartily as he did the ponderous humorlessness of the French realism with which Zola was then beginning to stimulate the long succession of followers who still urge upon us the dismal dirtiest of life as the most of it.

Mr. Riley could find a story to tell, or a poem to write, in any slightest thing on earth if it had significance. A rooster standing on one leg under a bush in a thundershower absorbed him; and, telling you about it, he stood one-legged himself and became so anxiously the very rooster that you felt the wetness of the rain upon him. Mr. Riley, not a satirist, didn't feel superior to the rooster, didn't jeer at him for holding up the leg; he loved him for it, and was delightedly excited by divination of the plaintive thought in the bird's head: "Well, maybe I can keep one of my feet dry, anyhow!"

Sometimes the poet came in the afternoon, stayed to dinner, took me for a stroll in the dark afterward, and, as we walked, would seem to consult me—always with the air of one man, or boy, to another—upon verses or phrases or, possibly, the whole of a poem that he was in the process of composing. In tremulous pleasure I walked beside him hushed, only murmuring my responses and, knowing my privilege, hoping for more and more from him. I wasn't puffed up by his seeming to appoint me to the office of critic; even at eleven and twelve and thirteen I had at least the sense to know that he was only "trying it on the dog," and I asked for nothing lovelier than to be the dog.

Mr. Riley's Collaborator

Mr. Riley didn't inspire me, as the phrase goes, to write or to wish to be a writer. I had no such desire, though long I'd not infrequently found myself writing something, usually a fragment—probably the pompous rendition of a thought I thought I had or the beginning of a story that stopped after a page or two. What I wanted to do was to draw and paint, especially to draw. School hours had become, permanently, interminable periods of tedium for me. Under cover of the pupil's back before me I spent the time drawing irrelevantly, and throughout almost the whole of suppositious study hours at home I covered the margins of my textbooks with clumsily fantastic pencilings instead of trying to digest instructive print. Mr. Riley helped me with my drawing, showed me anatomical relations in the human body I'd not even suspected, and encouraged me not to draw all of my people in profile facing left.

Sometimes he'd spend the greater part of an evening drawing with me, and once, while I was still a schoolboy, he went so far as to ask me for suggestions about the cover of his first "full-size book." It was to be a paper cover; and for it he'd designed an ink bottle mounted as a cannon firing a charge that exploded into the words that were to be the title of the book. When he'd sketched the design, I drew upon the paper an imp flying downward from the top of the page and, with the point of a long quill pen applied to the touchhole, firing the ink-bottle cannon. The idea pleased the poet; he made much of it and of me, and the book was printed with my imp upon the cover. Whenever he talked to me of *The Boss Girl* he spoke as if to a fellow workman who'd had much to do with the book's creation and rightfully shared credit in its modest success. I glowed, but didn't swell. In all my relations with the good and true poet, mercy from on high vouchsafed that I should know my place.

No other boy could ever have had precisely just such a friend—and yet there were times when I could wholly forget him and the fact that I knew him. That was when we saw him on the stage of a theater and he gave "readings" from his poems. Then he turned himself into other people—a middle-aged Indiana farmer, an old Civil War veteran, half a dozen different types of children—and cast a spell of such moving reality upon the transformations that the artist himself was utterly forgotten, though we, his audience, sat roaring with laughter, or weeping, at his will. Suddenly it would be over; like sleepers waking, we'd come from another world and there again before us we'd see Mr. Riley himself walking off the stage, a quiet blond gentleman in excellent evening clothes.

Never in a life somewhat experienced in such spectacles have I seen any other comedian or tragedian so accurately lead an audience where he would, and never have I known other poet or other author so loved by the people of his time. In Indiana we had great personages then. It was warmly to our pride that General Wallace had written *The Fair God*, and, with *Ben Hur*, was read throughout the whole world. In Indianapolis fellow citizens and neighbors of ours were political figures on the national scale. Governor Hendricks was to be Vice President soon, and Gen. Benjamin Harrison moved, in his stately way, toward the presidency itself; but first in the hearts of his countrymen, Hoosiers—and to remain there all his life—was their poet. He didn't seek to be first; he was.

There can't have been many better times or places in which to be a poet—or a boy—or anybody. Youth recollected in age always trickily casts its spell, of course; but I deduct this necromancy and still find that period to have been the Golden Age, with the last decades of horse-and-buggy days the best of it all. For myself, at thirteen and running into fourteen and fifteen, I was so dull in school, and such a butterfingers when we played ball, that the memory pictures of the evenings—the summer evenings at home—are what make recollection wistfullest.

Our house, shrouded in the ivies and Virginia creeper that my mother and father loved, loomed in the warm night under an Indiana moon, and all the neighborhood would be scented by the wild-crab tree in bloom in our back yard. On the side porch that was veiled by drooping vines, my father would sit reflective behind the garnet spark of his cigar. From the distance there'd be heard the cries and laughter of children playing Hi-spy after dark, and from the street the soft plod-plod of horses' hoofs on wetted dust as a family carriage or a surrey or phaeton lightly rumbled by, out for the evening drive. My mother, if she wasn't on the veranda swaying a fringed small fan beside my father, would be in the library reading—that month's *Century* or *Harper's* probably—beside the gas droplight; and in the large room we called the "drawing-room" there might be, besides my sister, another girl or two, attendant gentlemen, and all too possibly the egregious little brother, me.

I wasn't invariably perceived to be there. With all my outrageous curiosity I wasn't intentionally a spy, but had a deadly habit of lying on the floor to read, either under the piano or beneath a large sofa, my book pushed into the light that fell behind; and I was often unnoticed until I spoke out upsettingly when I felt called upon to improve the conversation with better ideas. I had none to offer, though, when my sister came to the piano and sang.

She'd always studied music, and her music masters had developed in her a soprano voice of grand-opera power, range, and dramatic capacity to express and produce feeling—a startling voice for a chance passer-by to hear coming from the open windows of a house in a midland town on a summer's night. When she sang, the plod-plod of the horses going by would cease to be heard; the family carriages and surreys and phaetons and buggies, halting one by one, would fill the street, all silent; and strolling pedestrians paused, listeners gathering in deep, still clusters all along the sidewalk, while the high moon itself seemed to stop overhead to listen to that lovely voice.

Under the moons of those summer nights all was well. Throughout the town and throughout the wide quiet countryside beyond, men rested after the hot day and with easy hearts thought of the morrow. No one was anxious for America; and all through the world—except, perhaps, where sporadic tribesmen raided on the Congo—there was peace. I hear again my sister singing on the summer nights of long ago and think of the good world we had then. Ah, yes, it was the Golden Age!

My sister had other gifts besides that of music, and one of them was so strange, and its discovery came into our placid family life so suddenly, and yet with so subtle an appearance of being a natural, matter-of-course reality, that we were amazed, but wondered that we were not more so. It changed the basic character of the thoughts of all of us, and still for me is a part of the ancient and eternal cryptogram, the schoolboy's question: "What is life?"

V. Where Do We Go from Here?

I was fourteen when the experiences with a force unknown to us began in our house. We'd sometimes heard prattle of such foldariddles and laughed when credulous souls told us of table tippings and inexplicable rappings on walls and tables—nonsense always easily to be explained by "natural causes," we were certain. Rats, the wind, creaky woodwork, or crackly knuckles and sleight of hand were the right answers to shabby miracles, we said; and I was the loudest in scorn of all spectral bugaboos. Had not I, with other boys, gone after nightfall to a half-decayed little cemetery? Had we not pushed through its shroud of underbrush; and, seated upon gravestones, hadn't we valiantly told ghost stories in the dark of the moon? It's not difficult to be brave against ghosts when we're sure there aren't any. He who's never met one can explain them all away.

It was on a bright Sunday afternoon and I was reading in the library when my sister and another girl and three young men came indoors from a walk and sat down about a table in the drawing room; whereupon I glanced through the open double doorway, became scornfully interested, then went to look on talkatively. They'd decided to see if they could "make a table move," and they bore my freshness amiably because they, skeptical, too, were only whiling away an idle bit of the afternoon.

The table, inlaid mahogany, was heavy, though not large; they sat with their arms outstretched, their fingers resting upon its top, but otherwise no one touched it. After ten minutes or so, as the table remained coldly immobile, they began to laugh at themselves rather boredly and would have given up; but someone said, "Oh, well, since we've started, why not give it a really good try?"

They did, and ten or fifteen minutes more may have passed before the table began to stir. It moved a few inches, then several feet, and they all stood up, keeping the tips of their fingers upon it and moving with it as it slowly progressed across the floor. All of them laughed, yet were puzzledly interested, as was I. The table moved over the thick Brussels carpet erratically; it would go four or five feet in one direction, then in another; then it would move back upon its tracks, then forward again. There was no tension visible in any of the fingers resting upon it; the young people were a little excited, not much, and the sense of what they exclaimed was that though they'd heard that tables could be made to move like this, they'd never believed it.

When the table had worked its aimless way across the drawing room and almost through the open double doorway into the parlor, somebody made the suggestion, "Let's see if it moves for any one of us more than it does for the others. Let's each in turn take our fingers off and see if it stops."

They did this; and, when it came my sister's turn to remove her fingers, the table stopped, declined to move another inch. When she returned her fingers to the table top, the thing waited some moments; then renewed its motion. Again experimenting, the others all took away their hands, leaving only hers upon the table, and its movement continued. With her finger tips upon it, the table passed into the parlor, came back rather quickly—so that she was walking backward, with the table pushing toward her—then it zigzagged wanderingly about the drawing room.

The Drawing-Room Riddle

My sister, like the others, was puzzled half laughingly—impressed, like them, somewhat as children are when for the first time they see a steel needle hop to a magnet with no visible cause for the hop. It's interesting for a while, but not forever. One of the young men looked at his watch; they were all expected somewhere else by now for iced tea and cake; so they gaily took themselves off, my sister with them, and I heard them chattering as they passed through the hall to the front door, saying things like "That table certainly was queer"; "I can't see any explanation at all"; "Never believed it before, but it really did"; and "Let's hurry, we're late!"

None of them wondered if my sister, by either muscular power or trickery, had made the table move; it was plain that she couldn't have done so. She wasn't athletic, she was fragile; and she wasn't a prestidigitator. Sleight of hand bored her; she never attempted even a card trick and was always mystified by the simple ones with which at times she patiently let me try to dazzle her. Broad sunshine had poured into the room through four large windows while the table moved; there was no possible illusion. My father was a muscularly powerful man, accurately adroit in the use of his strong hands; and I knew that with his finger tips he couldn't make that table move as it had moved for my sister's.

"Funny business," I thought. "I'd not believe it if I hadn't seen it, but it seems to be true that tables do move for some people, and Hautie must be one of them." That, for the time, was my whole thought upon the matter; and, within half an hour, having joined a group of contemporaries on the veranda of the house next door, I let the episode slide into an obscuring recess of my mind. A needle or bit of steel would move to a magnet without anybody pushing it, and a table would do much the same thing, on a larger scale; and that was all. Affairs of my own preoccupied me; at home I didn't happen to speak of the table-moving, and, during the next months, if I remembered the incident at all, it was but vaguely. I didn't know that my sister had several times repeated the original experiment, and then had shown my mother and father what happened if she sat or stood for a while with her fingers upon the top of a table. They could no more find an explanation than could she herself; but, their curiosity aroused, they'd had her "move tables" again and again—and these inspired pieces of furniture, content at first with mere motion, developed a new activity.

One evening late in the year, when I'd been somewhere about the neighborhood, I returned at nine o'clock, my curfew hour; and, as I left my hat and overcoat in the hall, I heard peculiar sounds from the drawing room: two or three people seemed to be tapping sharply upon wood, either with their fingernails or with the blunt ends of lead pencils, while another thumped heavily with his knuckles. These noises ceased, and I heard my father's voice slowly reciting the alphabet. Stumped, I went into the room, came to a halt, stared, and listened.

Under the lighted gas chandelier in the center of the room, my mother and my sister and Mr. Riley sat with their outstretched hands upon the inlaid-mahogany table, no other part of them—no knees or feet—touching it. At a little distance from them, in easy chairs, my Grandmother and Grandfather Booth looked on with a grave tensity; and my father sat a little nearer to the table with a pad of paper upon his knee. It was the table that was making the tapping and thumping sounds, and they seemed to come from its smooth surface, upon which nothing visible moved. There were no drawers in that table nor any loose part that could be made to rattle.

Nobody paid any attention to me; and I drew closer, strongly disapproving, but enough impressed to be silent. My father finished writing something on his tablet; then began to recite the alphabet slowly again, whereupon the table became noiseless. Suddenly its thumpings were renewed; father interrupted himself, and there ensued a dialogue that was, as nearly as I can remember, about as follows:

"Is G or H the letter you want?" my father asked. "Is it G?"

The table thumped twice.

"Not G, then," my father said. "You want H. Is that right?"

The table thumped three times.

Mr. Riley laughed. "Yes; I recognized it. That's my brother again." This I was to hear him say many times in the future; for those special thumpings were always to resound whenever he happened to be present at such sittings. "That H is for Hum," he said. "It's Hum Riley. That's you, isn't it, Hum?"

Thereupon the table thumped effusively; thumpings were heard all over it and under it and also seemingly within it. Almost riotously the table expressed pleasure.

I felt greatly annoyed. This was an affair I didn't like and in which, despite the evidence of my senses, I didn't believe. In particular I was disturbed by my father's seriousness over something that simply had to be pure nonsense; and this whole group of people, all dear to me and previously reverenced, seemed engaged in queer processes discreditable to their intelligence. On the other hand, the table was certainly peculiar. I sat down, watched, and listened.

The thumpings continued—obviously expressing to Mr. Riley the exuberance of his jovial brother, Hum, who had died young—and, with the aid of the recited alphabet, they thumped out a message. What it was I've forgotten, except that it was of merry import to Mr. Riley, who seemed to believe—as indeed he heartily did—that his dead brother was actually present. Not accepting this improbability, I nevertheless saw plainly that none of the living persons present was by any bodily means causing the thumpings. The room was brightly lighted and trickery visibly impossible even if it hadn't been morally so.

I perceived that my father had developed a simple code of communication: three thumps or raps meant "yes," two meant "no," and one, "I don't know." As with deliberation he recited the alphabet, the thump or rap came upon the letter desired by the thumper or rapper. Father wrote the letters down as they came, and the groups of letters formed words, and the words formed coherent sentences.

More than the thumpings came from the table. Supposedly made by the ghost of Hum Riley, they were frequently accompanied or interrupted by the other types of sounds I've mentioned—less heavy, but as loud as decisive tappings by lead pencils or fingernails. Sometimes they interfered with the recordings of the Hum Riley thumps—when my father would say, probably, "Just wait a few moments. We're talking with Hum Riley now, but we'll let you speak a little later." Then, when one or two thumped sentences had been completed, the other rappings would become insistent and he'd say something like this. "Very well. Walter and Lucius both want to talk, and so does Laetitia; you'll have to wait, Hum. Go ahead, Walter."

I comprehended that my dead uncles, Walter and Lucius, and Aunt Tish were supposedly with us, but I didn't think so.

Sometimes there'd be as many as seven or eight—or even more—clear, loud raps sounding simultaneously from different areas of the table upon which rested, motionless, the hands of my mother and my sister and Mr. Riley; and I began to realize that these raps were of different types and qualities. A few of them, like Hum's and those attributed to my Uncle Lucius, were hearty, even boisterous; others were quiet and dignified; some of them were light and dainty, recognizably feminine. That is, the raps were individual, differed from one another just as the voices and handwritings of all the people I knew differed; and I saw that my father and the others recognized my Uncle Walter's strong but neat and incisive rap, for instance, because they had learned, in previous sittings, to identify it with him.

A Bridge to Eternity?

What messages were rapped out upon the table that evening I don't remember. The process was, of course, inordinately slow and the purports were inconsequent—unless they served to establish the tremendous fact that the dead were present. The sentences written by my father on his tablet might have been a record of a disjointed and fragmentary short conversation during which relatives or intimate friends mentioned without detail that they were leading interesting lives, and recalled to mind a few past episodes; that was about all.

My sister began to look tired; whereupon my mother said anxiously that she thought the sitting should stop, and it did. I spoke privately to my father: "Father, you surely don't believe those—those people were really here talking to us, do you?"

Always reluctant to say "I believe," he looked like a man perturbed by the forced alteration of strongly held previous opinions. "Why, who knows—but what else can it be? I can't find any other explanation."

Since he took it that way, I gave up; but my almost first thought was a shabby one—I'd be just about ruined among even my closest friends if it became known that my family were doing such things as this and believing them. I didn't put my protest in precisely that way; I said that if this ghost business became known the whole town would think we were crazy.

Family Secret

"Yes, of course!" my father agreed, and reassured me. The table sittings with raps that produced messages were known so far only to relatives and to Mr. Riley, and weren't to be mentioned outside of this small circle. "Naturally, everybody'd think we're insane," my father said. "Other people would think of us just what we'd have thought of them only a couple of months ago, if we'd heard they were in the habit of sitting about a table, listening to raps. No, you needn't worry; we're keeping it in the family."

That night's session with the raps was typical, much like the many, many others that were to follow; and, with one exception, all the people who were present at any of the sittings—grandparents, uncles, aunts, cousins, and close family friends—accepted as most probable the conclusion that they were communicating with the dead. Uncle Newton, now done with politics and spending much of his time in travel abroad, stopped for a visit; and, agnostic citizen of the world that he was, found himself helplessly in my father's position—that, simply, there wasn't any other explanation. Just after he'd taken his seat facing the eloquent table, the first message to him came: "I'm the boy who braves all dangers."

Uncle Newton said huskily, "Walter!"

In their boyhood, he told us then, his brother, Walter, and he had shouted the quotation tauntingly at each other and had tussled over it, half irately, half jocosely, each proclaiming himself to be "the boy who braves all dangers."

This rapped reference to a bit of coltish fooling, known only to the two brothers and long forgotten, until the table's reminder, seemed pointedly significant; and when Uncle Newton returned to California, he spoke of his strange experience to a friend who was in deep grief. Uncle Newton suggested that he come to Indianapolis, and he did—a kind, sad old retired colonel, lost in a world that lacked his wife. My hospitable mother asked him to stay with us, and his visit, intended to be for a day or so, lasted three weeks. The first rappings the table addressed to him spelled out the opening verses of a song the dead wife had been wont to sing for him in the earliest days of their married life, long, long before; and after that, poor man, he'd have had the table going all night every night, except for the exhaustion the sittings brought my sister.

The exception I've mentioned—the one person who came to see the table's performance and didn't think the dead most probably responsible for it—was my Grandfather Tarkington. He didn't think the dead made the raps; he thought something else did. Grandfather Tarkington was a ruddy, husky-voiced, squirely man, powerfully agile like my father, and, like all the

Tarkingtons, given to cheerfulness and ready laughter; but he could be grim. Neither my father at fifty nor any of my Tarkington aunts and uncles was reckless enough to mention card playing, wine, the theater, or dancing in his presence. He thought tobacco abominable, breakfasted at seven, and, in his eighties, was on a horse at half past.

In his pioneer youth he'd had a disturbing spiritual experience, had broken with the Southern Tarkingtons' previous easy Episcopalianism, and, after soul searchings, discovered that he couldn't be a Roman Catholic or a Presbyterian or a Baptist. The theology he found in himself proved to be Methodistical; he'd become an early Indiana circuit rider and, in time, a presiding elder. Now, retired to his big sweet-smelling farm—always heaven to me whenever I got there—he preached only upon special occasions, but was unshakable in old convictions that included a necessary modicum of hellfire and brimstone. My mother's family, the Booths, deriving Congregationalism from Connecticut, had gone Presbyterian in pioneer Indiana, and this was my church and Sunday-schooling; but with both Booths and Tarkingtons the old orthodoxies were fading. Of all my relatives, the only one who hadn't lost faith in a personal Satan was my father's father, the Reverend Joseph Tarkington.

My father wrote him of what was happening at our house, and Grandfather drove the forty miles from the farm and sternly occupied a big chair throughout an hour of afternoon rapping. He spake not a word till it was over; then said, "Those sounds are not made by human trickery, but they cannot be from spirits in heaven. There is no countenance for them in the Bible. They are from the Devil."

One didn't argue with Grandfather Tarkington. This was his say, and, having said it, he drove back to the farm with what subsequent thoughts in his mind we never learned. No one dared speak of raps to him again, nor did he ever utter another word upon the subject he'd so ironly settled.

Behind the Veil

The sittings continued, sometimes desultorily, over a period of perhaps three years; and now and then the force that produced the raps did freakish things. Once upon an evening, when the table had been busy in the afternoon for a visiting uncle and cousins, I went upstairs after dinner and to my certain knowledge was the only person on the second floor. As I passed through Grandmother Booth's room on my way to my own, its walls, its floor, and its ceiling abruptly resounded with such raps as we'd never heard, though often the table thumpings had been easily audible beyond closed doors. They made an almost thunderous uproar for probably half a minute.

As they subsided I heard voices shouting from the drawing room below, and, going to the head of the stairs, found that my father and mother, my sister, and the visitors were rushing out of the drawing room, where they'd been talking to Grandmother and Grandfather Booth. They were all calling to me, wanting to know what on earth was going on upstairs. When I said, "Nothing; it was raps," they believed me for two reasons: one, that obviously I couldn't have produced such a multitudinous outrage singlehanded; and the other that they were habituated to miracles. So was I. Though startled, I hadn't been frightened at all; and never, never was I numbered among the brave.

For that matter, nothing in this whole long experience appeared to us as supernatural: it all seemed "just natural." Apparently we'd stumbled, as it were, upon phenomena not yet recognized by physicists and people generally as a part of the known order of Nature. Our ghosts were never in the least ghostly; they "talked," sometimes eagerly, but always cheerfully, with the amiable inconsequence of people who drop in for a while on friends; and, when we asked questions about the "life beyond" or about the space and time in which they lived, they replied they couldn't explain to us what we couldn't possibly understand. When we asked for prophecies, they said we knew as much about what was to happen on our "plane" as they did.

The Giant "Perhaps"

They seemed reasonable, and the only person whose nerves were affected by the sittings was my sister; she grew tired and wan when the sessions were protracted or too frequent. She felt that the drain upon her was less if other people's hands were on the table as well as hers; nevertheless, that her strength did wane became evident. Finally my mother talked to the family physician, and he said that in his long practice he'd known two or three other persons for whom tables moved and raps sounded, manifestations he'd had to believe genuine; and that in these other instances he thought the mediums' constitutions had been somewhat weakened.

After that the sittings were short and held only at considerable intervals; then came my sister's marriage, subsequent preoccupation with a household and children—and when she tried to make a table move and rap again, years afterward, nothing happened. The power was gone—like that of the great voice she'd had and lost when, for the care of children, she'd given up her singing.

In the meantime, for her and for my father and for all of us, there'd come doubt. We'd never made the experience scientific, had never even tried to prove with irrefutable tests the identifications of the unseen visitors. The phenomena themselves, the raps, though incredible to anybody without a real experience of them, we of course never doubted. They were beyond question, but what had been the intelligences that directed them? In time we were confronted by the Hudson theory that those intelligences are contained unwittingly in the subconscious of living people, and for this we hadn't any answer.

When we reviewed our apparent communications with the dead, we could only say that perhaps—perhaps—it was they. But this "perhaps" was to be with us the rest of our lives, and "perhaps" can be a giant. If perhaps there is no death, what then perhaps is suicide—or murder? Question most dread of all: What, perhaps, is war?

During all the time of this adventure I asked no such questions of the rappers or of anyone. Speculations upon the unknown possibilities among which man, like a bull on volcanic crust, walks his strangely confident way, weren't anywhere in my head. That fuzzy asylum, dismaying to the eye that now looks back into it, was all the while engaged with interrogations it found more absorbing. In particular it concerned itself with the vital question of beauty—my own.

As I floundered through fifteen, a yearning to know what I looked like exerted acute pressure. Feeling that I had to learn the true quality of my appearance and how nearly its effect upon the world approached my desire, I gave an incalculable amount of time to the pertinent research. The fact that my dressing-table mirror was exceptionally large lengthened the periods devoted to this study because, if one stood some distance away, almost a full-length view was afforded.

By retiring to the opposite wall and approaching studiously, I could even observe my gait, grace of carriage, and how I tipped my hat to ladies; but most of the work was done at close range and sometimes caused pains in the neck and eyes brought on by hard effort to discover my profile. The problem continued to confront me: Was I or was I not beginning to be rather a handsome person? I was too familiar with my face to answer this question for myself, but evidence collected from outside pointed to not.

Years of exercise were bringing results, developing my nose and ears, the rest not keeping up with them; but, on the other hand, I could look forward to whiskers as a remedy. Whiskers, at that time still frequent among grown men, could be used both as balance for protuberances and as the mask of deficiencies. Alone with my mirror and a burnt cork, I studied whiskering as an art, sketching upon myself the most favorable future possible, and striving, as a seer, to picture the romanticized face maybe I'd be able to have when, in fuller manhood, hair should arrive upon me.

Growing Pains

In fairness to my whole person I had to admit as much doubt of my figure as of my features. I still wore a Youth's First Base collar, size 13, but my face seemed nakedly farther above it than was desirable; and the length of my trousers didn't remain stable, shortening after a month or two of wear and descending only to high-water mark. I needed new shoes usually, because my feet were stealing a march on other members; but what most deeply concerned me were my shoulder blades. I stooped a little and was thinner than the thinnest of my friends; lawn tennis had arrived in Indianapolis and a serious player wasn't supposed to go into action wearing his jacket, or blazer. Contortions before the mirror made me suspicious of the impression my shoulder blades created in the minds of spectators, and one afternoon I confided my anxieties to a friend.

He and I were to play tennis with two girls, one of them a visitor all magnolia loveliness from the storied South; and my friend arrived while I was dressing for the game. Finished, except for a jacket, I asked him for his frank and honest private opinion.

"Well, since you ask me," he responded sincerely, "I guess I better tell you. I wouldn't say it except you asked me, but since you really want me to say right out whether I ever thought so or not, well, I have to say I have: they do. They do stick out too much and I kind of expect she'd notice it. If I was in your place I'd wear two shirts."

It was a painfully hot afternoon, but I took his advice and made this sacrifice. In addition to underwear, I wore two shirts, the inner one of flannel; and, though I suffered plenteously, I felt rewarded. On the way home my friend said he doubted if she'd noticed my shoulder blades much. Anyhow, he said, I looked a lot better in two.

It seems clear that the question for which I sought the answer—had I beauty?—was at least in part related to my effect upon girls. The trouble was, I couldn't discern any effect at all—either upon them as a class or upon a single representative. Still, as I believed girls to be secretive, I thought I could go on hoping that there might be some effect sometimes somewhere.

"Maybe," I thought—"maybe I've passed some girl on the street sometime—some girl I didn't know and that even didn't seem to notice me and had special kinds of taste—and maybe she was thinking to herself: 'Who is that handsome boy?'"

From my family I couldn't find out what I looked like. In their fondest moments and in their other moments this was a subject they never brought up. There wasn't anybody at all to whom I could put the inquiry, "Am I handsome or not, and if not—as appears pretty likely—how much not?"

I never fully discovered how much not, but finally let the matter come to rest upon the conclusion that while waiting for whiskers I was probably kind of queer looking. Of course I'd had eyes enough to perceive from the first that my looks could never put me in the group of outright handsome boys like Horace Hord. Horace, harmonious in feature, graceful in figure, had two intimate satellites—Bushrod Browning and me—and both of us were always loyally conscious of our privilege in being handsome Horace's constant accompaniments, or trailers.[1]

Horace wasn't only more agreeable to the eye than Bush Browning and I were; his debonair self-assurance when we were among girls at a party, or on someone's veranda of a summer evening, fortunately kept our ill-chosen imitations of it from being even heard. Horace's dash was so contagious that Bush and I, though not without many correct misgivings, dared to become musical semipublicly with him. Partly supported by a fourth friend who played the guitar—some—we several times stayed out as late as ten o'clock at night, ventured into the front yards of girls whose parents we thought we could count upon to remain quiescent, and injured the quiet night with attempted quarteting serenades. Diligent sensitive neighbors may have counted the chords that went foul in "My Bonnie Lies Over the Ocean," "Over the Banister Leans a Face," "The Spanish Cavalier," and "Aunt Dinah's Quilting Party."

The worst effect that Horace had upon Bushrod Browning and me was a treacherous braggadocio. Bush and I belonged to a type now almost lost, the bashful boy; but Horace made us feel up to a formal evening call upon an Older Girl. Horace, as hardy as handsome, had already called upon several of the Older Girls; but for Bush and me this was to be our first effort to make what could officially, as it were, be known as a "call"—and upon an Older Girl, a woman of the world at least sixteen or worse! All these things were different in that long-extinct age; and so were we, its young.

At the Older Girl's front door Horace jauntily made the proper inquiry, and Bush and I were received with him by the Older Girl in a room that became formidable promptly at its threshold. Horace said, "I think you've probably met Mr. Browning and Mr. Tarkington somewhere already," and the Older Girl said cordially, "Yes, indeed, I'm sure I have!" and Bush and I,

---

1. Horace Hord went on to become a successful attorney in New York. Bushrod Browning committed suicide in 1899, purportedly out of despondency at his inability to find employment.

keeping behind Horace, both said, "Yes, indeed!" and laughed to show that we were cordial, too, and of course fully at our ease. I thought Bush laughed too loudly and too long, especially as there wasn't anything to laugh at; and I felt hurt when he whispered, "Shut up. What do you want to keep on tittering for?" Then we both said, "Yes, indeed!" again and laughed again.

The Older Girl said, "Shan't we all sit down?" and she and Horace took chairs, but Bush and I didn't know how or where to lower ourselves. We somehow couldn't. We said, "Yes, indeed!" and remained standing close together.

Parlor Panic

The Older Girl said, "Mr. Browning, perhaps you and Mr. Tarkington'd like to sit on the sofa?" and, as Bush only laughed, I said laughingly, "Yes, we'd like to," and Bush and I, red and laughing, sat down on the sofa together.

Horace and the Older Girl began to chatter, while Bush and I sat and sat on the sofa. We didn't know what they were saying; we didn't know what it was all about; but it seemed to make a lively amount of noise, and Bush and I laughed because we wished to appear parties to it. I felt ashamed of Bush, he was so red and laughed so much, in an ignorant-sounding way. I began to hate him, too, for his stupidity and because every time he thought the Older Girl wasn't looking he dug his elbow into me and whispered out of the side of his mouth, "You're making a fool of yourself."

Horace and the Older Girl continued to chatter cozily, though now and then she'd ask, "Don't you think so, too, Mr. Browning and Mr. Tarkington?"

We'd say, "Yea, indeed, huh, huh!" and hate each other more and swivel our necks inside our collars and cough and look guilty. Whenever Bush stopped laughing he seemed to feel that he had to fill the gap with a cough. It wasn't natural, or etiquette, either, for us to cough so often at the same time; but he didn't once let me cough alone.

The muscles of my face were hurting me; I was too warm, and I suffered because when I sat down I'd crossed my right knee over my left, and after half an hour or so I wanted to get both feet on the floor again, but didn't like to try because I thought the action might look boorish. Horace and the Older Girl, thick as thieves, chitter-chattered unceasingly and even had a scuffle over a ribbon she was wearing and he tried to snatch from her. Bush and I sat in a kind of hell, glassy-eyed, hot, red, and making horrible laughing and coughing sounds. Unalterably affixed to the sofa and repellently coupled to each other, we had no hope; our condition seemed permanent.

Horace rose at last, "It's time to chase our freight," he said, in knowing argot. "Get off that sofa, jaybirds; we got to chase our freight for home."

Bush and I stood up, coughing, and the Older Girl said she was sorry we had to leave so soon; she hoped we'd come again. Bush and I said we'd certainly like to, and remained where we were, mumbling, making semi-bowing motions, and moving our hanging hands in little arcs, in case she intended to shake them.

She didn't, but said she was glad we'd like to come again; and we said, yes, indeed, we'd like to; and Horace said, "Well, for heaven's sake, come on; we got to chase our freight!"

Bush and I, still making little bowing motions, began to move backward toward the door together, saying, "Well, good night, huh, huh!" and then coughing. Every step or so we stopped because she'd say, "Well, good night; I do hope you'll come again!" and we had to respond, "Well, good night, we'd certainly like to!"

Our progress backward, accompanied by these courteous vocalizings, was impeded. We were too close together; Bush seemed to be both a little behind me and somewhat in front of me. I stepped on him and he stepped on me; our feet became confused, all eight of our limbs seemed to be interlockingly in the way of one another. Bush lost his balance and I mine, there were hopeless clutchings, and then we were both full sprawled upon the carpet, still entangled, and exclaiming scrupulously, "Pardon *me!*"

The Older Girl covered her face with her hands. Bush and I rose, each using the other regardlessly as a means of assistance, laughed loudly at ourselves, said, "Well, good night again," and, still laughing heartily, followed Horace out of that terrible house.

We laughed as long as we thought there was a chance we'd be heard from indoors; but false merriment died suddenly when we reached the sidewalk. Bush and I were instantly vehement in mutual accusations. All the way home each charged the other with not having enough sense not to trip a person up in a lady's house, and each vowed bitterly never so long as life lasted to make another call in the other's company. At intervals we appealed passionately to Horace for his testimony in the matter of who did the tripping.

Horace, indifferent to our troubles and fond of his voice, kept a few paces ahead of us, singing:

"The Spanish Cavalier
    Stood in his retreat
And on his guitar played a tune, dear."

Bush and I were sore with each other for days. Recriminations broke out between us illogically in the midst of conversation upon other affairs; neither could say the slightest thing in indirect praise of himself without the other's interrupting, "You're a nice one to talk! Look what you did last Thursday night!"

Follow the Leader

Bushrod Browning and I were often critical of each other, though never of Horace. On all subjects except Bush's opinion of me and mine of him, the three of us were always of one mind—Horace's. We were a trio, but he was the leader, and in the company of our peers—girls especially—Bush and I enjoyed the reflected prestige of being his entourage. Most of the time, however, there were just the three of us and we spent nearly all of it outdoors for a reason unconnected with sports of the playground, field, or stream.

Rightfully looking upon ourselves as youths—virtually young men of fifteen or sixteen sometimes addressed by even street children as "mister"— we were bigotedly regarded at home as much younger. Expected to go to bed at ten o'clock, and, if out earlier, to report where, we were surrounded by parental care and the difficulties it imposed on us. For instance, we were all supposed not to smoke until we should be twenty-one, whereas Bushrod Browning had first tried to smoke cigars at the age of five, and had succeeded, in the Brownings' stable, before he was nine. Later in life he'd given them up for cigarettes and exercise with Horace and me—exercise because the sense of well-being, while smoking, increased with the distance from home. We were great walkers and versed in the use of such herbs as pennyroyal, mint, and even catnip, to dispose of lingering aromas. We never ate cloves; it was notorious that a person who smelt of cloves had been doing something wrong—drinking, most likely.

One walking afternoon, when our topic was the future, Bushrod said gloomily that his was all settled for him, he'd have to go into business with his father; but Horace, looking solemn, was silent. So was I. I'd twice taken a series of drawing lessons, one from a portrait painter and the other from a French stonemason who worked on our new statehouse, and, as I spent most of my spare time drawing, and nearly all my time was spare, I habitually supposed myself on the way to become an "artist." I didn't say so now, because I was waiting for Horace to speak.

Footlight Future

As he didn't, I ventured to ask him, "What have you decided to be in this life, Horace?"

He stopped short, stood looking into distance. "During the whole of my days I've never once considered adopting any other profession except one."

Bush and I had halted too. Almost breathless with deference, we stared at Horace as he looked over our heads into the faraway sky. "Which, Horace?" I asked, almost in a whisper. "Which is the one you've never had any ambition except for?"

"The only one—for me," he said. "I've never even a moment considered anything but going on the stage. I intend to become an actor."

Suddenly a rosy footlight glory seemed to flare before me; Titian and Rembrandt were part of dull doings in the clouded past. "I'm going to, too, Horace," I said, in the deepest tones of a voice almost rid of adolescent quaverings. "I intend to become an actor, too, Horace."

In spite of Bush Browning's expression, this hypnotic moment seemed to settle, unalterably, my career. I knew what Bush was thinking, even without his saying, as he did, that a person who couldn't step inside a lady's house without tripping somebody up wasn't going to get very far as Romeo. Untalented and doomed to grovel in the drug business, poor left-out Bush was disregarded; Horace and I, with our new bond between us, began to talk inspiredly of Edwin Booth and Mary Anderson and life on the stage.

Determined to enter into that life, we decided to sweep away all difficulties—such as school, having to go to bed by ten, etc., etc., etc. Of what benefit would a whole lot of useless education be to us on the stage, we asked—so why wait till we were old men? Our families would be proud of us when we wrote home after achieving our success, we said reassuringly; and planned to select a supporting company in Indianapolis to tour the country as immediately as possible.

VI. Turning Out to Be an Idiot

Horace Hord and I made exciting plans for our future theatrical touring company; but, as we felt that the enterprise might be generally thought overambitious for two young men of sixteen, we didn't embarrass ourselves by speaking of it to others. The first practical step, we agreed, was to choose our own roles. Horace thought he'd be at his best as Romeo, Orlando, Macbeth, and Richelieu; my selections were Richard the Third, Shylock, the melancholy Jaques, and Tony Lumpkin.

It was in Richard the Third that I saw myself as most powerful; and, having learned the part, I became more than ever studious of my dressing-table mirror. Wearing eyebrows and sneering moustachios of burnt cork, and a costume of my own long winter underwear shadowed by an evening cloak of my mother's, I twisted one shoulder higher than the other, and put my sprouting features through gymnastics, muttering malignantly the while,

> "Deform'd, unfinish'd, sent before my time
> Into this breathing world, scarce half made up,
> And that so lamely and unfashionable
> *That dogs bark at me as I halt by them*——"

After inquiries called through the locked door one morning—didn't I know breakfast was waiting, and I'd be late again to school, and what on earth was I talking to myself about?—I'd perceived life would be simpler if I did my rehearsing *sotto voce*. Even with this handicap, I liked my rendition of the foully insinuating Richard's great scene with Anne, and my hissing sinfulness in such bits as,

> "Ha!
> Hath she forgot already that brave prince,
> Edward, her lord, whom I, some three months since,
> Stabb'd in my angry mood at Tewksbury?"

Horace and I asked each other for criticism, so to speak. I'd act a scene from *Richard the Third*; then Horace would say hurriedly that he thought I was going to be first rate, he'd like my opinion of how he did the *Macbeth* dagger scene, and he'd begin it before I could even sit down to listen. Horace rather baffled me by seeming more interested when he was acting than when I was. I feared, in fact, that he implied something like a trade—he'd listen to me if I'd listen to him.

Before long, however, we realized that Shakespeare employed too many dramatis personae for a company still consisting wholly of nucleus; so we decided that I'd better substitute for him and write a play—one needing only a few other actors. We couldn't think of any both talented enough to suit us and able to leave home, but Indianapolis had a large population and with most of it we were unacquainted. We'd keep our eyes open busily and be careful to pick just the right people.

The Play's the Thing

I began the play at once in a school copybook; and few playwrights, I think, have ever been more illimitably copious. At every opportunity, morning, noon, or night, dialogue and "stage business" flowed illegibly in a penmanship notorious in our high school as its worst. I filled copybook after copybook with what I know not, except that any end to it appeared more and more utterly impossible and that the part I wrote for Horace was heroic and that the one I composed for myself involved bucolic comedy. The ancient pattern was certainly there, with Horace the handsome lover superb in every peril, and me the faithful funny friend who'd get all the laughs!

We decided not to wait for the manuscript to be finished; I could easily, we said, write the end any day between rehearsals, and the thing to do, of course, was to settle upon exactly the right leading lady. Naturally, she'd have to be somebody still a stranger to us, because of all the girls we knew there wasn't one that wouldn't yelp, "Why, Horace Hord! What on earth are you talking about? I'm glad mother didn't hear you. You must be cracked!" No, we had to find an extra-good-looking girl whose family didn't amount to anything, especially with her.

It was I who discovered her. After school and on holidays I often went downtown to the city library to read old plays. I'd become familiar, in particular, with the seventeenth and eighteenth century English dramatists—some of them occasionally left me incredulous, Mr. Wycherley especially—and now that Horace and I needed a leading lady, I mingled with the populace when I finished my reading, and looked and looked for her. On crowded Washington Street, one Saturday, I came face to face with her.

She was frail, pretty, with notable black eyelashes; and she was what we then called "painted." To the best of my information, her rouge meant that she was either an actress or from the South. In the North it was believed that Southern ladies added this adornment permissibly and sometimes charmingly; and I supposed that actresses "painted" for both stage and street. Others, too, used "paint," a professionally "bad" class; but I was certain that this girl didn't belong to it. Neither did she seem a stranger in the city; so she couldn't be a Southerner. Then what was she but an actress?—or if she wasn't yet fully one, she'd like to be, and her family'd probably consent, since they let her "paint." Almost at sight, within the few moments of sidewalk approach, I inspirationally selected her to be Horace's and my leading lady.

She didn't seem to observe me as we came abreast of each other, and of course I didn't look noticeably at her, because I'd been brought up to know that staring is unpardonable. We passed on, but, much stirred, I felt that our theatrical destiny intended us to meet again. We did. I walked round the block and met her, halfway, coming from the opposite direction on Market Street. Again she didn't seem aware of me and I was careful not to stare; then, continuing, I once more encountered her, with the same decorum, on Washington Street. We went on, as before; and, as previously, came face to face upon Market Street.

How many times Horace's and my new leading lady and I walked round and round that block, meeting twice every round, but never with any forwardness, I'm unable to say: but finally she failed to appear on the Washington Street stretch of our promenade, and, retracing my steps to the corner, I saw her in the distance. She'd turned into Virginia Avenue, a thoroughfare that led to the South Side, a respectable area of shops and small houses unfamiliar to me. I had no thought of following her. Receding, she had the air of a person going tiredly home, and to follow would have been intrusive.

Maid of New Orleans

I looked for her vainly every afternoon of the next week; but on Saturday, suddenly, there she was, coming toward me, as before, on the Washington Street sidewalk. With tremulous wobblings in my upper inside, I repeated the performance of the preceding Saturday, and so, with the same propriety, did she. We walked round and round the block, meeting twice every time. Then she turned off toward the South Side, and I went home.

I couldn't possibly have spoken to her. Not only "home training" and the proprieties of the 80's prevented; I had that now apparently vanished handicap of youth, bashfulness. It was a misfortune in my character that unstrung me in the presence of all but completely ill-favored girls; and some months earlier it had done something to me that still rouses my self-pity.

Uncle Newton, upon one of his passages to California, had taken my Cousin Fenton and me with him on a detour to New Orleans, and, having enriched us, left us there to finish our holiday in the care of a severe old lady from Terre Haute. We stayed in a large boardinghouse where were many other old ladies and one alleviation with flaxen hair, an unprecedented precocity in beauty, named Helen. I couldn't even look at her without finding Fenton in the way; but there arrived what I took to be an ineffable opportunity.

In the boardinghouse parlor one of the old ladies mentioned that the poets, Julia Ward Howe and Joaquin Miller, were to give a joint reading from their works the next evening. A beautiful thought set me all aglow: I could take Helen and sit beside her for maybe two full hours without a single noisy intrusion by Fenton.

Of course I couldn't ask her to go without a chaperone—I didn't know how to ask her at all—but at the moment she was demurely on the arm of her grandmother's chair. In addition to the grandmother there were six other elderly women in the room, and I knew my manners. Blushing, I rose from the sofa where I sat with Fenton, who was gazing detestably at Helen, and, after coughing formally, I spoke. "Won't all of you, except Fenton, give me the pleasure of going with me to the reading by Julia Ward Howe and Joaquin Miller tomorrow evening?"

Helen's grandmother and the six others looked surprised for a moment; then all of them, in pleased but inscrutable voices, accepted. I went forth and bought nine reserved seats for seven old ladies, Helen and me—which somewhat depleted the fortune Uncle Newton had lavished in departure. Next day I was nasty with Fenton, explaining frequently that I'd had to leave him out because he wouldn't care for so intellectual an entertainment as Helen and I—and her grandmother and the other widows—had in prospect. Indifferent, he only sang Little Buttercup at me; and that evening, when Helen and I and my large party passed out to the street to go to the reading, he was with us.

I rudely asked him why, adding rather loudly that he perfectly knew I'd provided no ticket for him because he wasn't literary. "No, indeed," he said. "This is the evening Helen and I fixed two days ago to go and buy fireworks from the Chinaman on Canal Street."

Hand in hand, he and Helen skipped away, singing Little Buttercup, while Helen's grandmother took my arm and moved with me in the opposite direction at the head of my odd procession. Few poets have had a more dazed auditor than did Mrs. Howe and Joaquin Miller that night. No noble word they uttered reached my heart as I sat forever and ever among seven beaming beneficiaries who did their best to lengthen the hours with encores.

Stalking a Leading Lady

When we got back to our *pension* we found Helen and Fenton on a balcony over the courtyard, setting off the last fiery squibs of their joyous evening. Haggardly I tried to join them; but, by the time my seven friends finished thanking me for the pleasure I'd been so unusual as to give them, Helen's grandmother said that it was time to go to bed. . . . No, I wasn't capable of introducing myself to Horace's and my selected leading lady and informing her of her new status.

I studied her, so to say, for several Saturday afternoons; then Horace accompanied me to look her over. We met her—met her about five times, I think, before she turned toward the South Side—and Horace was enthusiastic about her. He said he could see she'd be good in the part. Dashing among the girls we knew, he was as incapable of audacity as I in the approach to a lovely stranger; and yet we both were satisfied that this one was to become our leading lady. I thought of her so, writing more and more scenes in my play, and, when I read them to Horace, we'd often say, "Yes, sir; I bet she'll do that just right!"

We weren't troubled about when and how she was to be notified. Like other dealers in vapor, we were pleased to feel that we were "making progress." Nevertheless, roused enough, we were capable of adventurous action. The Bennett and Moulton Opera Company, with Miss Della Fox, aged seventeen, as its prima donna, sang Olivette, La Mascotte, Giroflé-Girofla, and The Chimes of Normandy, at ten-twenty-thirty prices in Indianapolis; and, at first sight and sound of Miss Fox, our hearts turned over—Horace Hord's, Bush Browning's, and mine. At all of her appearances we were in the front row, and we made our farewell to her, on Saturday night, as brilliant as it was wistful. With three other boys, we took a stage box, fifty cents apiece; and, since that theater was ill attended by our parents, we treated Miss Fox, the other singers, and the ten-twenty-and-thirty public to an aristocratic spectacle—six sixteen-year-old men of the world in "full evening dress," white ties and swallowtails, a tableau of fashion well lighted by the glow from the stage. Scrutiny would have revealed suggestive misfits; but the remarkable thing about our achievement, pointing to skill and energy in time of real need, was the fact that not one of six fathers afterward even suspected that his evening clothes, shirt studs, and so on, had been borrowed for several hours and then quietly returned.

Horace and I talked more eagerly than ever of our coming tour: on the road we'd certainly be playing some of the same towns that the Bennett and Moulton Opera Company would, and no doubt we'd often find ourselves in the same hotel with Miss Fox. Fellow players, we could go right up to her in the lobby, begin talking and laughing, and ask her if she wouldn't like to join us in the new delicacy, soda water with ice cream in it. We built many rosy pictures into seeming actualness, and yet—unbelievable perhaps for those who've never possessed or have forgotten the mind of a boy—I was all this time making simultaneous plans for a wholly different future.

A Juvenile Five-Year Plan

Dan Calkins, contemporary next-door neighbor, was entirely for large outdoor adventure, didn't like cities—Indianapolis particularly—and I was in warm agreement with him. We both often felt unappreciated by Indianapolis, and I wonder how many times each of us said to the other, meeting with complete sympathy, "I'd like to just get out of this old town! Yes, sir; I'd like to stay away for about five years—and then come back!" When we said, "And then come back!" there was always triumph, not to say vindictiveness, in our voices.

Dan knew of a canvas canoe—old and a little bit rotten, but only five dollars. As soon as our savings—there weren't any—amounted to over five dollars, say seven or eight, we'd buy this vessel, stock it with crackers and sardines, paddle down White River to the Wabash, then into the Ohio, then into the Mississippi, and come out somewhere in the Gulf of Mexico. We'd wear sun helmets with white veils round them and go ashore at places like Memphis and Natchez and walk about mysteriously. Then—after the specified five years—we'd come back! We'd find "everybody" groveling about the old place the same as ever; we'd dazzle 'em and just laugh.

One of these plans was in my head while I talked with Dan, and the other, perhaps the same day, when I gabbled with Horace or wrote my endless play. I saw no inconsistency in expecting to carry both to fulfillment. What happened to them? Being made of nothing, they returned to nothingness. Dan became absorbed in roller skating in admiring rinks, and, during the fading of the theatrical project, I again once or twice saw Horace's and my leading lady on Washington Street and thought vaguely. *Oh, yes; I must finish that play sometime.* Did any obscure part of me know all the while that both of the great ideas were gas? No doubt; but as I look back into their container—that head so strange to me now—I seem to be writing of a congenital idiot.

Bright-browed youth has the illusion that it lives among certainties, seeing solids all round about it, far and near, in clear illumination; whereas it's like a complacent cocooned creature blown from its twig and unaware that it's being tossed vagrantly through underbrush in the dark. A worn-out police officer once said he thought the world would be improved if most persons between the ages of fourteen and eighteen, inclusive, could be kept under lock and key. That, with "proper instruction," might have been useful to me. Among my contemporaries, intelligentsia of sixteen and seventeen, I sometimes held argument, free will versus predestination, and thought I proved the case for predestination—that we are conscious of what we do, but cannot control it. If I'd applied this to myself, which of course I didn't—because I really thought that I myself had volition, even if no one else had—I'd have been only half right: I neither chose what I would do nor had perception of what I did.

Fate's crazy-quilt-making so casually used me for a miserable bit of patchwork that I hadn't an idea of what was happening. Consequences that were to pile upon one another for years began with an infinitesimal episode: the mere exchange of a morning's greeting with a friend.

Bushrod Browning had been taken out of school to do "collecting" for his father, who was under business pressure; and Bush's work, I enviously thought, was done in luxury. He had a horse and a high cart—merely drove about, smoking cigarettes, handed bills to people, and received money or checks or promises in return. So agreeable a life was in hard contrast to mine; for I still had two years and a half of high school before me. Dragging year after year had passed; I was no less a sloth at the tail of the class, and my ennui in school hours was like nausea. Creeping like snail unwillingly, that morning, with my strapped books swung from a lax hand, I brightened when Bush drew rein at the curbstone beside me, and leaned from his high seat to offer me a cigarette.

I glanced up the street toward home, then lighted the cigarette, smoked, and lingered. I was already late and would have to devise another of the old drudging excuses for tardiness; so why not make it a little later? I did, and presently climbed to the pleasant leather seat beside Bush for more convenient unimportant conversation.

He was the first to remember duty. "Well, I got to chase my freight," he said, and I, looking at my watch, was startled to discover entirely too much tardiness to be accounted for plausibly.

I'd never "played hooky" in my life, and I was now too old—and too dignified, I hoped—for such ignobly infantile deceptions; but to clump into my dismal big classroom in the dismal big high school an excuseless full hour late—it was to ask of myself the brazenly impossible. Helpless, I stayed where I was, drove about town with Bush, smoked cigarettes, and held his horse while he went into small drugstores to "collect." At the usual hour I returned home, swinging my strapped books and presenting the appearance of a scholar possessing fresh learning, his day's work done.

Behind this front I was embarrassed. After any absence a student had to bring to school a note from a parent or guardian explaining the hiatus; and I didn't see myself in a position to apply for such a document. I couldn't admit to either my mother or my father that I'd just driven about with Bush Browning all morning: some ignominies are too petty to be confessed. Thus the next morning found me leaving home with my textbooks swinging and myself in a predicament too much for me. I walked about till I found Bush Browning and his cart.

I did the same thing the next day. *Now it's gone this far, I might as well make it a week*, I thought. *I'll wait till Sunday. Then, of course, I'll simply have to go through it and tell father and mother. It'll be sickening, but they'll write some kind of excuse for me and I'll make a fresh start in school Monday morning.*

Steeled to Face the Music

That was a good resolution; but on Sunday our house was all day long, and all evening, too, so cheerful—except me, inside—that I hadn't the heart. Once or twice I made a faint start; but reluctance overcame me—and bright and early Monday morning I was desperately out in Bush Browning's cart again. I spent all the mornings of that week in Bush's cart; but henceforth had no thought of a confessional Sabbath. What had begun as a peccadillo was now an enormity.

When I didn't drive with Bush I spent the school hours in the city library, reading—and one noon, when I'd been truant a full month, the avalanche rumbled. On my way home from the library I had a distant view of the high-school building and before its ugly main portal a heart-stopping object—our family carriage in the act of leaving the curb where it had too obviously been standing. Stricken in my tracks, I watched that shape of doom grow slowly smaller as it rolled homeward. Nothing seemed plainer than that my mother or my father, or more probably both, had just come from within the building after an interview with the high-school principal, a deadly man weighing three hundred pounds and wearing bank-president side whiskers. Then all was over; some accident had exposed me.

I'd have to confront not only my father and mother. Grandmother and Grandfather Booth and my sister and my brother-in-law, but also Uncle Newton! My misfortune was that he, of all people in the world, happened to be visiting us just then; and with clarity I realized what shame the others would feel in my disgrace before him. The noon sun was calmly bright above me, but I crept home through a blackness shot with lightnings. I stayed in the stable until I knew that everybody was at lunch; then I slipped into the house by a back way and upstairs to my father's room, where I got out his enormous old Colt revolver and green bullets in its cylinder. I think I did this partly because I believed it correct under the circumstances and partly because I truly felt that extinction was the only neat way out.

Brief meditation, however, informed me that the revolver didn't seriously intend to do anything about my troubles, and I slid it back under my father's shirts in the bureau drawer. Then I went downstairs, and listened. From the open door of the dining room came sounds that astounded me—a confusion of genuinely jolly voices and laughter. They didn't know! Then what had our carriage been doing before the high school?

When I'd taken my place at the merry table, cautiously contrived questions to my mother revealed the coincidence that had unmanned me. My father and Uncle Newton had been walking up from downtown, and, driving from the same direction, she'd overtaken them as they were passing the school. When I saw the carriage they'd just got in and were driving away. The crisis had passed, but the dreary days of truancy limped on, each hour a prayer, my rosary. No embezzler incessantly contorting his accounts and smoothing his face for his family uttered in his soul any wretched gulp that I didn't.

Except those most concerned—the members of my family and the high-school authorities—everybody of my acquaintance came to have knowledge of the dreadful prodigy. A successful truancy of two whole months had no precedent; and, in many a hurriedly withdrawn glance at my face, I read that I was regarded as the hero of a fearsome exploit. Glances like that flicker in the death house. Everybody knew that I was condemned; all, except me, waited interestedly for the end. "Miracles can't go on every day forever," Dan Calkins' kind mother warned me one evening. "This entire part of town thinks you'd better get it over."

The suggestion only wrung my vitals; but my hour was at hand. At the end of the ninth hideous week my mother met an interesting woman at an evening reception—our high-school instructor in physics—and, with strange, maternal confidence, asked smilingly how I was progressing in that subject. The teacher stared. "What? I supposed you'd taken him out of school months ago! Didn't you?"

The End of Nine Weeks' Truancy

My father got my mother home somehow; and, when I came in, a little later, my brother-in-law thoughtfully met me at the front door. "If I were you," he said, "I wouldn't go into the library; I'd go upstairs and get to bed right away."

This kindhearted friend's implication was lost on me; curiosity took me at once into the library. Father, pale, sat looking at the wall, and my sister was trying to comfort my weeping mother. Only one thing was said to me: "I met Mrs. Marshall tonight and she told me! Oh, Booth!"

That was all. Neither then nor afterward did they either reproach or question me, and I wonder now what they thought I'd been doing with all that vacant time. They didn't ask for an explanation; they couldn't—not any more than I could offer one. For a while, a week or so, they were more silent with me than usual, and then tried to be as before, gay and pathetically interested when I hesitantly chattered. There was no suggestion that I should return to high school; it was arranged for me to study drawing, working from plaster casts, and to take vocal lessons to steady my uncertain voice. In the autumn I was sent to a New England prep school to prepare for college—Princeton, my mother hoped.[2]

At this school, so far from home, I was at first in a condition that I recognized as bewilderment. New England itself, and New England professors, and boys who seemed a new species to me—they were from everywhere over the country except Indianapolis—all, for a time, confused me. Then, after a groping month, I thought that I had the hang of things. I became easy and confident, and thenceforth lived in bewilderment without knowing that I did.

---

2. Tarkington entered Phillips Exeter Academy in fall 1887.

A Boy without Supervision

Earlier in this narrative I expressed surprise that small boys grow up; here I wonder how so many abruptly transplanted midland and Far Western and Southern youths survived some of the best schools of those ancient days. At mine, the New Englanders from nearby towns often went home over the week ends and were all the time easily reached by adult relatives; but—so wholly different from today's were such schools then—the rest of us had almost no supervision at all from anybody. By modern measure the faculty was tiny; the students lived in boardinghouses scattered about the town, and, for the first time in their lives entirely on their own, were free to tinker with any new experience.

After my high-school truancy and the hurt it gave me to see the hurt it brought at home, any human being endowed with reason must surely have said to himself, "I've had my lesson; henceforth my pupilage shall be diligent and conscientious. My parents, who can ill afford the costliness of this phase of my slow education, shall at last rejoice in me." Not I! Skillful professors did corkscrew information past tortuous resistances among my mental cavities; and, at the end of two years, I had a sheepskin; but my general behavior might have been Tom o' Bedlam's.

There were some semi-sane intervals and schoolmate visitings—eager hours in the Boston Museum of the Fine Arts and in the Metropolitan in New York; though most of the "exciting" objects of art then in both would probably be found in their cellars today. In Boston I ran to catch my first sight of a portent, one of the new streetcars not drawn by horses or mules; this strange thing astoundingly moved because of a pole rising from its roof to a wire overhead. In New York were fabled spectacles: the unbelievable Elevated; impossible twelve and fifteen story buildings; Fifth Avenue alive with beautiful glistening horses; that kingly "matinee idol," Robert Mantell, cauterizing his bitten arm with a red-hot poker in *Monbars*, Augustin Daly's glorious theater, and the splendor of Ada Rohan's hair; *Erminie*, in full furore, with Francis Wilson and that madding incitation to undergraduate dreams, Miss Marie Jansen.[3]

---

3. Robert Mantell (1854–1928) was an acclaimed Broadway actor who later found success in silent films. Augustin Daly (1838–1899) was a pioneering theatrical manager who opened Daly's Theatre on Broadway in 1879; Ada Rohan was one of his stars. *Erminie* was a hugely successful comic opera that debuted in New York in May 1886. It helped make the reputations of Francis Wilson (1854–1935), who was its lead, and Marie Jansen (1857–1914), photographs of whom cause one to wonder at the drastic change in undergraduate ideals of beauty.

Sometimes, in retrospect, I glanced toward the dull old days at home and had pangs of compassion for my formerly untraveled self. Good heavens! Back there in Indianapolis I hadn't even known how to dress!

Now, experienced, masterly, I'd learned at last to maintain an untouchably patrician countenance when the sight of me brought open demonstrations from the vulgar. This happened, indeed, for, like most of my intimate colleagues, I'd grown somewhat noticeable; and a stroll downtown during the Christmas holidays at home in my senior year had a perceptible effect on Washington Street. Apparently, nothing much like me had before been seen in that backwoods purlieu. I carried a shiny crook-handled walking stick an inch thick, wore pale spats, a puffed white ascot, a fore-and-aft deerstalker cap, and a long-caped tweed ulster that didn't quite sweep the ground, but just missed it. There was rude staring; plebeian voices were heard to inquire, "What is that?" and "Whose is it?" Also, I learned, with sang-froid, that I was hotly described in the Meridian Club, where one of the middle-aged members couldn't speak of me and my clothes without beating a card table in a kind of passion. Other citizens wondered whether my pleased-looking parents were crazy or had only gone blind.

The caped ulster and concomitants were but items. Utterly too-too in fashionableness, I parted my hair in the middle, with "bangs," wore sashes instead of waistcoats—sashes of black or green watered silk with long, dangling fringed ends—and these fantasies, popular among the knowing young, weren't too harmonious with my physical style. This was, to put it simply, large-nosed, stooping, and still glunky and twitchy. Thinnest of the thin, I had habitually what's known as a hacking cough and was generally expected by my classmates to finish erelong in a consumption accelerated by nonintermittent smoking.

My schoolboy tastes, meanwhile, had become as expensive as they were cheerfully asinine. I bought meerschaum pipes that cost thirty dollars, had running accounts at the livery stables, ordered cigarettes by the gross, clothes of every variety from metropolitan tailors, and I belonged to a club devoted singly to clandestine suppers, mainly champagne.

I had no consciousness of any hour but the present; whatever was idiotic engrossed me.

The Class Yearbook

As commencement approached, my mother's letters had a sad urgency: my Grandmother Booth's health failed and she wished to see me "once more." I must please get home as quickly as possible after my graduation. That troubled me; but I had other worries, one of them involving a letter hard to write. It was to my father, admitting that the large check he'd sent me to cover all final expenses fell short of the mark by some hundreds of dollars. He didn't send me the second check at once—I had the disturbed impression that he was unable —and when he unreproachfully did, he said I must get home as soon as I could, because my grandmother was feebler and often asked for me.

What happened to that second check stupefied me. I cashed it and set out to pay bills, did pay one or two of the smaller, bought a few things, drifted into a coaching party to the seashore, bought a case of champagne to celebrate a school victory—a few other odds and ends like that—and had no money. Startling evaporation! My debts, however, hadn't become ethereal, and there was another complication.

My class had decided to perpetuate itself in a yearbook. It was to be splendid, cloth-bound, and elaborately illustrated with many drawings and with dozens of photogravure reproductions, a memorial to the class. Seven editors, it was decided, would be needed for such an undertaking, but factions among us could agree upon only four. We who'd been elected held a meeting, energetically chose a chairman and a treasurer and at once got ourselves photographed together—for the frontispiece.

Having accomplished these tasks, we relaxed.

"Completing" the Job

The rest of the school had itself photographed in groups for the book, and the members of the class sent in contributions toward publishing it. Cully, the treasurer, took charge of the funds; all four of us frequently said we must really get down to hard work pretty soon—and then, unexpectedly, it seemed, our final examinations were upon us. The seven projected editors, like the ten blue bottles ahanging on the wall, dwindled decisively. The day after commencement two of the elected four were missing, one being in such a mess that he didn't even need to explain his flight, and the other, the chairman, writing from New York that he had to please his family, who wished him to spend the summer abroad. He added that he hoped Cully and I'd complete the book in handsome style.[4]

"Complete" was an ill-chosen word; what Cully and I had to do was to begin it. With a fund of about three hundred dollars, I think, we had to write, compile, illustrate, edit, and publish an edition that would cost, if memory serves, something approaching two thousand dollars; but these figures

---

4. "Cully" was Edward Cullinan, who went on to work in the insurance industry in New York.

didn't bother us. We airily supposed that advertisements and the sale of a thousand copies—confidently computed upon wishfulness—would more than pay the printer. In the emptied hot town, the day after commencement, Cully and I went to work, and I had a telegram from my father asking what train I was taking for home. The next afternoon there was another from my mother: "She died this morning surely you will come."

I wrote her miserably that I couldn't possibly come until the yearbook was finished, moved into Cully's room, and used his sofa as a bed. We worked all night every night, slept till noon; then worked again. We'd begun in June, and, about the middle of August, Cully had a shock. He was a Catholic from "up-state" New York, and his father was unable to credit Cully's letters explaining that a yearbook detained him. Cully's father had never otherwise heard of a yearbook, feared the worst, and sent the priest to bring Cully home. Cully convinced the good father that there really was such a thing as a yearbook and that honor required ours to be finished. The night-and-day work went on.

My letters from home had become more and more distressed and distressing; and then—a bad sign—they became fewer. Like Cully's father, my family had never before heard of a yearbook, didn't understand what one was or why; and when the priest came for Cully, there were surmises I had to drive from my mind or I couldn't work: Would someone have come for me, except that the journey couldn't be afforded because I'd spent so much—or were they afraid of what they'd find—or both?

In September we had the tough job done. I faced the creditors whom I'd twice had the money to pay—and the innkeeper's three months' account for two meals a day—and told them all they'd have to send their bills home to my father. I sold my evening clothes, my watch, and my banjo; but at the last moment settled a pressing small bill, and at the station we found that Cully'd have to pay for part of my ticket to Indianapolis. I reached home at night with a nickel left, and, when I got on the horsecar for our street, the driver said, "Thought you was never comin'! Your father had 'Welcome Booth' cut in big letters in the grass of your side yard way back in June. Kep' it there a good while; but it's gone a long time now. Where you been all these months?"

This was a question I proved unable to answer credibly at home. There they couldn't have been more gently forgiving; but this time I'd all along been offering true explanations of my mysterious absence—and they did their best, but just couldn't believe me. They didn't believe there'd been any yearbook at all. "But you'll see!" I insisted, less and less convincingly. "You'll see with your own eyes. I'll prove it by the book itself." I was sure of this. Everything, the whole mass of material, was in the hands of the printer and many plates had already been made from the photographs and from the illustrations Cully and I had drawn. He'd gone home; and after that to Harvard, where he was near the printer and would collect from the advertisers and take charge of the book's distribution. "Copies will be here maybe as soon as within a week or so," I plaintively told my mother and my father. "When you see them you'll understand."

They never did understand. My mother'd try to smile at me; but tears would come into her eyes, she'd look away and murmur, "Ah, Booth!" My father said nothing at all; and I knew that the bills he'd twice raised the money to settle were raining in upon him. The household was skimped, the stable vacant; times were hard again, and I realized that only a scanted table and a thousand other sacrifices had kept me in school till I graduated. One thing alone held a little redemption for me. When I'd place that splendid big yearbook in their hands they'd at least know I hadn't caroused through my grandmother's funeral and the whole summer long—far into September!

At first I waited confidently for the book; then I waited puzzledly. Cully didn't write to me—he was having his troubles—but one day in October I had a telegram from him: "Printer refuses go on until paid eleven hundred claims we already owe him if not paid immediately swears will hold all material sell it to next class school for their memorial instead can you raise amount or part hurry or too late."

I didn't speak of the telegram. I stopped telling my father and mother I'd "prove by the book" that I wasn't quite all they thought me. I never proved it; nor did they ever refer to my assurances that I would. Of the bills with which I'd swamped my struggling father he spoke to me just once. On a May night, eight months after my crippled home-coming, he and I sat late outdoors talking of the brighter stars overhead, and, when I rose to go up to read in my room, he detained me.

"Oh, Booth——" he said, and paused.

"Yes, sir?"

I stood still; and after a moment he spoke hurriedly, almost under his breath, as if apologetically.

"I thought you might like to know," my father said, "I got the last of those bills of yours paid today."

In my room that night I didn't read; I didn't light the gas.

What good such wretched dark vigils do helpless fools, who may say? But though I went on being foolish and helpless, sometimes dangerously, one single useful item for human conduct had been stabbed into me: Never afterward did I contract a debt that I didn't know I could pay. I seem to have been one of those who improve only through punishment; yet the thought doesn't now discourage me. Whole nations are like that.

VII. The End of Those Days

THROUGHOUT MY NEW ENGLAND school days I'd expected that in the autumn of '89 I'd be a freshman at Harvard; but more than lack of means kept me at home. I had reached there, pallid from night work, coughing, stooped, and emaciated; my family were so indomitable in their affections as to be frightened about me, especially when I dropped before a national epidemic as soon as it reached Indiana. At least in title new to us, it was called "La Grippe," and journalistic humor made merry both with the disease and its name until the hearses rolled too thickly. The Christmas holidays were over when I arose, an enfeebled shred only faintly curious about what was to become of itself.

A singular foreigner had drifted to Indianapolis—a man so reticent that gossipy investigation never unearthed his nationality; but he seemed able to teach anybody anything. He taught cheaply, and his great talent somewhat advanced even me in learning. I tutored with him the rest of that school year, and made unskillful charcoal studies from live models at the new School of Art in the building downtown that had once been Henry Ward Beecher's church.[1] By the end of the summer, thrift at home had again provided a modest educational fund for me; I was in better health, and my mother brightly planned that I should enter the sophomore class at Princeton. Once more I mystified her.

In August, at an Indiana lake, I'd played tennis with a girl whose opinion of Robert Browning and George Meredith differed spiritedly from my own.[2] Literary criticism, I have since observed, is dogmatic in propor-

---

1. The Indiana School of Art was founded by Theodore Clement Steele (1847–1926) in 1889. If Tarkington is referring to Steele himself here, he must be making a joke about the native Hoosier having recently returned, in 1885, from Germany, where he had been perfecting his craft. A member of the so-called Hoosier Group that included William Forsyth (1854–1935) and John Ottis Adams (1851–1927), Steele based himself in Indianapolis and the surrounding Hoosier countryside and became an accomplished Impressionist.

2. The lake was Lake Maxinkuckee in Marshall County, a little more than one

tion to its youthful lack of understanding—some of it remaining always young—and I was disturbed by the satirical gaiety, almost insulting, with which this opponent treated all my certainties. In particular, she was disrespectful of my announcement that George Meredith and Robert Browning ranked not among the great; for at that time I was encamped against such novelties in poetry and prose—especially when I was looked upon as an ignoramus for not appreciating them. Summer ended unsatisfactorily.

She returned to Lafayette, where she lived; but I could not let the matter rest. I hadn't a wish in the world except to continue the argument about Meredith and Browning.

At Lafayette was Purdue University, and I lost no time in discovering that a great instructor in pen-and-ink drawing was a member of the Purdue faculty. Sometimes I had designed myself to be a painter or perhaps a sculptor; but my dabblings in color and with clay were all prophecies that I'd never be either. Then I thought that at least I could hope to be the next best thing, an illustrator in black and white. What I needed now, I vehemently urged at home, was craftsmanship in the linear art; nowhere except at Purdue under Prof. Ernest Knaufft could I achieve this, and, in deep puzzlement, my parents consented to Purdue, for a year, instead of Princeton.[3] From the Lafayette station I drove, not to Purdue but to announce that I was present to talk about Meredith and Browning for at least a year; and seldom in my life have I caused more astonishment—or pretty laughter.

Enrolled as a student, I found immediately that others wished to talk to her for at least a year and that they included my nominal superiors, most of the unmarried professors and instructors in the university. The position of an undergraduate struggling to monopolize anybody's conversation and herself against the competition of his own faculty is disadvantageous, and, as I was at the age when one is timid this minute and too fresh the next, there were embarrassments.

George and John Liven Things Up

Despondent, I sometimes devoted myself to the curriculum and even, slightly, to athletics. Football in the Middle West being then indeed in its

---

hundred miles north of Indianapolis and a popular summer vacation spot, then as now, for well-to-do Indianapolis families. The girl was Geneve Reynolds. Her father James had gone to Asbury College with Booth's uncle Newton.

3. Knaufft (1864–1942) was indeed a young, highly regarded teacher whose pupils included, at the time, Bruce Rogers (1870–1957), later to win fame as a graphic artist, book designer, and typographer. He was the creator of the Centaur font.

infancy, I occasionally played on the Purdue scrub, a preposterous fact I'd forgotten until the other day I received a letter from a classmate: "I used to envy you the poker face, when, playing football, you carried the same expression when you made a thirty-yard run or got your head sat upon." The implication that I'd learned to conceal strong emotion surprises me; though it's true that at Purdue my secret sorrow wasn't guessed in the chapter house that had offered me shelter.

This cheerful spot, luckily for all the brethren, often held a special liveliness at week ends; there'd be a welcoming clamor at the entrance and shouts would summon the studious from their rooms upstairs: "Yay, it's George and John; George and John are here, everybody!" This meant that two youths, recent graduates, had arrived from Chicago, where journalism already supported them, and that until Monday we'd all be listening uproariously to George Ade and John McCutcheon.[4] Like Mr. Riley at home, these were brilliancies out of another world, and days and long evenings with them were amelioration for what I suffered from professorial and other rivals who talked better about George Meredith and Robert Browning than I did. In the end, however, the bachelor faculty was no happier than I; it was to a member of the board of trustees that her engagement was eventually announced.[5]

... A few days before the opening of the next college year I stopped at Princeton—to please my mother—on my way to Harvard. She'd stipulated that I was to spend a week at Princeton; then, if I didn't like it, I could go on to Cambridge. In Nassau Street I descended from a station surrey and looked across the front campus at Nassau Hall, determined not to like it. Something unexpected happened to me—gray-brown old stone, ivies, elms, the cupola of Old North high in the sunshine—suddenly it was with me as though my skeptical and inquiring glance had been returned, not by a stranger but with kindly warmth by a grand old person already my friend. Thus instantly Harvard, not inconsolable, lost a student whose description I have but now been reading.

Cousins I'd never seen lived then in Princeton; and a daughter of the family sends me, in 1941, a letter to them written by my father fifty years ago: "I write in the interest of our boy, Newton Booth Tarkington, who is destined by his mother to go to the College of New Jersey before devoting

---

4. Ade (1866–1944), Purdue '87, was one of the most popular and successful humorists of his day. McCutcheon, Purdue '89, would become nationally recognized for his work as a newspaper cartoonist in Chicago, winning the Pulitzer in 1932.

5. Geneve married William V. Stuart in 1896. He had been elected mayor of Lafayette in 1887 but would not become a Purdue trustee until 1899. With competition like this, it is easy to see why the young Tarkington became discouraged in his pursuit.

himself to journalistic art, or something of that indefinitive mode of procedure toward the poorhouse. I'd like him to be comfortably housed and to have plenty of substantial food, as he is long-boned and needs filling out. He is twenty-one, is five feet, eleven inches tall, dark brown eyes and hair, a long face and an ambitiously prominent nose with nostrils to please Napoleon himself. He is fine-tempered, gay and good. He is nervous, sympathetic and affectionate, and without pretense."

Except for the nose, my memory has almost no recognition of the person described; and in particular the comprehensive adjective "good" seems founded upon paternal indulgence only. The letter implies anxiety about my health, and this may account for the ascribed goodness: parents easily mistake an only son's flat chest and sonorous cough for nobility of character.

"It has been a question," my father added, "whether to send him to an exclusively Art school or to study broadening branches of learning first. I am afraid it was a mistake that he did not take a graduating course; but that is a past mistake."

My father never saw profit in dwelling upon past mistakes once they were understood, and neither did I; but the one here in question I had determined to rectify. It had been caused by an increasingly general belief that a classical education was useless to an American. Uncle Newton had been caught by this idea. He said that Latin and Greek had been of no value that he could see either to himself or my father; progressive American youth should study science and the live languages, not the dead ones; and, as Uncle Newton's lightest word was law to my mother, and my father never argued, I had "prepped" for "Harvard Scientific" and had stressed courses in biology and chemistry, as well as in modern languages, at Purdue. Now, arrived in Princeton, I thought to change all that, go academic and become a bachelor of arts.

With little Latin and no Greek thus far, I'd have to work like a farm horse; but that was what at least I wished to do. I presented credentials, was sent to professors for various examinations, and found myself finally in the presence of that great dean who has seen his own bronze statue in his own lifetime. I showed him the schedule that I'd prepared for lecture and classroom hours.

"You can't!" Andy West said.[6] "Thirty-two hours a week would bring nothing but brain fever to the student who attempted them. Sixteen hours a week is the limit. I'll let you try sixteen if you insist."

---

6. Andrew Fleming West (1853–1943), Princeton '74, was the son of a Presbyterian minister. A droll, heavy man who would later win an epic battle with school president Woodrow Wilson over the location of the graduate college (of which he was dean), he had returned to Princeton to take the Giger chair in Latin in 1883. The author

Thus, with the dean's assistance, I lost my bachelorship. I accepted his sixteen, found these classroom hours so congenial that they were more pleasure than work, and, admitted to the Class of '93 in its junior year, indefinitely postponed the extra courses that would make me eligible for a diploma. I never did find time for them, nor regretted that I didn't.

What took their place was absorption into Princeton life itself—the generous Princeton life of those easy days, with its love of the very place and its devotion to every symbol that expressed Princeton's everlasting warmhearted and high-minded meanings. For me, my first sight of Nassau Hall had been unexpectedly a vision of the Promised Land—nor ever has the vision faded or the promise failed. I think that only once did I hold a doubt of the wisdom that had sent me there. This was when I read the program for the first glee-club concert in my junior year and without warning discovered, half an hour before the event, that I was to be a soloist.

I could lurk obscure among my fellow bassos and boom through choruses confidently enough; but I had no belief that I could discharge my single voice into the faces of a large audience and remain in a standing position. Merely reading the program set me to shaking pitiably—an ague that continued, got worse with every moment of the solo, and repeated itself at all of our concerts throughout the next two years. Urgently entreated, the other members of the glee club, chorusing, stood as close behind me as possible during the solo, indulging my hope that the silhouettes of my vibrating legs might merge with those of their motionless black trousers; but I was often depressed to see auditors in the nearer rows before us staring surprisedly at my knees. Except in theatricals, when I was pretending to be somebody not myself, never after my confident infancy did I without palsy meet the gaze of an audience.

The new psychiatry, or its imitations, might dissect out fancy causes for excessive nervousness before and during a public exhibition of oneself; but I think that in great part my glee club and other jitters, and subsequent ones, were emphasized by a Princeton code. Princeton derision for the slightest hint of show-off was healthily extreme. Self-pushery, showmanship, self-conscious worth, and love of prominence—all worse than crime—were made ludicrous, raised mocking shouts and burlesque slogans on the campus; yet never was there a place where a little proficiency in anything roused heartier cheering. We hated, laughingly, a boy who thought he did a thing well; so, naturally, all of us had a horror of thinking that we ourselves

---

of *Alcuin and the Rise of Christian Schools* (1892), he was an eminent classicist and ardent defender of the study of Latin and Greek who went on to cofound the American School of Classical Studies in Rome (1895) and to become president of the American Philological Association (1901–2).

did anything well—and, as few important things are done well and those who do them are never satisfied with themselves, it's my present belief that we taught one another nothing more valuable.

Easy-going as Princeton life then was, the days were crowded, and so were the nights of writing and drawing for the undergraduate periodicals. My oil lamp burned often enough until dawn and I'd still be loath to stop, though I knew how inconsiderately my roommate would drag me by the ankles out of bed to hustle me, when he could, to my morning place in the chapel choir. Summer vacation came too soon—a sorrowful one for my family and me.

A Busy Senior Year

All of his life Uncle Newton had been more than the head of his clan. Either absent or present, and independently of his great generosities, he'd seemed the very life of it. With the midnight death message from Sacramento, a blankness came upon the least of us; and it was from a house of mourning that I returned to Princeton as a senior.

I think that may have been the busiest year of my life, at least until the college theatricals were over; my powerful roommate, Big Murray, daily announced, roaring plaintively, that my nightlong energies made life a curse to him.[7] When spring came I was idler and had only one desire—to stretch every moment of every passing day to last as long as I could hold it. Even undergraduates were sentimental about some things then, thank heaven! and Princeton seniors were inwardly solemn when they took the steps of Old North to sing through the twilights of their last days in college. None, I think, was sadder than I; for I knew that I was coming to the end of two years not an instant of which I would have changed, and that I was to part with friends not a day of whose merry and kind companionship I could bear to spare from the rest of my life.

My mother and sister came from home for class day; and then, when the hard hour of farewells was over, we went to spend the summer on Narragansett Bay. Whole afternoons I sat alone upon salty rocks, staring at the meaningless water; and I was heavy with dismay because almost suddenly the best of life—thus I bereavedly thought of Princeton—lay behind me.

The future meant nothing at all to me until we were home again, with the first frost, and I discovered myself to be an unemployed person in busy Indianapolis.

---

7. Harold Griffith Murray, who went on to found a New York advertising firm that specialized in advertising American products in Asia.

AS I SEEM TO ME

A Hard-Working Amateur

Ostensibly I was a somewhat elaborately educated young man who'd soon be on the job, profitably making a place for himself in his own world. This of course was correct expectation, and I'd surely be thought rather disgraceful if I didn't fulfill it. The community didn't lean to gentlemen of leisure—especially not to young gentlemen of leisure. For that matter, neither did I; but, unfortunately, I couldn't do anything except write and draw—or amateur-act a little and amateur-sing a little—and Indianapolis didn't much believe that a living could be made out of drawing or writing. Again, neither did I—not out of such drawing and writing as mine.

I wasn't ambitious. That is, I had no ambition to be anything or to be known as anything. I didn't yearn to be a novelist or a playwright or a distinguished illustrator. On the other hand, I did wish to do something. Having found that I couldn't paint, I mightily yearned to draw good pictures. Therefore I began to draw pictures in earnest—and almost at the same time I began to write a novel. This seems inconsistent and a little odd. I had no conscious wish to write a novel; I didn't deliberately, so to say, begin one or feel anything like the interest in writing that I did in drawing, and yet I began to write a novel. Perhaps it's nearer the truth to say that it began to write itself. It went on writing itself—I had no control of it—and, after wandering whither it would for several months, it banged its head into a stone wall at the end of a blind alley and seemed to die there. As it appeared to be through with itself, I thought I was through with it, and without regret put the self-willed scribblings away.

Most of my work was done at night. My mother lamented, but indulged me, and she and my father understood one unreasonable reason why scratching paper till after daylight was more than ever congenial to me. Already I'd begun to appear to be a loafer, and even this reputation was rather better, I thought, than letting it become known that I usually spent fourteen hours of the twenty-four trying to draw and trying to write. In seeming, the night was a cloak; if one had to do foolish things, 't were better they were done after dark.

When asked what I was doing, I had no good answer, but said, "Oh, just fooling around," and did my best to prove it with a pair of colts, a red-wheeled runabout, and amateur plays I wrote and acted in for charities and a cheery membership, the Dramatic Club. Thanks to Uncle Newton, I didn't have to prove to myself that I was no longer a financial burden at home. One of his sixteen residuary legatees, I could live on the rents of two small buildings in which my father invested the inheritance for me; and my experience as my own rent collector would prove to anybody that nature hadn't designed me for business.

One of my two tenants was a grocer who so thoroughly assumed an attitude toward me that for a time it convinced himself. His periodic emotion, at sight of me, was that of a hard-working man engaged in serious affairs and interrupted by a kept imbecile come to importune for allowance handouts. I grew to dread the grocer's truculent eye, postponed my timid monthly appearances before him; and one day, when I came, he burst out at me even before I spoke.

"You go home!" he shouted with passionate sincerity. "Hain't you got no better sense than come around here boddering me for money? Listen, I got debts to pay!"

Desiring a better location, he moved out, owing me four months' rent; and one afternoon not long afterward I was embarrassed to come face to face with him on the street. He blushed not, but, looking me full in the eye, laughed openly and loudly, passed on and was noisy in the distance behind me.

. . . I sent many too laborious pen-and-ink sketches to *Life*, that fine satiric weekly then to America what *Punch* was to Britain; but they all came back—hurried back, it seemed to me. I worked at short stories, too, many kinds of short stories and all laborious, like my drawings. I set them into various periods, trying to flavor different styles with phrasings suitable to the times and places and the types of people I used. The stories were of seventeenth- and eighteenth-century England, of eighteenth-century America, of Indiana in the early nineteenth century, of California in '49, of France under Robespierre. The splendid magazines of the 90's, the *Century*, *Harper's*, *McClure's*, and *Scribner's*, rejected all of these manuscripts so rapidly that sometimes I thought my poor things must have been stopped and returned from Philadelphia; they didn't seem to have had time to get all the way to New York and back.

Fool's Goldsmith

I strained and fought with writing, striving to accomplish styles and to chime style with subject; and all the while, though I knew that I worked at drawing because I liked to draw, I hadn't the least idea why I worked twice as hard at writing. My manuscripts pleased me no better than they did the magazines, but I couldn't see just what was wrong with them, nor, naturally, could the editors spare time to tell me. Printed rejection slips clarify only one point.

Without informing me, my sympathetic sister asked Mr. Riley to criticize one of my stories, and he, poor man, read half of it indignantly. It was an eighteenth-century stylistic imitation done a-purpose in the manner of Goldsmith; but this hadn't been mentioned to Mr. Riley. He made a few marginal attempts in pencil to modernize and Hoosierize the phrasing, reached the middle, and blew up. "Damn it, this is Goldsmith!" he wrote across the page—and we all felt the episode should close there without explanation. It's often best just to let things go.

A Successful Contributor

For a young man in the middle twenties, my lifelong earnings were unimposing. At ten, I had earned half of fifteen cents for shoveling snow—seven cents plus my share of a one-cent stick of candy halved with the other shoveler. When I was thirteen, my Grandfather Booth had given me a dollar to draw a charcoal portrait of him that hurt his feelings; and at Princeton I'd had fifteen dollars for a Lit. prize story and twenty-five for the words of a prize song. Now, out of a clear sky, *Life* accepted a drawing of mine, a burlesque of Aubrey Beardsley, with accompanying text satirizing a semi-prose style of Oscar Wilde's.[8] The check from *Life* was twenty dollars, in one bright flash bringing my total earnings up to sixty-one dollars and seven and a half cents—not counting my share of Punch-and-Judy takings in Marshall, Illinois, or my receipts from the play of Jesse James in our stable, sums later not precisely calculable. I wasn't vitally concerned with money-making, it's true; yet it can't be denied that the amount of one's earnings usually bears some relation to the measure of his usefulness to society. Since my whole previous life had shown only a trifle over forty-one dollars' worth of usefulness, the twenty-dollar boost was inspiring.

Squandering ink like water, I flooded the mails with drawings and bits of writing for *Life*, which seemed to have forgotten overnight that I'd successfully established myself as a contributor. Something more than thirty offerings, I think, brought rejection slips before my flush of hope subsided.

---

8. Beardsley (1872–98), three years younger than Tarkington, had illustrated Oscar Wilde's *Salomé* and self-consciously cultivated the decadent-eccentric, homosexual-aesthete image that characterized the Wilde set. Beardsley's bio reads like a late-Victorian cliché; he managed (1) to die young, at age twenty-five, (2) in France, (3) of tuberculosis, and (4) shortly after entering the Catholic Church. His illustrations were grotesque and frequently erotic. In short, he was a suitable figure for a Tarkington parody. Titled "In the Borderland," Tarkington's work appeared in the April 4, 1895, issue of *Life*. Tarkington biographer James Woodress judged the text and sketch to be "remarkably unmirthful today."

I'd been out of college two years when there came a second stimulation: my sister contrived to get one of my Dramatic Club comedies into the hands of a dramatists' agent in New York.[9] The agent wrote briskly of important actors almost certain to like the piece, and said I'd better come East to see her at once; but, when I hurriedly did, I was somewhat let down by her advice that before being shown to a manager the manuscript needed rewriting under her direction. I stayed through the autumn and winter, rewrote and rewrote the play, and drew more pictures and wrote more short stories; and, professionally speaking, got rather worse than nowhere. The agent's interest waned with every rewriting I brought her, though I slavishly followed all of her suggestions; and, when I presented myself to hear her opinion of the last edition I made of the tortured comedy, her manner with me was so absent-minded that I thought it tactful not to call again. Wondering, in fact, why I'd come to New York at all, I returned limply to my "fooling around" in Indianapolis.

There, recovering from an illness, I wrote in bed a story I thought rather better contrived than the others. Nowadays its manner might vulgarly be called streamlined, though here and there touched with eighteenth-century phrasing, as the setting was of that period. The theme was accidental, suggesting itself to me in a meandering moment of meditation upon *John-a-Dreams*. This was one of the aesthetic little magazines then unprofitably published; and my Princeton classmate, Robert Sloss, who edited and printed it was so hard up for illustrations gratis that for some time he'd been printing all the drawings I sent him.[10] Now and then I included verses, or perhaps a playlet, to accompany the illustrations; for I drew the pictures first and afterward wrote the text they seemed to suggest.

When I fell sick I'd just finished a small pen drawing for *John-a-Dreams*—two men in early eighteenth-century clothes, one large and irate facing a French-looking dapper young gentlemen across a gaming table, with some indistinct figures about a doorway in the background. Convalescing, I glanced over drawings on hand, came upon this one, and thought

---

9. The play was *The Prodigals*, a youthful, romantic effort set—somewhat improbably—in Trenton, New Jersey, circa 1790. The agent was Elisabeth Marbury (1856–1933). Tarkington does not mention her name, and his biographer Woodress mentions her only in passing, but Bessy Marbury was an important, trailblazing theatrical agent and producer whose clients would later include Tarkington's fellow Hoosier Cole Porter. Tarkington returned to Indiana in the spring of 1896.

10. Robert Sloss (1872–1920) was a journalist. Now quite obscure, his papers are held at Princeton. In his 1910 essay "The Wireless Century," he predicted with extraordinary prescience that in 2010 people would carry "wireless telegraphs" that function very much like today's mobile devices.

that Sloss might be pleased if I sent him text to fit it. So I wrote the story; but, by the time I was out of bed, *John-a-Dreams* had perished.

The manuscript, eleven thousand words, was of an uncomfortable length for any of the professional magazines; but couldn't be made shorter, though I rewrote it several times before naming it *Monsieur Beaucaire* and sending it forth upon its expected misadventures. It had them. *The Century, Harper's, McClure's, Scribner's, Munsey's*, all of course returned it with the accustomed rapidity and the printed slip. I put the shamed thing away, half forgot it, wrote more stories for rejection and another play or two for the Dramatic Club.

. . . As I review those years it seems to me that my family were heroic about me; their embarrassment must have been severe. A white-haired, greatly successful citizen spoke to me one evening on the country-club veranda: "Booth, I asked your father what you're doing. He says you're still trying to be one of these damn literary fellers."

I mumbled, and he looked at me pityingly; but I knew that his pity was for my father.

One day as I sat facing the fact that I'd been working for four years with blank results, I remembered the novel I'd begun when I came home after Princeton, and abruptly I saw why it had jammed itself into a blind alley. I got the manuscript out, began it again, found that I had some control over the story, and, though I was without any hope that it would ever see print—I couldn't imagine anything of mine doing that—I worked month after month after month upon it.[11]

A Thin-Skinned Hoosier

I tried to keep out of it any imitation of my literary gods, Alphonse Daudet, Victor Cherbuliez, Dickens, Irving, Henry James, Howells, Mark Twain, Stevenson, Thomas Hardy, Thackeray, and George Meredith—I'd at last grown up enough to come round to Meredith—but of course bits and echoes of all of them got into it. Mark Twain was the hardest to keep out, because I tried to pitch the style principally in the key of Middle West ordinary speech. My father's talk, recorded literally, was like Mark Twain's writing; so were the spoken words of most of the intelligent midland men I knew of that generation, and daily I heard that way of speech all about me. It was the native way, just as it was natural to Mark Twain, himself a midland man of the same period; and as he talked, so he customarily wrote.

---

11. This novel became *The Gentleman from Indiana*.

The texture of my novel thus couldn't wholly avoid being pseudo-Mark Twainish in spots if kept faithful, and, though of course romance and even melodrama got into the made-up events, I kept the telling as homely as I youthfully could.

There was something behind the story—a young hurt and a young championage. I'd first begun to feel the hurt, rather puzzledly, when from Princeton I visited Eastern classmates and their families, and observed that my Hoosier origin was ignored with conscious tact by these kindhearted people. It was as if I had a physical defect, they so thoughtfully avoided seeming to be aware of it. Later, in New York and elsewhere, I'd met several people of consequence who didn't warm up at all when cordially reminded that they'd been born in Indiana. Friendly girls spoke teasingly of the Middle West; gentle elderly ladies said forgivingly that they didn't think of me as Hoosier born and bred; I was more like one of them. Eastern newspapers then cherished the legend that Indiana was a backwoods state; our rusticity was an established mark for mechanized journalistic humor.

Senility Just Around the Corner

Sensitive and even resentful, I tried to make my novel answer all this nonsense. That heaven of my boyhood, Marshall, was just over the Indiana border and in Illinois; but out of fond memories I built it into an Indiana county seat and set the scene of my story there. A thing the novel tried to say was that in the matter of human character the people of such an out-of-the-way midland village were as estimable as any others anywhere, maybe rather more so—indeed, that even in its most bucolic aspect Indiana belonged to the beautiful and the good. This, in my sensitive young fervor, was my emotional tribute to the land of my birth.

I was as unconscious of the youngness of my thickening manuscript as I was of my own youngness, for I took the age of twenty-seven to be a movement on the downhill slope of life. Virtually middle-aged!—and what was I accomplishing? I couldn't draw and I couldn't write; yet here I was, digging away at a long novel that would never be a book. To have any life, writing had to become print, a transmutation that was never going to happen to any writing of mine—so why go on writing? I was at work on the last chapter when there came the first hint of a change.

My sister was in New York and had with her, though I didn't know it, a copy of the story I'd written to illustrate a drawing, *Monsieur Beaucaire*. She had also a letter to Mr. S. S. McClure, who had made the magazine that bore his name an influence upon American life. She left the note of introduction and the manuscript at his office for him, and, calling some days later, was told by a tired associate editor that Mr. McClure regretted his inability to use the manuscript because of its inconvenient length—too long for a short story, too short for a serial.

"Did he read it?" my sister asked.

"Well—no," the associate admitted. "I read it."

"You did?" my sister asked. "Didn't you think the poetic quotations at the heads of chapters quite good?"

"Oh, very," he told her, for he wished to be as kind as he could. "The poetic quotations were excellent."

"There aren't any," she said. "Where's Mr. McClure?"

I'd have been mortified if I'd known of the fuss she made in that editorial office, an unexampled to-do Mr. McClure gaily applauded for its sisterly gallantry. She telegraphed me: "Mr. McClure wishes to see everything you've written. Send him the manuscript of the novel immediately."

I sent it gloomily: she had too often been sure that manuscripts of mine were going to delight the hearts of editors. Two weeks passed; then the morning mail brought me a letter from a man I'd never met, an established writer whose work I humbly admired, Hamlin Garland. The letter began: "Mr. McClure has given me your manuscript, *The Gentleman From Indiana*, to read. You are a novelist."

I had only a half belief that I was reading Hamlin Garland's letter accurately or that his signature was genuine. I thought that there must be a trick to it somewhere; but the next mail brought a letter from Mr. McClure: "We accept your manuscript to be published in book form by Doubleday, McClure and Company, and we are considering it for serial publication in the magazine, though for this purpose you would have to cut it almost in half. If the idea interests you, perhaps you'd better come to New York as soon as you can."

. . . That day, marked for me by incredulity and a wondering gratitude to my sister and to Hamlin Garland and to Mr. McClure, was a pleasant one for my father and mother, though they were more serious than exultant; they'd always been, touchingly, more interested in my work itself than in its acceptance. Yet in one aspect the day was a culmination for them as well as for me. The end of my long struggle to be worth anyhow some of my salt was also the end of their equally long need to explain me to puzzled kinsfolk and commiserative friends. Looking back upon it now, I see that it was moreover the end, not of my youth—which lasted a long time afterward, too long!— but of a period in my life, the years with which this narrative deals. That day was like the happy ending of a story, and we were all to live happily ever afterward. Life is kindest when it permits these hours of completely cheerful illusion; necessarily they're but brief.

Indiana Is Not Amused

... *McClure's* began to print my Indiana story while I was still in New York compressing the final chapters of the long manuscript.[12] What I gladly did to it was drastic—"Effendi" Doubleday, who was to publish the book in full, usually referred to the serial as "the cablegram"—but as a workmanly experience the extreme condensing helped a novice hand invaluably. Before I finished, two installments had appeared—and without mention of this literary advent in any of the New York papers. No one spoke of it to me except a few intimate friends and the members of the staff of *McClure's*. Letters from my father and mother and sister reported that certain of my aunts and cousins had said agreeable things about the two installments; and I had the impression that nobody not personally concerned was reading the story. I was mistaken.

Newspapers from Indiana hadn't been sent to me; but when I reached home—somewhat bashfully because my novel too sentimentally bragged of home—I learned the truth. For that, indeed, I didn't need to wait to see the papers. On the very day of my arrival two people stopped me on the street, one angrily, the other derisively, and I was informed that my serial held Indiana up to scorn; I'd assaulted the sacred altars. Never was a young champion more astounded by a cursing from the championed.

Editorials mentioned me as a traitor, and a Hoosier-born officer in the United States Army wrote to the papers, asking why I wasn't run out of the state. A lovely lady, an old friend and a true Christian, said to me, almost with tears, "We had heard that you were writing a novel, Booth, and when *When Knighthood Was in Flower* came out we were all happy because at first we thought maybe you'd written it and that the name of the author, Charles Major, was a nom de plume you'd taken. Ah, Booth, Booth, if it only could have been!" I couldn't comfort her, or myself either.[13]

---

12. *The Gentleman from Indiana* was serialized in *McClure's* in May–October 1899. The book restores the material that Tarkington had to cut to suit the magazine's needs.

13. Charles Major (1856–1913), in fact, was the real name of Edward Caskoden, under whose name *When Knighthood Was in Flower* had been published. Tarkington may have meant to put the latter name into the mouth of his interlocutor, since Major was a prominent Indianapolis lawyer. In any case, the romantic, sentimental style of *Knighthood* was precisely what Tarkington had begun to leave behind in *The Gentleman from Indiana* in favor of something more like Howellsian realism.

Indignation with me seemed to be really of public proportions. Two short months had made me a prominent citizen, but prominent the wrong way; and again my family had to be heroic about me. Not that their grief was for what I'd done—they held up their heads as if they were proud of me—but they were hurt for me, of course, more deeply than I was for myself; and naturally that hurt me for them. Another installment of the serial appeared just after I came home, and the attacks, usually the more scornful for their brevity, increased in frequency. Except in anger, my story wasn't publicly mentioned at all, nor was I.

From the day of its acceptance by *McClure's*, I'd often wondered, with well-founded misgivings, what Mr. Riley would think of the novel when it was printed; for, though he hadn't seen any manuscript of mine since the unfortunate Goldsmith episode, I knew that of course he would read the serial—or at least begin to read it. He didn't speak of it to me at all; I doubt if he spoke of it to anyone. When we were together we talked of everything else—though one day, for a moment, I thought that he was about to bring up the subject. We were talking in a general way of contemporary writing when abruptly his face flushed and he rose and closed the door.

He's going to tell me, I thought; but he didn't.

Mr. Riley as a Critic

When Knighthood Was in Flower was in rich best-selling bloom with the reading populace and reviewers everywhere just then, and particularly in Indiana, which was proud to be the author's birthplace. What Mr. Riley, red-faced, closed the door to express as he strode fiercely up and down the room, was his private true opinion of that buoyant romance. I saw that he meant me to understand something he couldn't otherwise convey: he didn't like my serial, but it only made him sad; the other new Indiana author made him furious.

Another day I'd gone to see him when he was ill, and, as I sat by his bedside, he said a thing he may have meant for a consolatory bit of advice extracted from his own experience. His face on the pillow was never more like the death mask of Keats that it so strongly resembled. He'd been silent with his eyes closed, for some time; then he spoke suddenly. "Renown!" he said, and repeated the word in a resounding voice. "Renown! Renown! The higher you lift your head the more thrown stones will strike it!"

This was like a memorable sentence I heard that year from the recognized chief man of letters in America. Mr. Howells was in Indianapolis to give a reading, and, as I drove him to my sister's house for dinner, I made bold to ask him if in his supremacy he still gave attention to critics of his work. His reply wasn't heartening to a young man just beginning to be printed. "It can't be helped," he said. "They can still hurt you—long, long after their last power to please you is gone."

... When the later installments of my serial were published, the anger against it and against me abated. Those who read the story, at first naturally irritated by thinking that the rustic setting was only one more of the stale old gibes at Indiana, began to comprehend that at least I'd meant well. They perceived that I'd tried, however ineptly, not to knock down but to set up; that what I'd made, clumsily enough, was really intended as a wreath of laurel, my votive offering. When the book appeared, reproducing the original manuscript in full, it was received with a friendly indulgence. My family were able to look pleased with me not defiantly.

The book didn't extort anything from Mr. Riley, though. He didn't speak of it, nor did he speak of my next one, or the next, or the next, or the next. When I was at home we were as gaily and affectionately intimate with each other as of yore; but I wrote book after book, play after play, and not once did any word of his admit recognition of the fact that I had become professionally a writer. My feelings weren't hurt. I went my own varied and stumbling way, observing with regret that my work held no interest for either of two great literary artists I most delightedly admired, Mr. Riley and Mr. Howells; for Mr. Howells's columns of superb criticism omitted me as patiently as Mr. Riley did.

Fifteen years after my earliest magazine acceptance, there had just been published the first novel in which, through actual human character, I began to seek the nature of man;[14] and one morning, as I sat in my workroom, I glanced through a front window and saw Mr. Riley's limousine stop before the house. He was past sixty now, an invalid unable to walk without difficulty; and he sent his driver to beg me to come immediately and speak to him. I went out hurriedly, wondering what was on his mind.

"Yesterday and last night," he said, and his face was bright, "I read your new novel. I've come to tell you what I think of it."

Fifteen years!—but the blessed man came as soon as he could.

That was the integrity of a great literary conscience in those days; its benison was bestowed the first instant that it could be an honest one.

... As I said a little while ago, however, these confessions really close with the day upon which Hamlin Garland's and Mr. McClure's letters reached me. Of course, at the time, I mistook that day for the conclusion

---

14. Tarkington is speaking of *The Flirt*, which was serialized in the *Saturday Evening Post* from December 1912 through February 1913, and published in book form by Doubleday, Page & Company in March 1913.

of an apprenticeship better seen as unending; but I'm not mistaken now in observing that a course of my life ended there in a decisive change.

These pages have examined the creature that I was while centered upon the home of my boyhood. From the first of that time to the last of it I see the creature loved, pampered, and fought for by three too generous hearts that had never any reward except their own goodness.

PART TWO

The World Does Move

I

THE THIN YOUNG MAN who had come East to seek his fortune stood upon the steamer's forward deck with the sea breeze blowing upon his eager face and hastening the combustion of the Sweet Caporal cigarette he had just lighted at the spark of its predecessor. Before him the immense castellated sky line that amazed the world swam to meet him as the steamer rushed toward it over the flat water; and, stirred by the wonder of this great sight, he exultantly whispered to himself, "New York! New York! New York!"[1]

There was nothing else like it in the universe; and that startling invention, the skyscraper, gave it the air of being not real, but a prophetic vision of what cities might strangely come to be in the Twentieth and Twenty-first centuries. Yet there the new Cosmopolis was actually before him; and already he knew something of its miracles, learned in holiday visits during his New England school days and in week-ends away from Princeton. These week-ends were not of the long ago, having concluded only a year or so earlier; but at his age a year or so appeared to be a tremendous amount of time; he was returning to the glamorous city after what he felt had been a vast absence.

To him, as to most Westerners, New York meant Fifth Avenue and the Park, with long processions of romantically elegant ladies driving behind noble, sleek horses glitteringly harnessed; it meant an endless choice of theatres, with brilliant new plays done by superb actors; it meant a splendour of restaurants, with oysters and partridge and Burgundy unknown to the "cafés" of the great flat land behind the Alleghanies. It meant the Metropolitan Museum, the opera, the new Waldorf, the Holland House, Delmonico's, Wall Street, Richard Harding Davis, John Drew, Weber and Fields, Tiffany's, the *Sun* editorials, and the New York World Building.[2] For that supreme

---

1. This was the autumn of 1895, two years—not one, as he says later—after he had left Princeton. Tarkington had come to New York at the behest of agent Elisabeth Marbury to work on his play, *The Prodigals*, under her supervision. See page 104. Tarkington stayed in New York until the spring of 1896.

2. Davis (1864–1916) was a famous, and dashing, war correspondent and journalist.

skyscraper floated its dome upon the very clouds; high over all it was the ever-exhilarating, ever-dumbfounding symbolic monument that loomed before the passengers from the West as the Cortlandt Street Ferry carried them across the Hudson from the great terminal station of the Pennsylvania Railroad in Jersey City; and if there were only seven wonders in all the tumultuous great modern world of the *fin de siècle*, here was surely one of them.

But to the thin young man upon the ferryboat's forward deck, New York now meant something special that had not concerned him during his school and college adventurings there. Somewhere in the great hazy buildings north of Cortlandt Street there were fateful thresholds inaccessible to him; yet he must try to cross them, for they led to formidable desks where sat men of unlimited power dealing out destiny as coolly as a whist player deals cards. The thin young man's future was somewhere obscurely shuffled into the pile of destinies at the disposal of these potentates—they were managers who produced plays, editors who produced magazines, and publishers who produced books; and in the young man's trunk there were the manuscripts of two plays, of an unfinished novel, and of a now-forgotten number of short stories. The arrival in New York of that Cortlandt Street ferryboat, moreover, took place upon the bright morning of an autumn day a little more than thirty years ago; and the thin young man's name coincided with my own.

I go back to that day now not because I am engaging in an autobiographical writing—for this is not a personal memoir—but because the end of the last century was the beginning of the end of an epoch not coinciding precisely with the calendar years of the Nineteenth Century; it is of the change into the present new epoch that I am writing, and I can but picture the change as it has been visible to the person most familiar to me. That day of his landing at Cortlandt Street with a luggage of hopes and manuscripts was well back into the older age, with its life and thought so different from our lives and thoughts now; and I choose—as they sometimes say in Vermont—to begin there.

We did not know, in those days, that we were approaching a new epoch; we could not possibly have imagined then the change that has come in what is relatively so short a time. In fact, we who have lived in both periods—that of the *fin de siècle* and that of the Twentieth Century—do not ourselves yet fully realize how profound is the alteration that has taken place. It has been going on from day to day, even from hour to hour, like the growth of a child

---

Drew (1853–1927) was a Shakespearean actor and the uncle of John and Lionel Barrymore. The New York World Building had been completed just five years earlier, in 1890, and at approximately three hundred feet was one of the tallest skyscrapers in the world.

to manhood; those who live with the child thus growing do not find him startling when, at thirty, he weighs one hundred and sixty pounds instead of the seven that was his weight at their first acquaintance with him. But the Massachusetts life convict who went to prison in 1896 and was pardoned in 1927 came back babbling to the penitentiary gates, clamouring piteously for readmission after a week of freedom, dumbfounded and panic-stricken. From the very moment of his release he might as well have been thrown out upon the surface of another planet.

Not one person alive in the world when that convict was sentenced, or when the thin young man reached New York with his scratchy manuscripts, could possibly have prophesied what America would be like to-day. There were a few fanatics who believed that horseless carriages were coming; there were even some ridiculous star-gazers who thought men would be seen flying over head within the next five hundred years—perhaps within a hundred; there were devotees of teetotalism who predicted, in the face of general jocose scoffing, that "temperance legislation" would some day be enacted in Washington itself; other devotees predicted something of the kind for "female suffrage"; here and there were persons who foresaw individual advances in science or a coming change in a certain custom or in a certain type of established morality; but there was not on earth a mind that could have foreseen the whole vast change as we are living with it now.

The absence of such a prophet was not a misfortune. A complete view of this future now existing as the present would have staggered the *fin de siècle* mind, possibly to its unseating. If by some miracle of prevision the world of to-day, completely as it is, could have been seen by the people of that day, there were those among them, particularly among the older clergymen, who, like the friar Captain Brazenhead confessed to, would have "died that same night howling like a wolf."[3]

---

3. The reference is to *Brazenhead the Great* (1911), by Maurice Hewlett, a prolific English novelist.

II

YET NEVER DID AN epoch more placidly believe itself the last word than did the *fin de siècle*—and every country newspaper glibly used that phrase, so sophisticated was our whole nation in those days. The *fin de siècle* was the last word in scientific achievement, in modern inventions, in literature and the fine arts, in good taste, in luxury, in elegance, in extravagance, in dress, in cleverness, and in the art of being blasé. Civilization had gone about as far as possible; we had reached the summit of the peak and after us must come the decadence, which was, indeed, already setting in with Oscar Wilde's writings and the strange drawings of Aubrey Beardsley. Thus the *fin de siècle* thought of itself when the young Midlander walked ashore from the Cortlandt Street ferryboat and went to live on the top floor or a brownstone-front boarding house with three friends who, like himself, were only a year or so out of college.[1]

Of course, that brownstone-front, which had previously been the ample and pleasant residence of New Yorkers of some quality, no longer exists. Even now the neighbourhood is not wholly unfashionable, and a handsome, tall apartment house of inhospitable appearance stands upon the site—stands there temporarily, of course, for it will naturally be replaced before long by another one, taller, handsomer, and even more inhospitable. To live in an apartment in that street costs many thousands of dollars a year nowadays; but in those other days money was scarcer and more valuable. The "first floor front" of our boarding house was occupied by a lady who paid forty dollars a week for her pleasant lodging and three excellent meals a day. Startled when we discovered this, we of the top floor thenceforth spoke of her as the Baroness Rothschild. We lived opulently ourselves, upon fifteen

---

1. The top floor of the brownstone on West Fifty-Seventh Street cost Tarkington and his roommates fifteen dollars a week. One of these roommates was James Barnes (1866–1936), who having distinguished himself as editor of the *Nassau* and as president of the Princeton Drama Association, had graduated from Princeton in 1891. He went on to become a magazine editor, war correspondent, Farragut biographer, and, from 1918 until to his death, president of the Naval History Society.

dollars a week, and had college friends in New York who made themselves comfortable enough, in agreeable neighbourhoods, for half as much.

When we went to the theatre we paid a dollar and a half for an orchestra seat; though when Sara Bernhardt came over that winter the impressive charge for such a seat was three dollars. A silk hat cost seven dollars, and of course we all had silk hats and skirted coats for Sundays, "teas," and afternoon calls. The best derby hats cost three, four, and even five dollars; soft hats were rare east of Kansas, except on farmers and politicians. There were table d'hôte dinners with wine for thirty-five cents at Italian restaurants; a dollar and a half paid for a Sunday evening table d'hôte, with music, under the great gas chandeliers of the best hotels in the town.

For it was still the age of gaslight, and how dark an American city of that period would appear to us if we could see it now as it was then after nightfall! Paris was the only *Ville Lumière*; but city of light as it was, its famous illumination of the Nineties did not light the clouds above it with half the glow of any lively American county seat after dark in 1928. Electric light was on the way; already sputtering white globes hung from long arms at the crossings of many American streets; but the lamplighter with his ladder would still be seen hurrying through the dusk for years to come. Theatres had begun to use electric lighting. Until then they had always smelled faintly and not unpleasantly of gas, for the footlights released a little before catching the flame, one from the other, and so did the upper lights over the stage and the invariable huge chandelier at the top of the house. The mildness of that light did not increase the eye repairing of oculists; and, moreover, the very craft of the actor did not suffer from it. Electric light made a lamentable change in that.

Of all our excursions from the boarding house top floor to the theatre, none was merrier than that to see Joseph Jefferson in *The Rivals*. Jefferson was an elderly man, but there was no elderliness in his "Bob Acres."[2] A fresh-coloured country youth came before us, inimitably the funniest young coward ever seen on the stage, and not until he played that part with increasingly fierce electric light glaring upon him was the illusion of youth dispelled. Maggie Mitchell, at sixty, played "Fanchon" in *The Cricket*, and what we saw was an elfish young girl;[3] old men played "young parts"; there were youthful actors, who were specialists, playing "old parts."

But nowadays the manager stares at an actor in the light of an office window and puts him on the stage to look—and usually to act—much as

---

2. Indeed, the brilliant comedic actor Jefferson (1829–1905) would have been sixty-six years old would Tarkington saw him reprise his famous role as Bob Acres.

3. Mitchell (1832–1918), in this role, was the subject of Henry James's first published work.

he does in that same illumination. Painters would feel that something had gone badly with art if old men's portraits could be painted by old painters only and young painters were limited to the portraits of young sitters. And if the thing went further, limiting painters to portraits of themselves—which is not so far from what electric light and "realism" have done to the art of acting—portrait painting might seem to be on the way to become not an art at all.

But the passing of gaslight changed many things besides acting and lighting fixtures. The gas fixtures were not beautiful—heavy chandeliers of bronzed metal, "drop lights" with long green snakes of flexible tubing feeding gas to them, side lights that were merely iron pipes protruding from the walls—and usually the more ornamental these strove to be the uglier they were. Their passing made matches less a necessity, did away with the vases of spiral paper tapers rolled by frugal housewives, altered the plans of suicides, and destroyed the most useful stock joke of the humorous weeklies and newspaper comedians.

This destroyed national joke was founded upon fact. It is not so easy to lay a gas pipe through the ground as to run a wire through the air, so there wasn't much light on the farms and in the villages; all over the country the farmers and villagers used oil lamps and candles. Some collector of antiques may already possess an oblong of cardboard whereon, in heavy black letters, is printed, "Don't Blow Out the Gas"; and it is curious to remember now that hotel-keepers usually displayed such a warning in every bedroom. For years the weekly and daily press humorists and draftsmen profited by a vast, continuous burlesquing of bucolic mishaps with city gas; and asphyxiation made into comedy was staple ware, too, for the vaudeville joker.

For the rustic sufferer himself, asphyxiation was as truly tragedy as was a fractured skull to the victim of a bicycle speeder; but the farmer had become too fixedly a stencil of urban humour to receive much sympathy. He was a bewhiskered backwoodsman and cheered another Roman holiday when all his savings were exchanged for a satchel confided to him by a well-dressed city stranger; our *fin de siècle* sophistication had only derision for him. It was otherwise with the unfortunates run down by the ruthless bicyclists; we became indignant for their sakes and sympathized with the constant editorials in the newspapers denouncing the speeders. For among other madnesses of the *fin de siècle* was the new speed mania.

But the bicycle craze was not quite yet at its maniacal maddest; all the world was not yet awheel, though most of the cities were passing ordinances forbidding the sidewalks to the wheelmen. School children were warned not to cross the streets without first looking carefully to see if bicycles were approaching from either direction; and out in the country farmers were indignant because their chickens were in frequent danger on the roads, and because horses became hysterical and ran away at sight of the miraculous new vehicles.

What was most *fin de siècle*, however, scandalizing some communities, sending some into furies of argument and others into uproarious public laughter, was a sporadic revolutionary daring in bicycle costume. Here and there a violently modern woman or girl wore divided skirts for the new sport; these were to the ankles, though brazen enough, at that; but this was not the peak defiance of all the old conventionalities. In one or two cities women riders had been seen wearing no skirts at all. Instead, they wore heavy bloomers and gaiters; but of course they did not dare to appear in the more populous streets, and they rode rapidly. When such a rider whizzed by little children they were sometimes so dazed that she would be almost out of hearing before they began to yell.

Our boarding house in New York discussed these outbreaks of the New Woman as it discussed everything, and on the top floor our decision was that we were glad our sisters and the "girls we knew" felt as little sympathy as we did with such immodesties. We held long and vehement debates upon the question of Ruskin's value to Art; but we had no argument over the wearers of bloomers and gaiters, for there we were unanimous.

It was the only subject upon which we were unanimous, I think; especially as the youngest of us was a law student and a willing debater, precociously adroit. The medical student and the young engineer, the other inhabitants of our heights, suffered themselves to be made into a plaintive and sometimes profane audience, while the law student for hour after hour used me roughly as a feebly opposing counsel. We fought over free trade, of course, and could not have imagined a time when that and "free silver" would not be the most vital of public questions; we fought interminably the battle between "realism" and "romanticism"; we wrangled long over young Stephen Crane's indebtedness to Zola's *Débâcle* for analysis of a soldier's perceptions and feelings during battle, and we were increasingly in opposition concerning the beauty and value of classical music. But here the law student always became intolerantly authoritative; he was a patron of the opera, never missed a concert of the new Polish genius, Paderewski, and was so ardently and openly in love with Madame Melba, though he had not the pleasure of her acquaintance, that he caught a dangerous cold by standing for an hour in a blizzard to see her descend from her carriage at the door of her hotel. After that, the rest of us never dared challenge his opinion upon anything musical.

III

ONE EVENING WE HAD our own gaslight accident on the top floor. An Irish housemaid used a spiral paper taper to light the gas in the hall bedroom; then she dropped it to the floor and put her foot over it to extinguish it. But there was still a flame from the taper, and the girl's petticoats, which of course were so long that they touched the floor, caught fire, and instantly she blazed from foot to head. The medical student and I heard her making strange moans of protest; but she was already in flight, a wild torch with her long thick hair aflame high over her head. We chased her down two flights of stairs before we caught her, and the medical student wrapped her tightly in a heavy curtain he had torn from a doorway as we ran.

She recovered, after a painful siege in the hospital; but the kind of accident she suffered was not infrequent and sometimes was fatal. Nowadays she would not use a taper to light the gas; she would not light the gas. She would not light the gas and drop the taper on the floor; but, if she did, her skirt would not catch fire. And, if her skirt did catch fire, her petticoats wouldn't, because she wouldn't have any; but if she did wear them, and if her skirt and petticoats did catch fire, her hair wouldn't. No matter how they may look, girls are at least safer from fire to-day than they were then.

On the other hand, we all have diseases now that we didn't have then; or at least we didn't know the right names for them in those days, and that was half the battle, giving us a much better chance to get well. But the right names were being developed, and almost every evening the medical student told us a new one. Appendicitis had not really arrived; but the medical student gave us advance information about it, and so thoroughly made us understand the symptoms that we were uncomfortable all the rest of that winter. Nevertheless, his lessons were of the greatest use to me when I had a series of violent and unmistakable attacks. During the last one a physician was summoned to examine me and he dug his thumb into me precisely upon the point at which the medical student had taught us the appendix had its unpleasant situation.

"Does that hurt?" the doctor inquired.

It did. It hurt so unbearably that only the complete horror of operations I had developed by listening to the medical student enabled me not to shriek.

"No," I said. "The trouble seems to be more on the other side and higher up. It seems to be more in the left upper chest, as it were, doctor."

So he prescribed calomel and poultices, and I got well and began to be grateful to the medical student; and yet he had been enthusiastic about the new operation and maintained that under the best surgery a patient had almost an even chance for recovery.

For the medical student told us of all the new and strange doings in his branch of science, and one evening he arrived upon the top floor with a startling bit of scientific news.

"There's been a machine invented," he said—"a machine that will let people see spang through solid matter. They can use it to look right through a wall, or a door, or a person's clothes, or whatever's in the way."

We couldn't believe anything so fantastic as this, but he insisted that he was serious.

"It's the absolute truth. What's more, they can look through your skin with it. They can see all around in your insides with it as much as they please."

"Not in mine!" the law student said sharply. "Not in mine!"

"Why not?"

"In the first place, because I got anyhow enough out of the physics course I took in college to know that such a thing isn't possible; and, in the second place, because I wouldn't let anybody look at me through an instrument like that, even if he had one. Why, there'd be laws against manufacturing those things! Nobody's got a right to be looking through the walls of other people's houses, or through their clothes, or into their insides. What'd be the good of such an instrument anyway?"

"Well, suppose you'd been playing marbles and swallowed one and—"

"Who?" the law student asked quickly. He had been graduated from college the preceding June, the youngest of his class, and since he had fallen in love with Madame Melba he had become sensitive about his age and suspicious of insult. "Suppose who'd been playing marbles?"

"I don't mean you personally; I mean anybody—a little boy, for instance. If he'd swallowed a marble, or a dime, maybe, or a collar button, or tacks, they could turn this X-ray on him and find out just where to operate. Why, this invention is going to lead to more operations"—the medical student's eyes brightened with his enthusiasm—"it's going to lead to more operations than all the accidents and diseases people have ever had in the whole history of the world! Because now, with this X-ray, a surgeon can show his patient an actual photograph of what's the matter with him.

"'Look here!' he'll say. 'Here's a picture of what you look like inside. Heavens and earth! You don't want to go on looking like that, do you?'"

But we thought that his eagerness had made him credulous, that he had been gulled by a fairy tale; and we refused to believe in the magic ray until he produced an article clipped from a scientific journal and overwhelmed our skepticism by the power of print. We were awed by this culminating wonder of the day of necromancy we were living in, and we felt that the human mind had reached the limit of its powers. Within the lifetime of an elderly man, the age of invention had touched the ultimate, so fast had been its development!

For it had begun, really, with the railroad and the telegraph. My grandfather, who lived under every president until McKinley, beginning with Washington, had told me of his first railway journey. The train worked up to a speed of sixteen miles an hour, and he got off at the first stop and hired a horse; he was appalled, unable to endure such a hurtling through space. And my father had told me how Governor Ray, of Indiana, was defeated for a reelection to Congress because he had voted for a reckless governmental appropriation of several thousand dollars to stretch an experimental wire between Washington and Baltimore for the purpose of making little clicking sounds at each end of it.[1] The voters were indignant that their representative could believe in such nonsense and waste public money upon it.

Since then the world had become a New World, indeed. We of the top floor were in our early twenties, yet we had seen the first electric lights, the first telephones, the first phonographs, the first cable cars, the first trolley cars, the first rubber tires, the passing of the universal household bootjack and winter high boots, with the better paving of city streets; we had read the first cabled news of Pasteur. Telephones and electric light were not yet in common household use, but were coming more and more to be so; rubber tires were still a luxury, though all bicycles were now made with them; but, as for the phonograph, many people felt that Edison had rather wasted his time. The machine was too squeaky to be long endured, and the waxy records were too perishable. Children played with the thing for half an hour, when it was given to them at Christmas, and then broke it.

---

1. James Brown Ray (1794–1848) was governor of Indiana from 1825 to 1831. Tarkington seems to have some facts wrong here. Ray never served in Congress. He ran in 1837 but was defeated. And whether or not he was an enthusiastic supporter of the telegraph, he was certainly an ardent backer of the railroads, and for this opinion he was indeed castigated roundly.

Nevertheless, the phonograph, like everything else, was being improved and could take its place as one of the miracles of the triumphant *fin de siècle*. And now that the X-ray, performing the incredible, penetrated to the mysterious heart of solids and brought human vision to bear upon what had been immemorially secret, so that a living man might see his own skeleton, what more was left to be done? No wonder we thought that after us must indeed and inevitably come the decadence!

And yet, within gunshot of our comfortable boarding house, there were slums more tragic than any to be found in New York now; and the "Tenderloin," like the "Red Light" of all American cities, renewed a vivid, septic life with every nightfall. The top floor had little curiosity about the "Tenderloin" and never entered it; but we knew something of one miserable tenement quarter, for we had a Reverend comrade who was in charge of a mission there. So we learned something of mission work—so much more desultory then than now, but no less devoted—and even tried to help the missionary in small and easy ways. And after all these years it is still not difficult to remember the smell of that district; it was a smell to be rivalled now only by the smell of some quarters of the cities of Araby. American cities no longer contain such smells; municipal health officers are providentially more effective than they were in the Nineties.

The top floor had other comrades, some of them highly plutocratic, and these asked us to dinners and dances, congenial gaieties, but not directly helpful to surgery, law, engineering, literature, and the drama. These last two advanced most slowly of all; for the thresholds of managers, editors, and publishers remained cold and uncrossed by the top floor aspirant.[2] The medical student, the law student, and the engineer made visible progress; they followed straight roads symmetrically set out with milestones; their destinations were fixed, and they knew always just how far they had come on the way. But the young man who was trying to write groped in a thick mist, not knowing whether his feet were upon a road or walking circles in a desert.

His stories all came back promptly from the magazine offices; he rewrote them and they came back again with the same printed rejection slips. His plays never reached a manager; they were returned by the dramatists' agents to be rewritten; and, rewritten, were returned again. The top floor was sympathetic, and a non-resident comrade, who had already become an actual newspaper man on the advertising end of a journal down in Park Row, tried to bring the aspirant into contact with people who could advise

---

2. Tarkington now begins to refer to himself in the third person.

him to his profit.³ The undergraduate nickname of this friendly helper was "Big," which applied both to his heart and his body; and he was so long that when he spent the night with us on the top floor, as he did sometimes, a chair had to be placed, for his feet, at the lower end of the adjustable bed where he slept.

"You've got to meet some of these people and ask 'em what's the matter with you," he said. "You'll never find out by just sending manuscripts around. You've got to talk to 'em face to face and then they can tell you."

"Yes, but how do I—"

"I'm going to take you to a dinner at the Lantern Club," he said. "Irving Bacheller's the toastmaster; Steve Crane's a member and he knows Harold Frederic. Has anybody ever written a better novel than Frederic's *Damnation of Theron Ware*?"

"No, it isn't possible to write a finer novel; but—"

"Well, Crane could probably help tell you what's the matter with you— he's been having a fairly rough time himself, though it's true people are beginning to talk a lot about his writing. But if he couldn't, Frederic could. But that's not all. Edward Eggleston is coming to this dinner and they have hopes of getting William Dean Howells himself. I guess he could tell you what's the matter with you, couldn't he?"

"Good heavens, yes! But—"

"Begin asking at the top," Big said. "If Howells comes to that dinner, go right up to him and tell him all about it and ask him what's the matter with you."

Mr. Howells did come to the dinner, though Stephen Crane didn't, having gone away from New York just then in search of a cheaper place to live; but the literary young man from the boarding house failed to make any inquiries of the chief practitioner of his adopted vocation. The apprentice was reverentially in a state of nerves to find himself at the foot of the long table at the head of which sat that gentle and most unleonine of lions. The aspirant could not possibly have asked him any question whatever; it was too frightening merely to be in his presence, remembering what he knew about writing; and, besides, there befell a disaster.

With coffee, the toastmaster, who was the president of the club, rose urbanely. "Before we proceed to the speechmaking," he said. "I will announce that we have with us to-night a young man, lately out of college, who sings."

---

3. Harold Griffith Murray, Tarkington's Princeton roommate. See note 7 on page 100.

Then, to his utmost horror, the nervous guest perceived that Mr. Bacheller was looking down the table at him. Stricken instantly with stage-fright, he heard Mr. Bacheller request him to rise to his feet and burst forth in song.

It wasn't possible to offer any excuse or to decline; there was nothing on earth for it but to get up and make sounds. Without accompaniment then, the dazed and shaking young man lately out of college put forth a quavering voice upon the air. He was irrecoverably off key; he squeaked and blatted on misplaced octaves and knew that although upon occasion he had sung villainously before, he had never equalled this. Somehow, though it is still an unexplained mystery, he lived through his own performance and sat down, praying for unending oblivion thenceforth.

"Well, did you get a chance to ask Howells what's the matter with you?" Big inquired as we walked home after the dinner.

"Good heavens, no! I didn't go near him! He'd have thought I meant my singing!"

IV

IN THE FINE ARTS and literature American apprentices knew then that names of true masters shone high above them. In literature we had Howells, James, and Mark Twain, fixed stars no matter what later ephemeral fashions in reading and criticism might temporarily make of them. We had Joel Chandler Harris, Stockton, Cable, James Lane Allen, Miss Wilkins, the exquisite Bunner, Thomas Nelson Page; we had a people's great poet, Riley; Bret Harte, outliving his vogue but not his enormous influence upon the short story, was a consul in Britain.[1] Over the water, two surpassing novelists were writing, Meredith and Hardy, and in the South Seas the master craftsman of writing, Stevenson, was dying. Kipling had emerged over the Far Eastern horizon; and a lively Irishman named Shaw was beginning to puzzle London with its own laughter, though he had yet to wait for an American actor, Mansfield, to awaken general audiences to a first comprehension of his plays.[2]

"There were giants in those days." It is a fashion among the vulgar now to fall upon the body of the giant and rend it the moment he is dead; and in Paris the young vultures, screeching to be talked about for their daring and their originality in following the fashion, feared to wait until Anatole France was buried; eagerer vultures might have flown in ahead of them and stolen the advertising.

---

1. The "Stockton" here is likely Frank R. Stockton (1834–1902), humorist and author of fairy tales. "Cable" is George Washington Cable (1844–1925), most of whose work was based in his native New Orleans. "Miss Wilkins" is Mary Eleanor Wilkins Freeman (1852–1930), novelist, short-story writer, and private secretary to Oliver Wendell Holmes Sr. "Bunner" is Henry Cuyler Bunner (1855–96), poet, novelist, and influential editor of *Puck*.

2. Richard Mansfield (1857–1907), one of the most celebrated actors of his generation, would later star in the American production of Tarkington's *Monsieur Beaucaire*. He was at least mildly interested in playing the lead in the rewritten *Prodigals*, but during this trip to New York Tarkington eventually gave up revising the play to his agent Elisabeth Marbury's satisfaction.

What aids the vultures is Nature's technique in the production of progress. We are carefully so constituted that the generation just passed must ever appear ridiculous to us, its thought both pretentious and primitive, its taste abhorrent, its manners absurd, and its fashions ludicrous. Our own generation, we feel, is the only one truly sophisticated; that of our parents must be picked to pieces, though that of our grandfathers, dimmed and prettily remote, cannot threaten our new ideas or our revolt against everything from which we are struggling to emerge; and so we look upon it more leniently, investing it with a captivating air of quaintness, and buying what remains of its furniture and ornaments. And in its art and literature the rediscovery of beauty begins.

This present new generation, obedient to that ancient mechanism of progress, has found a word to express its hatred of the musty absurdities preceding its own enlightenment—a word curiously sprung out of Anglomania and inappropriate in the Western Hemisphere—"Victorian." Our "young intellectuals" have a habit of using it as an eraser; and with a lively historical and geographical recklessness they will tell you that the United States of America, during the reign of Edward VII in Britain, was Mid-Victorian. Almost the wickedest of their printable words is "Mid-Victorian"; and what they mean, usually, is something their fathers and mothers believed in or liked.

Thus those giants we revered are now "Victorians" and "Mid-Victorians," obsolete to the young, along with the mansard roof, the tandem bicycle, and the two-step. The new generation lumps together the great men, the songs, the dances, the manners, and the clothes of the *fin de siècle*, and, with the derision of established superiority, laughs at all. The *fin de siècle* was less sweeping and more courteous; we did not scorn great men lately dead; though we did laugh—among ourselves—at the songs and the dancing of our elders; we laughed at their photograph albums, at the clothes and whiskers there portrayed; we laughed at their sports; we were beginning to laugh at croquet.

When the young gentlemen of the top floor went down to the mission to sing for the entertainment of the missionary's protégés, they did not sing "To-night You Belong to Me"; they sang "Workin' on the Railroad," medleys from *Robin Hood,* and college nonsense jingles. When we went forth to dance we dressed almost precisely as youths lately graduated would dress to-day, except that our collars were circular walls of linen three inches high. We kept a distance between us and our partners (it was the fashion just then to make the distance as great as possible) and we danced—glidingly, not wriggling or hopping—only waltzes and two-steps. Square dances had disappeared except from pastoral and proletarian fêtes where the lancers and quadrilles might still sometimes be capered through for the benefit of middle-aged or old-fashioned people. The polka and the schottische were dropped early in the decade.

The girls with whom we danced had hourglass figures. Tiny feet and hands were adjuncts to beauty, but the small waist was a necessity. Schoolgirls, not yet allowed to wear stays, sometimes secretly strapped torturing belts night and day about their middles to prepare for the hourglass fashion they would follow when they "came out." Physicians attacked the hourglass bitterly and persistently, with complete futility. The race was being ruined by this abominable harnessing, they said; and they had no more effect than did the moralists who scolded when the girls, long after, left off the rigid harness entirely and made themselves into slim sacks with no waists at all.

The hourglass girls danced gracefully in spite of their harness; indeed, they danced more gracefully than do their sack-shaped daughters and granddaughters; for dignity, which may still be maintained in consonance with the airiest lightness, is ever a part of grace; and dignity vanished when the tight clasp and the negroid and Oriental dancing began with the incredible turkey trot. Moreover, the hourglass girls, apparently not incommoded, played tennis; they rode horses and bicycles; they were known to sail catboats and paddle canoes; and even the ladies of the ballet and those of the circus were hourglasses. But of course the girl with stiffly armoured body, balloon sleeves upon her upper arms, and her sacred and mysterious legs lost in petticoats and skirts that touched the ground, was not easily an outdoor girl. To be, even moderately, an athlete was not part of her destiny.

She was still, even that little time ago, the sheltered dependent—and therefore the diplomat—that she had been through all the Christian centuries. We of the top floor were well-brought-up young men; which means that we revered her and had no idea she was a human being. For us she was a lady, and that was something higher, finer, and more ethereal than no matter how good a gentleman. Bodily, she consisted for us of a head of hair, a face, an hourglass of silk or satin or cloth, gloved hands, and multiplex bells of stuffs that hung from the squeezed middle of the hourglass to the ground. Within these her locomotion was somehow mysteriously accomplished; it was not permissible to imagine how, and the nearest we came to that was in our verses about the "rustle of her skirts upon the stair." She had no feet—that is to say, she had slippers and at the most an instep. At a dance she had actual arms and shoulders and coquettish hints of bosom. Spiritually, she consisted of perfection—that was a matter of course—and mentally she consisted of mystery, which we had no great concern to solve.

Ourselves being of clay, we could only try to atone to her by the utter respect we paid her. No one except a "mucker" had any other view of her;

and yet, as we knew that there were "muckers" here and there among our own sex, so we knew that there were members of hers who had forfeited public respect, exchanging it for contempt from some and compassion from others. That is to say, there distinctly appeared to be two classes, or castes, of girls. There were the "girls we knew"—the sheltered, perfect, and revered girls, whom we and our comrades would one day marry—this was one class; and the other consisted of all the other kinds of girls.

Sometimes a girl of the upper caste was forced by family misfortunes to go to work; and there were a few kinds of genteel employment—governessing and teaching principally—that she could accept without descending substantially out of her caste; but work that brought her much into contact with men was thought roughening, at the best; it was not advisable. Something was pardoned to a girl of special talent; she might be admired and feted, but even in such cases the word "Bohemian" threatened her if her gift made her professional. Her talents were best confined to the amateur field, it was felt; and, if she must have ambitions at all, the single correct and useful one was to fit herself to be the inspiration and helpmeet of the man she would wed. Her true business, of course, was to get herself satisfactorily married, though that was the last thing in all the world she must permit to become visible.

Sometimes, when we went to dinners given by the mothers and fathers of the hourglass girls, sherry and claret were served, though sparingly; sometimes, at the more plutocratic dances, there was champagne with the supper; but usually both dinners and dances were "dry." There was a general prejudice against offering even the milder intoxicants to young men, and it was thought better not to put temptation in their way. There was no feeling about the girls in this matter; they were out of the question entirely; for they were not conceivably affected by temptations of any kind whatever. Cocktails and potent distillations were unknown at the dinner for young people, except among hosts willing to be called "fast," or here and there in the South, where Eighteenth Century hospitality still lingered in the mint julep. In general, when a young man appeared among ladies, his breath could not be aromatic of alcohol without damage to his reputation.

Our boarding house top floor had no concern in such a matter. At remote intervals we spent a temperate evening in a respectable big German beer hall where there was a good orchestra; but most of our evenings, like our days, meant work; and the literary aspirant, who was arriving nowhere in spite of his struggles, burned gas latest of all.[3] This was hard for the law student, who roomed with him; for the writing frequently went on until

---

3. Here Tarkington again refers to himself.

three in the morning and sometimes even later. The law student didn't mind the cigarette smoke that accompanied the writing; but he couldn't sleep with the gaslight full on his eyes, and he was too chivalrous to insist upon its being extinguished; so he developed a technique to meet the difficulty successfully. At eleven, his customary hour, he amicably opened two large black umbrellas, placed them upon his couch, and retired to sleep in peace within their shadow. Quiet would settle down upon the house and upon the street outside; and except for the far-away rumble of Elevated owl trains and the spasmodic tootings of distant ferry-boats in the river, there would be silence. There was no Subway, there were no taxicabs; building went on in daytime; New York had only a million people then, and nearly all of them went to bed at night. The great modern night roar of the metropolis had not developed; strangers could sleep in quiet in almost any part of the city not too close to the "L"; and for hours the scratching of the thin aspirant's pen would be, barring expressions of feeling from an occasional cat in a brownstone areaway, the noisiest sound on our whole street. So the gaslit windows of our top floor front were the only windows bright after midnight on that street, while the unfortunate thin young man went on writing and rewriting and rewriting and getting thinner and thinner.

At last, when there were hints of coming summer upon the winds of the city and evening sunshine began to linger upon the roof of the church opposite the top floor windows, he perceived that instead of approaching the thresholds he had come to cross—those forbidden entrances to editors and managers and publishers—he had slid even backward from them; and he was now so thin he feared that if he lost any more weight he would alarm his relatives when he went home. Therefore, ere this might happen, he thoughtfully packed his new rejected manuscripts in a parcel with the old, and one rainy morning went down on the Ninth Avenue "L" to recross the Cortlandt Street Ferry, going West.

Thus the top floor had a vacancy, but the companions did their best to provide a substitute. The medical student had long desired an articulated skeleton; when I left he bought one, and the law student and the engineer went with him on a drizzly evening to bring it home. They put a raincoat upon it and carried it through the streets, not without arousing comment and being somewhat earnestly questioned; but they brought it successfully to the top floor.

They attached it to the wall, supplied it with a cigarette, and gave it my college nickname. It had only one defect, the engineer wrote me—the law student couldn't argue with it.

V

Here then was a young man rather emaciated by his siege of New York, and returned to write until dawn, most nights, at home in a placid town among the green, far inland flat lands. No great discontent was involved, however. On the contrary, it was a luxury to live pamperedly again in the pleasant house in the friendly neighbourhood where he'd been born and had grown up. The whole town, except for the business district, was made of friendly neighbourhoods, in fact; and so was like a hundred other just such towns of the Midlands and of East and West.

The great change had not shown its first beginnings; though now, looking back upon those peaceful days and those quiet, seemingly settled and completed American towns, we can see that it impended imminently. We see that the shadow of the change loomed close over them, like the ceiling shadow of a lifted war club over one of the pioneer settlers reading his Bible by candlelight in the log cabin out of which the cities grew. For no catastrophe of earthquake, of war, or fire, or flood, or tornado, or all combined, could have done more to those towns than the change has done. Of the pleasant smallish city I lived in when I came from New York in that year of the *fin de siècle*, there remains about as much as the Roman left of Punic Carthage when he drove his ploughs over its site before building his own city there.

No one could have dreamed that our town was to be utterly destroyed; such a thing was as unbelievable as that the pioneer's Bible would be dismembered along with the town. At the centre, we had finished the building of our great monument to the men of our state who had fought in the Civil War, the War with Mexico, and the War of 1812. The shaft rose two hundred feet and more in the air, a mark to be seen all over the countryside, far and wide. Forever it was to dominate; forever it was to stand high above the tallest buildings of the city; for it was higher, even, than the noble green dome of the State House. Straight northward from the monument ran the "principal residence street," parallelled by four other "principal residence streets" of rival merit. These avenues were amply broad for the family carriages, bicycles, phaëtons, buggies, and light delivery wagons that formed the traffic; and they were shaded by maples, by sycamores where lazy bayous from the creek had been, and by old elms, hickory, and black walnut trees, relics of the original forest. By mid-Maytime, on many of the streets, leafy branches had crossed and mingled above the roadway, so that the movement below was through cool green tunnels and emerged into sharp sunlight only at the crossings.

Most of the houses facing upon the "principal residence streets" were built solidly of brick and trimmed with white stone; the windows were all plate glass; the ceilings were high—eleven to fifteen and even sixteen feet; the staircases were walnut and the verandas were of stone or painted wood. The lawns were broad, often generously without fences to mark dividing lines; there were shade and orchard trees in every yard; some yards had fountains, and one or two cast-iron deer were left, though these were disappearing.

From some of the verandas, after dark, there came on summer evenings the tinkle of mandolins and guitars, or the twanging of a banjo; young voices might be heard softly singing "Answer, Bid Me Good-bye" and "Go, Love's Sorrow," or the livelier measures of "Mandalay" or of a new "coon song"; for in the milder seasons the verandas were the foregathering places of youth and courtship. The elder folk were usually indoors after nightfall, but with open windows; though on hot evenings they would sit out upon the lawn in wicker chairs, fanning themselves and murmuring against the heat. There was not obviously an official chaperonage, but, by the very custom of that simple way of living, the older people were usually within earshot of the young.

Bicycling had begun to give the latter more range; though not beyond the lamplight of the streets after dark, for the roads were too rough. Phaëtons and dogcarts and runabouts permitted tête-à-tête driving by daylight; but not to great distances, nor with roadside parking in the dusk—an idea completely unknown to the hourglass girl of the higher caste. She lived within strict boundaries both of conduct and of manner, and she was sufficiently her own chaperone. To have offered her a cigarette, except as a rather feeble attempt at humour, would have disturbed her as with something near an insult; and a rumour that she slyly used a little rouge, or artificially coloured her lips or eyebrows or lashes, would have frightened her as a threatening of intolerable slander. And if such a thing as that she sometimes liked a drink of gin could have been imagined and actually told of her, she might as well have cut the throat of her baby brother in his cradle.

Yet who shall say she was less care-free and less buoyantly happy in her youth in that pleasant town than are the liberated maidens of the place to-day? Pleasures were simpler then; but that has never meant less pleasure. Life was slower; but that means there was time to enjoy it a little copiously. When the first country club was built, far, far out among the woods and farms, it took us almost an hour to drive there from downtown, unless we had a light vehicle and a fast horse. Even upon a bicycle the going was slow; there were ruts to ride, and bumpy, dusty country roads; and, after all, when the club was reached there was nothing to do except to sit upon a veranda and look down upon the river below the bluff. Yet the young people did it, and so did their elders, and believed themselves delighted. A lovely landscape was there, something to dwell with a little in those leisurely days when there was time to talk and even time to think.

But that same summer the landscape at the country club was artificially altered. The alteration was so slight that it was almost imperceptible from the veranda; nevertheless it was a forerunner of the change into the coming age, the first to touch the countryside. It was the feeble beginning of a prodigious thing, yet we who watched the making of that little alteration at the country club thought no more of it than if it had been the laying out of a bowling green. At best it meant the appearance of a slight imported fad, we supposed; a curious game that the followers of fads in games might play for a season or so and then forget, since it was too bothersome ever to get a grip of people and attain the stability of tennis or croquet, or even quoits.

Two young men, members of the club, returned from a journey abroad, and, hiring a few puzzled farm labourers from the neighbourhood, constructed something they called a links. But if ever that word may be used in the singular, what these two travellers made should be spoken of as a link. It consisted of a square deposit of lumpy sod, imaginably a green, and, at the distance of a hundred yards, a clay platform. That was all, but the place soon resounded with conscientious cries of "Fore!" And when these first golfers were ardent in sport upon their stretch of ground, members of the club and visitors, glancing that way, would be stricken into attitudes of still amazement. All summer and autumn there was one question that had to be answered, or else given up, continuously:

"Are those people crazy?"

VI

THUS AN UNSUCCESSFUL YOUNG man, painfully engaged in the pursuit of letters, had one of the earliest opportunities afforded in this country to become a golfer instead of a writer. This might well have been a temptation, because having no career at all, nor any visible business, profession, or employment, was never a way to popular esteem among the descendants of the hardy Western pioneers. In the remote, decadent East, where the Anglomania of the later 'Eighties still had sway, there were known to be, here and there, gentlemen of leisure; but west of the Alleghanies only tramps were fully comprehended as representatives of such a class.

Moreover, the parents and relatives of a persistently rejected writer have the constant embarrassment of trying to explain his occupation to inquirers; nothing could be more difficult, nor, when the inquirer is of an especially practical turn of mind, more mortifying. Therefore, as time passed and passed—and continued to pass—an effort to display something more plausible than an exhaustive collection of printed rejection slips from magazine offices, as proof of actual labour, seemed more and more advisable. Unfortunately, this young man had now so thoroughly acquired the habit of collecting these slips that he seemed to have become unfitted for anything else.

In this strait an old family friend favoured him with an encouraging talk. This was an elderly gentleman, professionally a lawyer, but one of a varied career.[1] He had done extraordinary writing and important soldiering, though he had interrupted his writing, for a time, to become our ambassador to a European power. As a soldier, he had fought his way in a war to a Major General's epaulets; and as a writer he had published a novel that found as near a universal reading as any print may well attain.

"What are you doing?" he asked one day. "You seem to spend most of your time driving a pair of trotters to a red-wheeled runabout."

---

1. This conversation with Lew Wallace (1827–1905), Indianapolis's most famous resident and author of *Ben Hur* (1880), took place in 1896 or shortly thereafter.

"That's only in the afternoons. I work at night."

"What for?" the General asked.

"Well, it's quieter and it draws less attention to the fact that I'm trying to learn to write. I—I don't get on very well, General."

"So," he said, "I suppose you think you'd get on better if you got something printed?"

"Well, yes," I answered. "At least it would be a sign that I was getting somewhere. It would be a sort of justification for the embarrassment I'm causing my relatives and friends when they try to explain me, wouldn't it?"

"I'm not so sure of that," he said. "in fact, I somewhat doubt it. We are a very practical people, and, though it's considered pretty disgraceful not to do anything, every community has a few loafers and is accustomed to see them hanging around the saloons or pool rooms, borrowing tobacco, and drifting down to the station to sit languidly on packing-boxes when the trains go by. Our people look down on them, of course, but understand them, because laziness and drink easily account for them. It's a type that developed even among the early settlers, and we've always had it among us. But the fact is that although for some reason we are a reading people and comprehend the reading of books, we don't understand anybody's writing 'em except peculiar strangers from far away. We can't imagine one of ourselves writing a book unless there's something idiotic or ridiculous about him."

"But, General, there's Mr. Riley. Surely he——"

"Yes," the General admitted. "The whole state has a great tenderness for James Whitcomb Riley, that's true; it even brags of him, but always with a note of indulgence, the sort of chuckle with which one mentions a whimsical character whose drolleries make one laugh. Listen to any public orator extolling the great men of the state. You'll hear our ex-President's name bellowed, and the names of a dozen senators, governors, and industrial magnates; but you won't hear Riley's—not if the orator considers himself a serious man speaking seriously. You'll find the same thing in the newspaper editorials. As for myself, the publication of my first novel was almost enough to ruin my law practice. Whenever I took a case into court for a jury trial, the opposing lawyer knew that all he had to do was to mention my authorship and I was demolished. He would rise with an air of solemn waggery and address the jury: 'I trust I may bring my wreath of laurel to be placed upon the poetic brow it should rightfully adorn. You may not know this, but it is a fact, gentlemen, that the learned counsel upon the other side has become an author. Yes, gentlemen, you are in the presence of an author! Yes, gentlemen, my learned brother has written a novel——' But that was about all he needed to say. As soon as the jury of farmers and village merchants heard the word 'novel' they uttered hearty guffaws, and after that I had no weight with them whatever. When I addressed them their eyes bulged with derisive merriment, no matter what I said. Merely to look at me roused an inward hilarity that flushed their cheeks and bedewed their foreheads. I might as well have appeared in court dressed as a circus clown."

"But after you had written *Ben Hur*, General——"

"Oh, yes," he said. "The church people approved of that, and I'm taken seriously on other accounts, no doubt. Also, our fellow citizens are more liberal than they were at the time when I wrote *The Fair God*. Nevertheless, they are not wholly changed in their feeling that an author, to be highly respectable and of some importance, ought to spring from a distant community. If he is an American, he should come from New England; but if he is English, he will impress us more. If he is French, we will be almost ready to believe him a great man; while if he is Russian, we will be sure that he is. Russia is so very, very far away; but an author here at home—— No, don't be discouraged because you can't prove by print that you are one. And, as for the embarrassment of your relatives about you, don't be unduly troubled; their difficulty might be worse. Remember, a great many of our fellow citizens would rather have a loafer in the family than a writer."

Undoubtedly this talk with General Wallace helped, and so did the light, red-wheeled rubber-tired runabout and the pair of lively young trotting horses. Being young helped, too—though the young seldom know how much their youth helps them—and it was a pleasant and easy time, historically, to be young. There was a cheerful placidity in American life then. The "free-silver scare" had passed and the issue was dead; Europe was so far away that it still seemed an adventure to voyage there; Asia was infinitely remote; all the world that we knew was at peace, and a great many enlightened people were sure there would never be another war of any consequence. It was a quiet world, a respectable world, completed, unhurried, unpuzzled, unrebellious.

VII

IN THE MIDLAND TOWN, as elsewhere over the country, almost everybody—among the native born—went to church either regularly or at intervals. True, there were atheists and materialists here and there; and there were scattered agnostics, followers of Ingersoll; but the church governed the customs and prevailed in the established conventionalities of the people. Moreover, the universal rule of the church, and these customs and conventionalities, were not even slightly disregarded except by daring people willing to risk interdiction. There was a terrible and excluding word that excommunicated them—"fast." In the age of bicycles and family surreys and "livery-stable rigs," this word, with its implication of rapid movement, was almost the worst that could be said.

Divorce and rouge were "fast" and as rare as a game of whist on Sunday; late hours were "fast"; French novels were "fast"; a girl was "fast" if she mentioned her stockings; a young man was "fast" if he mentioned them; a married woman who went to a concert with a man not her husband was "fast," and so was the man; Welsh rarebit cooked with beer was "fast"; people who went to evening concerts in German beer gardens were "fast"; people who played games of cards, or any other games, for stakes, were "fast"; a woman who wore a low corsage was "fast"; it was "fast" to be interested in the ballet, to read Ouida, or to have read Byron's *Don Juan*; it was "fast" to give lively dinner parties on Sunday. On Sunday, indeed, even fast horses were supposed to repose; it was no seemly day for the red-wheeled runabout.

The churchly rule of the elders prevailed unchallenged by any "young intellectual." Everywhere, even among those who were not churchgoers, there was an abiding and accepting, not a questioning. One night a milkman expressed his sense of this acceptance to me and spoke reverently in the very spirit of the times. A friend of mine died; I had been spending the night beside his coffin, and just before dawn had gone out to walk up and down upon the lawn in the moist spring air. The milkman, coming into the yard, observed me, and having filled the household can upon the back steps approached for a hushed conversation.

"Is this where the fine young man's dead that I read about in the papers last night?"

"Yes."

He sighed thoughtfully. "Well," he said. "I ain't a churchgoing man myself, I'm sorry to say; but I'm an abiding man. My wife's a church member and all, but I can't claim to be. I don't know whether it's going to keep me out of heaven or not, because that's something that nobody can tell beforehand, not even church members themselves; but, on the other hand, I reckon being an abiding man's pretty safe to keep me out of hell. I like to read James Whitcomb Riley and Bill Nye, and I can't claim I read the Bible anywhere like as much as I do them two; but yet I never did claim there's any comparison in a religious way between James Whitcomb Riley and Bill Nye and them old prophets like David and Goliath and Elisha and Job and Jeremiah, and all them. No, sir; I read James Whitcomb Riley and Bill Nye for pleasure; I can't deny it; but when it comes to abiding, I abide by them old Bible prophets. Don't you believe us abiding people got a pretty good chance to get in?"

"In? You mean into heaven?"

"Yes. That's my opinion, anyhow. We can't all be church members—got too much to do that prevents it. Me, for instance, when I get back to the dairy farm after my route on Sunday morning, why, it couldn't hardly be expected I'd clean up and get on my Sunday suit and go to church. Night watchmen, they can't get to church, either; but they're just as likely to be abiding men as any. Pretty much everybody is either a church member or at least abiding, when you get right down to the facts. Ain't that your experience?"

"Yes, I think so."

"Yes, sir," he went on, "that's pretty much the way of it. It's just the same all over the country, too. I've done considerable travelling; I've travelled on every railroad in this state, and I've been on excursions to Niagara Falls and Washington and Asbury Park; I've been in Cincinnati time and again—I got kin living there—I've been to Keokuk, and I've been twice to Chicago. Well, you naturally always get to talking to passengers on trains, and, after you find out where they're from, and all about their family, and how the crops look in their part of the country, and what business conditions seem to be out there, why, nine times out of ten you and them get to talking about religion. Well, sir, I never come across but one infidel yet, in all my experience; and even he wasn't so much of one—said a good many parts of the Old Testament was too much for him. Except for that, he was as abiding a man as anybody. But I expect he might go to hell on account of them parts he said he didn't believe in. He's the only one I've run across, myself, though of course I know there's some others here and there that don't believe in the Bible at all; but there ain't many willing to take such a risk. No, sir, not many. Of course I know there's plenty that'll take a chance sliding off to one side now and then, like pitching horseshoes out behind the barn on Sunday, or getting drunk Saturday nights, or cussing around up an alley, maybe; but they know they can get back into line by repenting and abiding again before it's too late. Yes, sir; if you leave out saloon keepers and gamblers, and such like, the United States is a pretty good pious sort of country, by and large. The children respect and honour and obey the laws, and where there's a few like me that can't hardly make it to get to church, why, anyhow, they're abiding. Ain't that the way it seems to you?"

In general, though there were exceptions, that was the way it seemed to anybody. There was a tremendous universal respect for respectability. People who did not abide by the rule of the church and the law of the land were not within that respect, and, unless they were very powerful and adroit, they were outcasts if their disobedience became known. And almost universally children honoured their parents, believing them to be perfect in goodness, perfect in dignity; and the parents of that day took infinite pains to present only this aspect of themselves to their children. Less strict with the young than their own parents had been, and much more liberal in everything, they nevertheless retained authority and knew that they must never weaken it by endangering the complete respect their children had for them.

The churches ruled over all the outward part of life, and, although there were depths within the social body where they did not rule, even in the depths they were feared and the infractions were stealthy, like night poachings in the king's preserve. Even the legalized saloons dared not be open enemies of the churches, and groped obscurely, under cover, for a little local power in dirty small politics. But the rule of the churches was not the rule of the Inquisition; it was neither early Puritanism nor early Wesleyanism; it was not militant, except when the corruption of brewery politics became too brazen. The children did not challenge the church or the faith of their parents; usually they accepted that faith themselves as a matter of course. Moreover, respectability did not make the town gloomy; and, looking back upon it now, it seems to have been not only a contented and peaceful place but a fairly happy one.

Beauty was there, outdoors, and in the tranquil, friendly life of the people. By June, if you ascended to the top of the monument and looked forth from that high vantage in the air, you seemed to be upon a tower rising from an island of stone surrounded not by water but by verdure. There were just glimpses of roofs and windows among green leaves, for the shade trees marched down the streets all the way to the State House, the Courthouse, and the Circle, where stood the monument. Beyond the town, a lazy silken creek wandered among great sycamores; and there were other waters—a crystal river below high bluffs and a canal that was like a long straight strip of green looking-glass. And all the air was pure; only the clean white dust of the country roads blew a little in the sunshine, and the sky over the town was unflawed blue in winter and in summer.

Upon a summer evening, if you walked abroad, there was the multitudinous rustle of leaves as if you walked in a woodland—as indeed you did; there was the quiet murmur of voices from the verandas, or from where the people sat out upon the lawns; there was the plod-plod of horses passing with surreys for the evening family drive; there was the tinkling of the little bicycle bells and the gliding passage of the wheelmen's lamps, whiter small lights than the gold pencillings of the fireflies among the shrubberies on the lawns. Sometimes the surrey drivers would draw rein and pause, and the foot passengers upon the sidewalk would stop; a quiet audience thus would gather outside an open window where a girl with a lovely voice sang to her piano. It is true that the song was likely to be sentimental, even sentimentally pathetic, and the theme was nearly always a variation upon the topic of constancy.

> Oh, love for a year, a week, a day!
> But alas for the love that loves always!

Or it might be the audience gathered on the sidewalk and in the street beyond a picket fence about a lawn where young people danced upon a waxed platform and an orchestra played by the light of Japanese lanterns strung among the trees. The young people danced happily, and, although they sometimes danced as late into the next morning as two o'clock, they began—even when they were under seventeen—at about eight. They danced for sheer gaiety and without other stimulation, though liquor was obtainable openly at any bar. When the young men drank they kept away from the "girls they knew"; and, if they were known to drink often, the "girls they knew" kept away from them—permanently.

The music to which they danced was made by violins, 'cellos, flutes, harps, triangles, and bass viols; sometimes there was a clarinet and sometimes mild drums and cymbals were heard; and again no one can deny that most of the sound these instruments made was sentimental. What seems incredible now, it is a fact that in those days old people could bear to listen to the dance music that was modern then. Not only could they bear to listen—they loved to listen; they could listen all evening long without bleeding at the ears. For one reason, saxophones had not yet been ejected by the volcanic insides of hyenas in eruption.

There were even midnight serenades, in those days, of a summer night; that dashing custom had not quite disappeared. Young men would hire an orchestra and an "express wagon," as the horse-drawn truck with a big canvas top was called; musicians and gallants would drive to the house of a pretty girl, encamp themselves noiselessly upon the lawn, and presently, after a faint and covert tuning of instruments, dulcet melody would ascend to her window. When she was sweetly thus awakened, she would slide out of bed, crawl on hands and knees to the window and lower the shade, raised for the passage of air. Then she would light the gas, and the bright window in the dark night was the serenaders' reward, the assurance that their music was heard and accepted. After a while they would move silently back to the "express wagon," the wagon would creak away, and the window would go dark again; yet for a time a breath of romance would linger within it and upon the air.

No serenaded lady could have thought to say she "got a kick" out of such a thing. Beyond question, it was a sentimental age! It was the age of sentiment, of faith, of leisurely days and quiet nights, of reverent children, of dignified parents, of placid newspapers, and of settled and contented living at home.

There the town lay, then, peaceful and completed, warm and green and a little drowsy, upon a September afternoon, when the strangest sight of all the *fin de siècle* —a sight even stranger than the photograph of a living man's skeleton—came rolling forth from within the cavern of forge and fire where it had been conceived.

The languid town awoke. Children, playing in back yards, ran shrieking into the street; coloured servants, glancing from front windows, yelled with surprise and bellowed for those in the kitchen to come and look; old ladies were roused from naps and fluttered to the windows. Horses snorted, reared, and could not be soothed; dogs barked themselves insane, and well they might.

Well, indeed, might those jolly old dogs bark; well might those kindly old horses prance and run away! For what they beheld that day was their Juggernaut; they might as well have cast themselves beneath its wheels then and there. But for more than horses and dogs the monster rolling through the street was to be the destroyer. Yet a little time and it would have down those sturdy, strong-built, big old brick houses with their broad plate-glass windows where faces stared, half startled, half derisive, at the monster's first passing. A little time and the monster would have them all down, every one of them; it would have them down and their trees down and their green lawns devoured. It would have the whole town down, and more; it would have the *fin de siècle* down and extinct, only the memory of it surviving in belittling laughter.

More, the monster and its adjutants would have the very spirit of that age down. The old faiths were to be put at bay; the old abiding was to vanish; the universal rule of the churches was to vanish; the old content was to vanish; the old romantic sentiment was to vanish; leisure was to vanish; the old reverences and dignities were to vanish; the old authority of parents was to vanish; even dance music was to vanish and be music no more. From the moment of that first apparition upon the streets of the placid town, Death waited for the God of Things as They Are.

And yet the monster that was to erase the world was no great shakes to look at when we goggled at it that September day. It was only a topless surrey with a whirling belt and other inexplicable machinery beneath it, emitting vapour and hideous noises. But there were no shafts for a horse—there was no horse—yet the wheels turned and the ridiculous miracle moved.

In the front seat a jarred and vibrated man, reddened in the face by his dreadful conspicuousness, held a crooked rod that seemed somewhat uncertainly to guide the forward wheels. And along the sidewalks and even at the tail of the monster, raced crowds of vociferous, mocking boys and girls.

"Git a hoss!" they shrieked continuously. "Git a hoss! Git a hoss! Git a hoss!"

VIII

Driving that pair of light trotters, one beautiful bright afternoon, far, far out in the wooded country, almost as far as the city now extends, I heard an inexplicable sound of thunder and a few minutes later encountered a farm hand who was in a state of nervous upset. Electrified, himself, by the unusual manifestation, he had left his plough in a furrow, vaulted a snake fence, and was standing all of a tremble between the ruts of the dirt road when the runabout approached. He made gestures of amazement and seemed wishful to communicate.

"Out of an empty sky!" he said hoarsely, and he pointed to a shattered tree, solitary in the centre of the wide field he had been ploughing. "Lightning! Right out of as bright and sunny a sky as ever I see! Not a cloud in it—not a single cloud! Dog-gone if it don't look kind o' like it was reachin' fer me and mighty near got me! Lightning out of an empty sky! Who'd ever dream such a thing could happen?"

It may have been an omen. More than lightning can come out of an empty sky when nobody dreams such a thing could happen. Thus, quite as dumbfounding as the strange flash that shattered the solitary tree and the ploughman's composure, there arrived with no forewarning a letter from the most interesting and adventurous editor and publisher of that day.

"We have read the ms. of your novel and shall be glad to publish it in book form," this startling letter said. "Also, if you will come to New York we should like to talk with you about using it as a serial in the magazine."[1]

In those first moments of mystification it was not easy to believe that the words were actual. Five years of printed rejection slips had not prepared one to receive even an encouraging letter of rejection from an editor, much less a letter of acceptance. Such a letter must be read several times to make certain that the reader's eye is not deceived, and then at intervals to be sure

1. The novel was *The Gentleman from Indiana* (1899). The editor was Hamlin Garland (1860–1940), author of *A Son of the Middle Border*, among other works, and a passionate proponent of the local-color movement. The publisher was S. S. McClure. Tarkington closes "As I Seem to Me" with a briefer discussion of this episode.

that his memory has not been tricky. But no; all these readings having confirmed the accuracy of the first, it became clear that the thin young man, however embarrassing he might be in his new capacity, was definitely no longer a loafer.

"And so they were married" used to end all the troubles of the fictitious lovers; and similarly, "So his manuscript was accepted by the great publisher" might be thought to signify that the literary aspirant lived happily ever afterward.

On my arrival in New York the great publisher said, "Just condense your novel to one half its present length; then we'll have space for it as a serial in the magazine."

It seemed to me that he might as well have asked me to condense the Brooklyn Bridge to half its length; yet Mr. McClure had every appearance of believing that such things could be done; that they were done every day, in fact; and that, as a matter of course, I knew how to do them.

I didn't. I hadn't the remotest idea of what should be done to that ponderous bundle of manuscript to reduce it to half its weight. Nevertheless, I carried it to a lodging on Madison Avenue—for the comrades of the brownstone-front top floor were now dispersed to follow their achieved professions—and there I nervously began the amputations. At first they were a little dismaying, but before long the surgery became interestingly vindictive. "Out you come!" seemed to be the very pleasantest thing one could say to a chapter; and so emaciated grew what remained of the manuscript that the new serial began to be known in the magazine office as The Cablegram.

Several of the installments had been published before I finished the work and came timidly home in the late spring—I had reason to return timidly, even blushingly. In the story appearing monthly in unalterable print, I had dealt with a pastoral aspect of my native state. I had been romantic, sentimental, and enthusiastic about the beauty of this aspect; I fear I had appointed myself its champion. Moreover, I had expressed a great deal of feeling for the populace; and, of course, it is an embarrassing thing to meet people face to face when you have just been making known—without their solicitation—your admiration and affection for them. I feared they might think I had overpraised them; that I had said too much, putting their modesty to trial. So, as I walked homeward from the station, I was not surprised but a little abashed when I encountered a middle-aged friend whose expression first showed that he was somewhat startled to see me and then became one of grave reproach.

"I almost wonder," he said slowly—"I do actually wonder, in fact, that you've had the courage to come back here."

"You—you mean my serial?"

"I certainly do! How could you have written such a thing?"

"I—I don't know exactly. I suppose it isn't very good writing, but perhaps some day I can——"

"Perhaps nothing!" he interrupted. "You'll never wipe it out—not if you live a thousand years!"

"I—I can't?"

"No, you can't!" he said. "There are some things that are not forgivable. When you strike at the sacred altars of a people——"

"When I what?' I asked, for I began to be mystified. "When I——"

"When you throw mud upon the altars of a great people," he said. "As a friend of your family, I'm sorry you have chosen to begin your career in such a manner. Good-bye!"

He walked on, and so, not a little enfeebled and disconcerted, did I. Then I met another friend, a person of my own age with whom I had some intimacy. He was still willing to shake hands with me, I discovered, though his expression was partly inimical, partly compassionate. I mentioned that I had just got off the train, after my long absence, and he made a rather disturbing inquiry.

"Has anybody seen you?" he said.

"Yes, I met Judge Martin a moment ago, not far from the station. He didn't appear to be very pleased with me. He said something confusing about my serial's having attacked the sacred altars and——"

"You look as if you didn't understand what he meant."

"No, I didn't—not exactly. I know, of course, that some people would think I've been too enthusiastic—perhaps even rather gushing——"

"Gushing!" he interrupted. "Do you mean to say you don't know what effect your serial has been having?"

"No. It didn't seem to be having any at all in New York, you see. I supposed that out here more people naturally might read it, and——"

"I think you'll find that enough of us have been reading it," he said grimly. "Didn't you really know that every paper in the state is broiling you alive?"

"Why, no. I haven't seen any reviews."

"Then it's because your family have been too considerate to write you about it. But these aren't reviews; most of 'em are editorials."

"I was afraid of it," I said. "I do wish I hadn't been quite so gushing!"

But at that he shook his head. "I see you don't understand," he said. "You'd better go on home. It would be best to have a member of your family explain what's happened to you. Go find somebody that'll stick to you no matter what you do, and ask 'em to break the news to you."

His advice was excellent; nevertheless a considerable time elapsed before I understood what had happened to me. What had happened to me was, indeed, a thing so significant of the times we lived in then that the perspective of years and change was needed in order to comprehend it fully. For it is true—and possibly, in the long run, fortunately true—that we are almost never able to comprehend during the actual moment of any happening the meaning of what is happening. The meaning of "what had happened to me," the rain of denunciation that fell upon a dazed but well-meaning young head, is clear enough to-day and marks how sharply changed are the times we live in now.

In that final period of the Nineteenth Century, the country at a little distance outside the cities was rustic. So were the small market towns characteristically rustic; so were the villages and many of the smaller county seats. The interurban trolley lines had not formed their enormous network; and, except by rail, ten miles was a long distance. It was long even for good horses because it had to be travelled over roads that were a continuing dust heap in dry weather and sloughs of mud in wet; only at intervals were there stretches of well-kept turnpike between toll gates. People still believed that "a straight line is the shortest distance between two points," and were to wait many years to discover that between two points the best made and best kept road is the shortest distance.

More, the metropolitan newspapers had almost nothing of their modern circulation among outlying townlets and villages; there was no Rural Free Delivery; great weeklies and the monthly magazines were almost unknown to farm and village. Small local newspapers gave the people of the farms and little towns some news of the world from which they seemed almost infinitely remote; the Bible and the Almanac made the staple of reading, crops and politics the staple of discussion. When the day's work was over there was nothing to do except to sleep; and, when the week's work was over and the farmers drove to town on Saturday and hitched their teams to the courthouse fence in the Square, there was nothing to do, after their trading, except in the saloons. The farmers' wives were predominant in the hospitals for the insane.

Naturally, the remoteness and comparative isolation of the country people sharply distinguished them from city people, who, of course, tend to become much of a pattern. The manners, the dress, the habit of thought, and the speech of a small and sequestered county seat were something of a pattern, too, but the pattern was rustic; and it was with life in such a county seat that the berated serial principally dealt. The berating, however, came from the people and editors in the cities and larger towns and thus proved as mystifying as it was painful to the serial's author. It was not until one of its assailants used a personal pronoun that the resentment it had roused began to be comprehensible.

"You've maligned the people of your native state," this critic said.

"I only wrote about a few of 'em, and I did that as truthfully as I could. I praised them; I didn't malign them."

"But look at what your serial is making the East think of this part of the country!"

"I haven't heard of its making the East think anything at all. I haven't heard of anybody's reading it except the people hereabouts who read it in order to make themselves more and more indignant with me."

"We've got a right to be indignant," he said. "You're making the East think of us as an absolutely uncultivated backwoods people. They think that of us too much already, and here you go, adding to the slander!"

It was his using the pronoun "us" that gave me the clew I needed. "What had happened to me" was what had happened to Edward Eggleston after his publication of *The Hoosier Schoolmaster*, and it had happened sometimes, though more mildly, to Mr. Riley because of his poetic studies of the Hoosier dialect. "We" were afraid that such writings would encourage the East in its belief that we were unsophisticated and uncultured. The East wouldn't know how to distinguish between our obscure, bucolic communities and our brilliant and forward cities.

There was some ground for this fear, moreover. Just as Europeans seemed to believe that bison, Indians, and Bret Harte's gamblers might be found anywhere inland from the Atlantic Coast, so did New Yorkers. Bostonians and Philadelphians appeared to be under the impression that the axe of the pioneer still rang in our flat-land clearings. We were sensitive; we could ill bear the sting of Eastern impressions; and in like manner the East, too, was sensitive to oversea impressions; in particular to British. And here we come to a significant matter—our whole country was sensitive to foreign impressions of us.

We were more than sensitive; we were thin-skinned enough to be jumpy. Criticism from abroad sent us into furies of vindictive denunciation of the critic, as Charles Dickens had long before discovered. When a travelling Englishman reported in print that not only a large proportion of our male populace but many of our statesmen and jurists chewed tobacco, and that spittoons were prevalent in our hotels and public buildings and were not unknown in private houses, we said he had dried eggs on his coat. We entreated him to tell us what he thought of us; but if he uttered anything except platitudes of praise, we showed our hurt by jeering at him.

We wanted praise, unlimited praise; we could endure nothing else. We begged praise from the traveller before he landed. "What do you think of America?" we asked him eagerly, and our eagerness was our hunger for flattery.

We still ask him that, but there is a difference. The country had no confidence in itself in those days when it raged if it wasn't flattered. It had not become self-sufficient; it had not discovered its place in the world; and it bragged of power that it was not sure it possessed. We had not become complacent enough to endure criticism.

Our orators understood perfectly that we could endure nothing but flattery. The orator went to the people, then, not with a microphone, but directly, with larynx, lungs, a "Prince Albert" coat, and with a white pitcher and thick glass goblet on a deal table. First, he flattered the audience before him; then he praised the community they lived in; then he offered tribute to the state of which that community was a part; then he paid his compliments to the country; and often his peroration was addressed to the national banner.

Of course, if his oration was political, his flattery was addressed only to that portion of the community, state, and nation constituting his own party; all members of other parties, especially the Presidents, senators, and governors they had elected, were treated as worthless. Thus an observer might have thought that criticism of the country was, indeed, permissible, since certain millions of the populace, the Democrats, cheered loudest when aspersions cast upon certain other millions, the Republicans, were most poisonous; but the observer who came to such a conclusion would have been deceived. Party criticism has ever been understood as sometimes half-humorous buncombe, as sometimes yearning for power, money, and office, as sometimes genuine desire to "save the country." And always it has interpreted itself not as criticism of the country but, on the contrary, as the highest and most enthusiastic patriotism.

"Our native land and its people are noble, magnificent, grand, incomparable on the face of the globe," it says. "But those feeble-minded, self-seeking and largely corrupt creatures of the opposition will damage all this perfection if they are put into office. Do not trust them with so priceless a charge."

Emigrants from other countries came in millions to seek a better fortune among us. We nodded benevolently, and, when they became citizens, congratulated ourselves on their appreciation of us; but when an American went abroad to live and changed his citizenship we damned him on every street corner.

"What? We aren't *good* enough for him, the green-spined descendant of a magenta-whiskered tom-cat?" we said. "We aren't good enough for *him*?" And when his friends explained that he had moved to foreign parts for the sake of the climate we felt the insult no less unendurable. Love me, love my dog! Find fault with my climate? Jackass!

The unfortunate young serial had innocently wandered into the jumpiest area of Midland sensitiveness; and, although before the issue of the final instalment the truth had appeared that the author's intentions were anything but critical and the denunciations somewhat abated, he still had much the general sensation of a person ridden out of town on a fence rail for saying the wrong thing. Tar and feathers had, indeed, been among the practical suggestions of reviewers from the larger county seats; and so, a little later, when another and much shorter serial was printed in the magazine and then as a book, there appeared to be, not in the flatlands but beyond the Atlantic, an area of probable sensitiveness where this story, too, might lead to similar practical suggestions. Wisdom gathered from bruises advised against its being printed there.[2]

It was a romance in miniature, no longer than a short story, written a few years before the novel that had just appeared, and even more in the fashion of its time; for the younger a writer is the more likely he is to write in the fashion of the time, even when he does not know he is doing it and believes that his writing is actually a revolt against the fashion. Romanticism was the fashion then; a romanticism somewhat sentimental, but more concerned with the continuous movement of incredible "characters" than with sentiment. What the action of my own small outright romance in the fashion required was that nearly all the secondary characters should be inimical to the principal figure; and I had happened to conceive this principal figure was a sympathetic French gentleman sojourning in England. Therefore the inimical characters were all English, and, as the action was based upon snobbery, all the English depicted were shown to be virulent and ruthless snobs except one. And for consistency's sake it was explained that this exceptional gentleman had been improved by a French strain in his ancestry.

Altogether, here was a yarn to make any patriot British heart murderous—a Frenchman, symbolically beautiful in all respects, exploited at the expense of caitiff Englishmen. Even the English heroine was a snob; great English nobles were represented as worse than snobs; they were brutal, cowardly, fawning, treacherous, clumsy, and impenetrably stupid. It was impossible to imagine allowing such a thing to be printed in England, or the play that had been made out of it for the American theatre to be presented

---

2. Tarkington now refers to *Monsieur Beaucaire*, ultimately published in New York by McClure, Philips & Co. in May 1900.

there. I wanted to go to England some day without simultaneously taking my departure therefrom upon a fence rail.

An English friend wrote me that I was mistaken to be apprehensive; and deciding that I could, after all, keep to the Continent when I went abroad, I nervously consented to make the experiment. The British reviews of the book were sent to me. They were blandly benevolent. Some of them mentioned the fact that all the English characters were extremely horrid; but went on to say that English memoirs of the period of the story easily justified the author in this usage, and for that matter there was undoubtedly still a great deal of snobbery in Britain.

When the play was produced it received a flawlessly cheerful approval; it had a thoroughly undeserved and inexplicable run of several years, and afterward was frequently revived. The King had a command performance of it at Windsor; nobody ever resented anything about it, not even its absurdity, and nobody ever inquired whether it was written by a foreigner or by somebody from home.

Thus it seemed to be astonishingly revealed by this small episode that the British wholly lacked our kind of sensitiveness, and, as a matter of fact, they did lack it. They had good reason to lack sensitiveness. They knew their predominant place in the world; their confidence was perfect; they were sure of the power Britain possessed, and therefore, instead of bragging of it, they almost never mentioned it. This confidence, this warranted, easy assurance on the national scale seemed admirable; but here, on this side of the world, we were often irritated by it. We were irritated because we hadn't anything like it within ourselves—and that was so short a time ago that already we were in the Twentieth Century.

IX

THE OLD OUTRIGHT ANTIPATHY between Republicans and Democrats, heritage of the Civil War, still lingered in elderly hearts, and was not wholly extinct elsewhere, though the newspapers no longer talked of the *fin de siècle* and the Twentieth Century had arrived. Moreover, with this feeling there still existed among the best citizenry the habit of political activity. Most of the elderly men whom I knew had been soldiers during the War for the Union; and most of them were, or had been, in politics. Having fought for their country and saved it from dismemberment, they naturally felt that they were the people to "run" it, or at least to see that it was "run right." Their children, the youth of the next generation, had politics with every meal; a United States senator was a great man; and every little boy was told on his birthday that he might live to be President. By the time he reached college—if he went to college—he had usually given up that ambition as beyond him; but, if he won some distinction in undergraduate oratory, it was still predicted for him that he might one day become a senator. Politics was the field for greatness.

During the *fin de siècle*, however, this feeling had begun to alter, and, with the Twentieth Century, the change was more decisively apparent. Nevertheless, in the Midland country, at least, it was still true that to some extent everybody was in politics and, for my own part, I found myself quite naturally, though not ambitiously, a member of the State Legislature. The experience was lively, enlightening, and in one or two particulars infuriating—for there were operations that could not be viewed with humour—and when it was over I published as short stories some studies founded upon observation. Straightway I was in trouble again, this time with a powerful and authoritative critic. He was at that time the President of the United States, and he sent for me to come to Washington.[1]

---

1. Tarkington refers to Theodore Roosevelt, whom Tarkington visited in the White House just before Christmas in 1904. The stories were published in book form as *In the Arena* (1905).

"Do you understand what you're doing to politics?" he inquired.

"Why—why, no, sir. I haven't noticed anything. I've only been in the State Legislature and nobody seemed to——"

"I'm not referring to your membership in that assembly," he interrupted with some sharpness. "I'm speaking of the stories you're writing about politics and politicians. Do you understand their effect?"

"Well, I—I hadn't heard of any. One of my aunts told me she'd been reading them, but that's all I——"

"Never mind," he said. "Everything published in that magazine has some effect, and what you're publishing in it now is the darker side of politics. Do you deny it?"

"No, I——"

"Certainly you don't. What's your object?"

"Well, I thought that perhaps if people could be made to realize some of the worst things that do go on they'd want to remedy them. I thought they'd——"

"You're absolutely wrong!" he said with his well-known decisiveness. "It's precisely what they don't do. They say to themselves, 'Ah, I thought so! Politics is too dirty a business for any decent person to mix with; I'll keep out of it.' That's precisely what they say and that's what you're helping them to say. Too many people feel that way already. Too many fine gentlemen have begun to say they won't soil their white hands in muddy waters. They wouldn't mind accepting ambassadorships, but they despise knowing how to swing their own wards, and they wouldn't shake hands with a precinct committeeman to save the Union! You're feeding the satisfied conviction of such people that superiority to politics and politicians is the correct posture. You're helping to crystallize the feeling that politics is no 'business for a gentleman.' You believe that's a dangerous and damaging feeling, don't you?"

"Yes; but I'd hoped to——"

"It's infinitely worse than dangerous and damaging!" he went on with his accustomed vigour. "It's absolutely destructive and what it may destroy is incalculable. Not only have people begun to say that politics is no 'business for a gentleman,' they've begun to believe that politics is no business for a business man—except as his business may sometimes make it necessary and therefore excusable for him to be a dictator and corruptionist. The old ambitions of able young men are disappearing; the enormous fees awaiting adroitness in the professions and the disproportionally vast rewards obtainable in big business are changing all that. The best talents, the best minds are abandoning politics to the smaller professional politicians, and, unless that is checked, the country will some day see precisely that kind of politician prevalent in the United States Senate itself. There are actually hundreds and even thousands of men in the country to-day who won't even take the trouble to vote! What you're writing now helps to make them say, 'Well, why should I vote? What difference will my vote make in all this boss-controlled turmoil?' Well, between the boss and the gentleman in the club window who won't even soil his gloves with a ballot, give me the boss every time! And if I have to choose between the reformer too dainty to know his own subject by experience—between the man who stands aside and yet criticizes and the man who takes his coat off and goes in to swing his ward, I'll take the one that sweats in his shirt sleeves! You're giving countenance to the gentleman in the club window; you're helping the stand-aside reformer to shout 'Dirty! Dirty!' at the best men in politics as well as at the worst, because the stand-aside reformer never knows the best from the worst. You're giving all the stand-aside people more chance to feel that they're right in holding aloof and feeling superior! Anything that encourages asses in their asininity is harmful; but it's infinitely more damaging to give able young men reason to say, 'Politics is too dirty; I'll go into the law or into business, and leave it to the swine to run my country!' That's precisely what your gloomy pictures of politics are doing—making people say, 'Leave it to the swine!' Excellent! It it's left to the swine, how long do you think it will be before only swine come to the meal?"

He had a way of saying "swine" that gave the simple Jacobean word a damning powerfulness: the swine he had in mind seemed to be incomparably more swinish than the ordinary swine other people sometimes had in mind; and he was so severe with me that even though he was giving me an excellent luncheon while he scolded me, I had a fear that he might possibly suspect the presence of at least a few porcine bristles somewhere upon my person. On the contrary, he was entirely benevolent, and the scolding was only a manifestation of the Colonel's great kindness to young people who were "trying to write." Moreover, he had said some things to be remembered; it is possible to look back upon them now and believe that they were at least a little prophetic.

X

THERE WERE PEOPLE AT that time who thought the automobile might be developed until some day it would become a vehicle of common use. A friend of mine even thought it would displace horses altogether.

"You'll live to see the day when there won't be any horses in the street and the horseless carriages are as ordinary as surreys are now," he said.

But his prediction seemed to be fanciful. The machines were unreliable and the early enthusiasts who owned them led laborious and exasperated lives. They spent hours lying upon their backs in the street, or in the mud or dust of country roads, striving with the inwards of perverse metals above them; they were never sure of arriving anywhere, or even of starting for anywhere. They often found themselves helpless at critical moments, and all moments were critical. They were mired in mud and had to hire horses; they hired horses on gentle hill slopes; they hired horses ignominiously in crowded streets; they bore conspicuous derision and sometimes leaped for their lives from explosions, or from flames that encompassed them without warning.

The strange-shaped horseless grotesques were propelled by the action of steam or electricity or explosive gas; there was conflict and argument over which served best, and there was further argument over what name the things should bear—"horseless carriages," or the French term "automobiles," or "cars," or just "machines." And, when an attendant mechanic was hired, there was other debate upon a title for him. Should he be called "mechanic," or "mechanician," or "driver," or "chauffeur"? Mark Twain, with the many horsepower of the elephant in mind, suggested "mahout."

When the gas machines moved they did it with outrageous uproar, and the vibration of them shocked the spines of the hardy experimentalists who rode in them. In 1903, in the early spring, I was stricken with typhoid fever which harried me until the summer; and, to soften the noises that came into the open windows of the sick-room, the street was covered with fine sand to the depth of two or three inches for the distance of half a block. In the daytime no automobile would enter the sanded area; but sometimes, after dark, one that had not wandered into that shrouded street before would come chugging and snorting into the sand and be caught there like a fly in soft glue. Then there would be blasphemous metallic roarings, accompanied by simple human cursings, for half an hour perhaps.

But the new locomotion improved from month to month; engineers in creative frenzy designed and experimented; stranger and stranger new shapes clattered, banged, and spat fire upon our streets; more horses ran away every day; and the upset citizens wrote fiercely to the papers demanding ordinances excluding motor-driven vehicles from the public highways. Nevertheless, the improvements went on, and, in that same year, having added a sea voyage to convalescence, I drove from Brussels to Waterloo and back in a device called—by the attendant Italian mechanic—an "automobilly," and was only slightly prostrated by the journey.

This automobilly was very high and shaped like an English brake; the engine howled in a ponderous box at the rear, and the front seat was protected by a tremulous leather dashboard from which one missed the whip socket. The driver steered with a bent rod, and the brave passengers mounted to their seats by means of a little stepladder which was afterward stowed away under the rear seat. The large wooden wheels had solid rubber tires, and their passage over an ancient stone-paved road would have been stimulating to the spinal ganglia if the performance by the engine's two large cylinders had not already attended to that. The return to Brussels was safely accomplished by four in the afternoon; the passengers walked into the hotel unaided; but having reached their rooms retired instantly to bed and did not rise again until noon of the next day.[1]

Thereafter, for a time, we forswore horseless vehicles, let use them who would; they were intended evidently for people with rubber backbones and no fretful imaginations. When you were driving a horse and ran into anything, the impact of collision was with the force of a single steed, not thirty or forty; if you ran over a pedestrian, he endured the passing weight of some hundreds of pounds, not of several tons; if you ran over a dog, he got up and went home, terrified but usually not ruined. Moreover, if things went wrong when you were driving a horse, you had somebody to blame; a horse could hear what you said to him and be brought to repentance. You could never reform an automobilly or get any relief by abusing it.

Europe was beginning to use the machines nevertheless, and more of them were seen there than in America; they were improving more rapidly

---

1. The passengers were Tarkington, his wife, and his parents. They arrived in Europe in 1903. This trip was in summer 1904.

there than in America, too; and in France we found that everybody talked about them excitedly.

"It's going to be a craze—and more," an elderly American who lived in Paris predicted one night at dinner. "It's going to be a craze on this side of the water first and then in America. It will be a craze in Europe first because of the splendid military highways and the improved roads generally. No sane person would attempt to do any touring in such machines on the horrible American roads; but when the craze becomes furious over there it may do a good thing; it may improve the roads so that one can drive about the country with horses in some comfort. Outside of that, I regard the self-moving vehicle as one of the most terrific visitations our old earth will ever endure."

"You're sure that a craze for it is coming?"

"It's in the air," he said. "Just now, to operate one of those outrages is the distinguished thing to do. Every few days one or another of my friends informs me that he has made the great investment. 'Well, I'm in for it!' he says, and his eyes glisten with pride and adventurous excitement. 'I have bought one!' Then he proceeds to boast of its horsepower and swears that he has already driven it from Versailles to the Louvre in twenty-eight minutes. He has one hand in a bandage, a torn ear, and a bruise over his eye, and he is delighted with these injuries. The women will help make it a craze because of the special costumes the sport requires—the wonderful hats, the veils, the pongee coats, and the gauntlets. And for the vanity of men, already it is a greater distinction to show automobile goggles sticking out of your breast pocket than a ribbon on your lapel. With these symptoms evident, the diagnosis is simple—within a very few years nobody's life will be safe the moment he steps out of doors."

"You aren't serious?"

"Try to cross the Champs Élysées when the crowd is returning from the Grand Prix," he said. "You will find that little task sufficiently preoccupying now, when all but a few of the vehicles are drawn by horses. Imagine the horse traffic complicated by great numbers of these roaring, darting machines. Of course I'm serious! Les autos are man's most dangerous invention, and I am not forgetting that his inventions have brought him the blessings of gunpowder and nitroglycerin. So far, the automobilists have contrived principally to get only themselves killed, and usually when they have been racing their dreadful contraptions; but as the craze spreads there will be massacres of innocents on every city boulevard and country highway. The new machine is simply a locomotive; but remember this mortal difference: a locomotive runs only upon the rails provided for it. Send not a few but thousands of locomotives wandering irresponsibly over the face of Europe and America at a hundred kilometres an hour and you will have an idea of what this certainly coming contagion is going to do. And yet all the slaughter and destruction will be only a part of the curse that is to come upon the world."

The others at the table were amused by this prophesying, as preposterous as it was gloomy, and one of them asked, "What worse can a craze for horseless transport do than to massacre the innocents?"

"It can make a change in the life of the people," the prophet said, not relaxing his gravity. "It will do more than mock the speed craze of the bicyclists; it will obliterate the accepted distances that are part of our daily lives. It will alter our daily relations to time, and that is to say it will alter our lives. Perhaps everybody doesn't comprehend how profoundly we are affected by such a change; but what alters our lives alters our thoughts; what alters our thoughts alters our characters; what alters our characters alters our ideals; and what alters our ideals alters our morals. When the horseless craze becomes universal it is not too much to say that the world will be inhabited by a new kind of people—and again I am serious."

"What kind of people will they be?"

"To themselves, they will of course represent an advance," he said. "They will look back upon us with a pitying contempt; but to us, as we are now, I think they would seem almost grotesque; they would appear to be machinery mad and strangely metallic. They will be unbelievably daring; they will be reckless of life—fast, materialistic, and yet incredibly prompt and efficient; therefore they will be richer than we are. Everything will be changed, because when a man accepts a new idea that revolutionizes his daily life, his mind becomes hospitable to every other new revolutionary idea. We are just entering the period when most of what we have regarded as permanently crystalline will become shockingly fluid—that is to say, we are already in the transition period between two epochs. We have seen the one and most of you here to-night will see something of the other. Your point of view will shift with the universal change; and, if you live, you will yourselves become strange inhabitants of the new world. A quarter of a century from to-night you will be taking as an accepted matter of course, and without a shiver, things that are simply unthinkable to you now. I cannot tell you what those things will be. I am only a reasoner and not an inspirational prophet, but I am sure that if you could have a vision of yourselves twenty-five years older you would be startled and incredulous. And in the meantime, within only two or three years, every one of you will have yielded to the horseless craze and be the boastful owner of a metal demon; you will talk nothing but machines, and as you are being removed to the hospital you will babble to the stretcher-bearers of horse-power and kilometres per hour. Restfulness will have entirely disappeared from your lives; the quiet of the world is ending forever."

The pessimist gave us two or three years to begin our transfiguration into strange inhabitants of the new epoch but for my own part I did not need quite so long. The fair golden sunshine upon the boulevards became more and more shot with the blue vapours; the smell of burnt oil and gas grew tolerable to the nostrils and then actually enticing. Simultaneously, the trains to Paris from the country suburb where I had gone to live appeared to become more and more inconvenient until at last the day came when I perceived that the contagion was irretrievably upon me. Excited by the discovery of my condition, I lost no time but hurried to the office of an automobile agent on the Champs Élysées and asked him to be my friend. He had various kinds of automobiles to sell, on commission; I left it to him to choose which one was best suited to my circumstances and my ambitions.

When most of us who are elderly or middle-aged recall the purchase of our first automobile, in those early days of motoring, we feel the forget-me-not breath of an ancient pathos upon our hardened cheeks. There seems to have once been something touching about us.

XI

The agent appeared to be a little puzzled by my request for his friendship; but, after looking at me thoughtfully for some moments, he said that nothing would give him greater pleasure. And when I explained that Providence had entirely denied me any talent for comprehending machinery, and that all I could ever hope to know about an automobile, through my own study and observation, was what colour it had been painted, he became enthusiastic.

"You ask for my friendship," he said. "You shall have it; already I feel myself drawn to you. You need disinterested advice. Excellent! I am your friend and I will advise you. I have precisely what you want. I have a superb automobile for you. It is not entirely new; but that makes it all the better, because a little usage imparts elasticity to the operating devices. It has been owned by a friend of mine who feels himself compelled to part with it, though he has grown so fond of it that he will not give it up except to a person able to appreciate it. You will obtain a great deal of happiness from this superb vehicle. It is as fast as your heart could desire, and the joy you will experience as you drive it at ninety or a hundred kilometres the hour——"

I interrupted him, though I liked what he was saying: "No; I—I don't think I'd better try to drive it myself. I have patiently to learn what makes these machines move, and I believe that I have succeeded in mastering the fundamental principle. My understanding is that an explosion of gas within a rigid compartment makes a pressure on something that is obliged to go up or down, or both, and this motion is somehow converted into a turning of wheels. Friends have tried to teach me how the motion is converted; they have drawn diagrams for me and I have faithfully studied them, but without any result whatever. To every mind there are certain things that cannot be conveyed, and this is one of the things that cannot be conveyed to mine. And as it seems to be established that unless one knows what takes place beneath one when one pushes a lever operating certain machinery over which one is sitting, one isn't justified in pushing such a lever, I have concluded that it will be safer for myself, and for people generally, so to speak, if I refrain from pushing the levers of this superb vehicle you have been so kind as to select for me. I think I should employ a chauffeur."

"Excellent!" the agent said. "But let me advise you, as your friend—first complete the purchase of the automobile we have selected. If you engage the chauffeur before you own the automobile, you will be embarrassed, because he would immediately ask you, 'What species of automobile am I expected to drive?' You would be confused and perhaps mortified to reply that you have no automobile. A certain amount of pretentiousness may attach to a person who, lacking an automobile, possesses a chauffeur."

"I hadn't thought of such a thing," I said hurriedly. "Could I see the automobile this morning?"

"Perfectly! Naturally, you should see the automobile before you purchase it; but I tell you confidently you are going to be delighted. We will go at once." He took me to a garage and there displayed to me a red car which he patted proudly and affectionately. "Behold it! This is what I have promised you. Have you ever seen anything more perfectly fitted to your special requirements? Think how you will look in it in the Bois de Boulogne! And observe, you will not need to buy any equipment or accessories except some tools. It already has a covering, which can be elevated in case of rain, and two splendid oil lamps with reflectors; you will not be annoyed by having to purchase a top and lamps, nor by the delay of getting them fitted to the machine; they are included in the price. Did I not tell you it is superb?"

Some workmen had joined us and I wished to appear intelligent. "What horse-power has it?" I asked.

"Forty—forty horses would be needed to do what it will do."

"Ah—what kind of a car is it?"

"What kind? It is a touring car."

"I mean what make."

"It is Italian, a magnificent Lux."

"Is it, indeed?" I said, impressed. "A genuine Lux?"

"Genuine? It could not be more so. Observe it!"

I did. I went to it and looked at it carefully. There was a narrow door in the middle of the rear wall for the entrance of passengers, and when this door was closed a little seat could be swung down from it, thus allowing three people to sit in the tonneau. Moreover, a long wicker hamper was strapped to each side of the car, above the rear wheels, and these arrangements pleased me.

"It is very convenient," I said. "People can get in by the little door and these hampers seem to me a great improvement. Luncheon could be carried in them, or almost anything."

"Yes," the agent agreed, "luncheon, maps, an umbrella, a cane—anything you wish. I was sure you would be delighted with the baskets. Are they not charming? As you say, they are a great improvement, and only a few of the very finest automobiles are equipped with them. Every convenience you can imagine accompanies this superb Lux. Have I been correct? This is perfectly the car you wish to buy?"

"I—I think so. I believe——"

One of the mechanics who stood by interrupted. "Don't you care to look at the engine?"

"Indeed, I do," I said. "Where is it?"

"It is in front," the agent explained. "All the most modern automobiles have the engine in front under a protecting hood nowadays." He opened the hood. "Observe it! Have you ever beheld a more perfect mechanism? Isn't it a masterpiece?"

"I'm sure it must be," I said. "Could we take a little drive?"

"A drive?" he repeated thoughtfully. "A drive? You would prefer to drive in it before completing the purchase? I will see if that can be arranged."

He spoke to two of the workmen and withdrew them to a corner of the garage, where the three engaged in a long conversation, gesticulating earnestly, while I again examined the baskets and the little door, becoming more and more pleased with them. Finally the agent returned to me.

"You shall have your drive," he said benevolently. "First, we shall go to lunch; after that we shall come back and then you shall have your drive."

When we came back, we climbed into the car through the fascinating little door and sat in the tonneau, while a serious-looking mechanic occupied the driver's seat and another went to the crank in front of the car, to start the engine. The agent chatted gaily, speaking often of the charming wicker hampers; but the seriousness of the workman who was to drive appeared to increase, and so did that of his companion, who was for some time violently engaged with the crank.

"Do not be discouraged," the agent said. "Often the best of automobiles—even a Lux—will require several turns of the crank before the engine——"

He was interrupted by a shattering roar; the engine had gone into action and the mechanic leaped back from the crank, then climbed back into the seat beside the driver.

"Do not be disturbed," the agent shouted in my car. "The noise is rather loud because we are in an enclosure. In the open, you will almost not notice it at all. Also, there will be much less vibration as soon as we are in motion."

When we were out of doors I persuaded myself that he was correct. We sounded like an itinerant battle and we undeniably vibrated; but we moved with startling rapidity, the wind hard in our faces; and I found the experience so exciting, even so exhilarating, that when we returned I decided that this superb Lux must be mine. I had a final moment of hesitation.

"You remember," I said to the agent, "you said you would act as my friend, my trusted adviser. I appeal to you now as you stand in that capacity. Do you sincerely advise me to buy this automobile from you?"

He looked me in the eye. "I will reassure you," he said earnestly and gently. "Listen well to what I am going to tell you. It is simply this: I give you my word of honour that I would sell this automobile to my own brother."

That settled it. I signed the purchase papers on the spot; but, when I engaged a chauffeur and we attempted to take the superb Lux home, I began to comprehend that the agent's brother at some time in their lives had done him a horrible injury.

The chauffeur and I, seated in the superb Lux, left the garage thunderously at three o'clock of a bright May afternoon and covered a dozen blocks before we had our first breakdown. Fortunately, we were near a repair shop and were delayed only an hour. The subsequent breakdowns were more serious and the last one happened long after dark in a deserted portion of the Bois de Vincennes. There were sounds of breakage, of things hurtling through the air, and the machine stopped violently. This abruptness no longer disconcerted me, as already I had learned that the superb Lux knew no other manner of stopping; but the chauffeur's mutterings had what young people sometimes like to speak of as an air of finality. He went forward, groped laboriously in the dust of the road, and returned with what seemed to me, as he held them up for inspection, some fragments of a heavy chain.

He confirmed my impression—a chain, apparently needful for locomotion, had been broken and dispersed; now it lay sprinkled upon the surrounding terrain in the darkness.

"But even if I could find it all," Victor said, "how could I reunite it?"

Victor was an Alsatian; he spoke French in a manner all his own; and in this he was no more individual than I. We had need of a great deal of conversation between us to arrive at small communication, but we finally came to an understanding. It would not be sensible to remain throughout the night as we were, Victor said; the locality was favoured by *les apaches*. He proposed to sit in a clump of bushes near the road and watch the car. If *apaches* arrived and stole it he would remain quietly in the underbrush, and I agreed that the superb Lux would be what the scoundrels deserved. If they did not appear, Victor would await a relief expedition, and I went forward to arrange it. After walking two miles, I found a pair of horses and a truckman willing to accept the commission; but I did not return with them; I drove the rest of the way in a hired carriage. The superb Lux, Victor, the truckman, and the two horses reached home at two in the morning. They had passed wine shops in several villages, but the two horses were still sober.

XII

Pedestrians had not developed then a precautionary sense that they possess now almost as if it were an instinct; they had not learned to time the approach of an automobile. People walking along country roads and crowds on the crossings of city streets were alike in this respect; despite an occasional reckless bicyclist, they were accustomed to vehicles moving at speeds of from three or four to seven or eight miles an hour; and, even if a fast horse came tearing down on them at nine or ten miles an hour, the sound of his hoof beats was the well-known signal to hurry a little, but not unduly. It was difficult to understand, when we were on foot, that we must begin to calculate upon less time to get out of the way, since throughout the centuries a fast horse had been the fastest thing upon any highway; and we would need years of indignant experience to teach us that the combination of old human nature with the new power for speed made inevitable a basic change in the mental attitude and bodily action of all pedestrians. When automobiles formed a slight proportion of the traffic and there were hundreds of horse vehicles where there was one automobile, the one automobile often appeared from among them like a charging demon, horrifying and unexpected. The demon was noisy; but the noise was so unfamiliar and so startling that foot passengers lost their heads in the crisis of his approach.

When the superb Lux was not in a repair shop, we drove either about the countryside or into Paris; and at night, after these excursions, when I went to bed, that half-awake interval preceding sleep would be crowded with pictures reproduced out of the events of the day just passed—pictures of terrified peasants escaping dimly into clouds of dust beside the road and crossing themselves; pictures of open-mouthed children screaming as they ran from our path at the last possible moment; pictures of enraged people who cursed us as they became unwillingly active on city crossings; pictures of scared women with baby carriages trying to go both ways at once; pictures of aged men and women in every attitude of sudden undesired haste and futile defence; pictures of pompous fat men outraged by the necessity to leap backward; pictures of faces in every distortion of fear and fear's close companion, hatred.

Often I remonstrated with Victor, and when I did he looked at me pityingly. "You think this Lux knows how to move sweetly?" he inquired. "It is impossible to its nature. Either this Lux is in complete repose or in complete action; there is no middle ground. By supposition only there are two speeds; but after he is cranked—on such days as he consents to be cranked at all—and I have mounted to my seat and thrown in his clutch to the lower speed, there is always a period when I must wait to ascertain if it is one of the days when he consents to allow his clutch to operate. If he consents, it will always be at a moment when I have concluded that it is not to be one of the days. He decides abruptly, gives a great leap, and within the instant he is forcing himself through a pile of stones half a kilometre down the road. If people do not get out of our way the Lux must stop, and when he stops you are well aware there arises always a great question: Will he ever move again? If he will, then when will he? To-morrow, perhaps."

When I engaged Victor he did not appear to be a drinking man; but his close companionship with the superb Lux had an evil influence upon him, and they formed the habit of becoming incapacitated together; though it must be said to the chauffeur's credit that the Lux always set the example. Victor was a handsome, tall, soldierly person of commanding presence. When we were travelling and stopped for luncheon or for the night, the innkeepers always first addressed themselves deferentially to him, bowing before him; and he would have to explain that I was his patron, not an attendant. However, when he was slightly in wine he sometimes seemed to forget this relation.

"I have discovered a thing," I shouted to him as I sat beside him one day in hilly country. "I have discovered that although it is difficult to make the Lux move slowly, there are nevertheless some moderations of speed that can be accomplished with care, when you choose. Why do you descend this hill on gas?"

"In order to get up the next one," he replied. "Great speed is necessary to surmount this next hill."

"But rather than go fast I would prefer not to surmount it. This speed has made me so nervous that my feet are cramped from pushing an imaginary brake and my fingers from clutching an imaginary wheel. Now I have bitten a filling out of a tooth and we shall have to find a town that contains a dentist. He will be the second to repair me on this one excursion."

"Disregard all that," Victor said airily. "You are acquiring new sensations."

"I have no desire for them," I shouted, and with as much severity as I could command in the French language I gave him the positive order to slacken speed. "Sweetly! I wish to travel more sweetly! Compel this Lux to a sweeter movement. The wind does not permit me to breathe and I wish to remain alive."

Through his goggles he gave me a benevolent glance. "The ozone will do you good," he said calmly. "The most distinguished scientists recommend it."

That was one virtue of the superb Lux, certainly—it copiously provided ozone to its occupants; for this was long before the day of windshields. Goggles and "automobile costumes" were almost necessities, but many of the automobilists wore the costumes with a little of the consciousness that sometimes attaches to a yachtsman dressed expressively for the deck. Ear muffs and pneumatic clothes would have added to the pleasure of travel in the Lux, it may be said; for the roar of the engine, the machine-gun explosion of the exhaust, and the vibration of the whole fabric of the car were such as would be intolerable and incredible to-day.

But the superb Lux was not immortal; its own imperfections and the destined progress of mankind were in operation to supplant it. That mischievously inspired machine, which had destroyed all the temperate inclinations of one human being and brought upon other human beings so many tedious and unexpected miles of walking and so many mortifying tardinesses, had at last one inspiration too many. In a valley of Touraine, at the foot of a long hill down which it had charged, swaying, bounding, crashing, roaring gloriously, and deafening the very birds of the air with the artillery of its exhaust, it uttered a peculiar shriek and a moment later sullenly came to rest, oblique in the road. This was familiar—all except the peculiar shriek—and we descended as usual.

"The town of Chinon is only about six kilometres from here," I said. "I will walk to Chinon and send back mechanics."

But Victor, examining the engine, shook his head. "This time," he said, "send horses."

The next morning I left Chinon by rail, Victor and the Lux remaining there in a repair shop. Then, having returned home, I waited, sending remittances at intervals; but after two months I had a letter from a friend who had gone to Chinon:

> I have seen your chauffeur, but he did not seem to comprehend what I said to him. The innkeeper here explained that the unfortunate man has been intoxicated continuously for the last six

weeks, and, after talking to the mechanics who are working on your automobile, I cannot say that I blame him very much.

I decided that neither should I blame Victor; there was no cinema in Chinon in those days, and the pleasures of that interesting town were for the archaeologist and historian rather than for the chauffeur. I sent him another remittance; but by the time he did finally arrive with the restored and still vociferous Lux, I had a new machine and a new chauffeur.

The new chauffeur was a teetotaler and meek; and the new machine was a glittering, smooth-spoken French thing of the very moment, just from the factory and unbelievably obedient. The new day had begun; people could travel all over Europe by motor without stopping at a single dentist's.

I sold the superb Lux to a training school for chauffeurs—and when the pupils could drive it, they were graduated.

XIII

THE MOTORING CRAZE HAD spread over the civilized parts of the world by this time. Everywhere there was what might have been called—if we had known the word—"stunt" motoring; there were races on oval tracks and country roads; races from one capital to another, races across Europe, races across Asia, races round the world. Everybody talked of speed, horse-power, cylinders, and models; and the names most upon the tongue of the populace were those, not of statesmen, but of manufacturers. Ardent debate upon the comparative speed, power, and durability of the automobiles that bore these names was heard at the little open-air tables of Paris; it was heard in Neapolitan restaurants, in Bavarian beer gardens, in London clubs, in Vienna cafés, and in the lobby of the Garfield Hotel at Kamchatka, Michigan. Most of the talkers did not own automobiles, and their talk was only a by-product of the craze; motoring was still a sport for those prosperous—or reckless—enough to afford it. But more and more people did somehow afford it every day; and even then there were scandalized rumours of houses mortgaged for money to buy cars.

People were stimulated by the mere talk of high speeds to which they had not become accustomed; and to all this exhilaration and excitement over the automobile there was coming to be added a general divination that a greater marvel was at hand. The thoughts of many men were longingly in the air; and, out in the open country, east of Paris, every summer afternoon we could see what appeared to be great pale bubbles rising slowly, one at a time, from the distant profile of the city outlined by the Eiffel Tower, Notre Dame, and the hill of Montmartre with its cathedral coronet. The bubbles floated dreamily toward us and passed overhead, silent and peaceful in the evening sky; we envied those people up there, so high and cool and quiet in their drifting balloons.

Balloons not so placid had been constructed and were discussed at the sidewalk tables of the boulevards; balloons shaped like fat cigars and driven by engines and propellers—things that could be steered, though clumsily.

Men had actually navigated the air a little in one or two of these absurdities. This was wonderful, but it was not flying, and now, at last, after all the ages of skeptical ridicule, the automobile had brought with its own coming a portent: the ancient wild prophecies were to be fulfilled. Mother Shipton had not been so crazy, after all; Langley and Lilienthal had not lived in vain; for somehow everybody knew—it was in the air—that men were about to fly.

Then, one evening, the Parisian papers hurried excited extras to the streets and the cables sped to the four quarters of the earth. Santos-Dumont had lifted himself from the ground that afternoon in a machine that was heavier than air. It was a kite with an engine and a propeller; it had lifted him for only a moment, in a little skip of a few feet; nevertheless, the thing was done and he had been in the air, the first man of all the earthborn to rise from the ground in a flying machine—unless that fantastic American rumour of men in the air near Dayton, Ohio, could be true. But, of course, no serious person believed that story; the Americans were great projectors of the fantastic; they were given to that boastful sort of practical joking. It was said that the men up in the air of Ohio were brothers named Wright; probably their machine was lifted by wires, or, what seemed more likely to be the fact, by their imaginations.

Little more was heard of the Wrights just then; Santos-Dumont got himself off the ground again before long, in what the papers began to call a hop; other air adventurers hopped, too; and one exultant day there came a hop of an eighth of a mile. Meanwhile that humorous story about Dayton, Ohio, was generally forgotten; and probably the most curious manifestation concerned with the first flight of men was the apathy of the first flyers' neighbours. For, before Santos-Dumont hopped, the Wrights had done more than hop—they had flown—and the last place in the world where you would find anybody in a state of excitement over that miracle was precisely Dayton, Ohio.

As it happened, in the autumn of 1907, the necessities of a comedy in rehearsal in New York brought me back from Paris for a while, and the subsequent nursing of this play, during its earlier presentations on the road, took me to Dayton for a night.[1] I had little time to spare from the theatre, but found opportunity to ask a number of people what they knew about the Wrights and the rumour that had reached Europe about them and then had been discredited there. Everyone answered my inquiries in the same way, with a laugh first, and then: "Oh, yes; there've been a lot of wild stories going around town." No one that I saw believed the stories; but what surprised me

---

1. The play was *The Man from Home*, a popular play co-written with Harry Leon Wilson. It debuted in 1908. Film versions were made by Cecil B. DeMille in 1914 and George Fitzmaurice in 1922.

was that no one seemed to have taken the trouble to investigate them. Every heart in Paris had leaped with the hop of Santos-Dumont.

A lady who lived in Dayton at that time explained to me, long afterward, why the city that was the home of the Wrights showed this curious flaccidity when a stupendous event had taken place in its environs.

"The feeling wasn't peculiar to Dayton," she said. "It would have been just the same in other American cities, especially in other Middle and Western cities. You know the strange mixture of championship and self-doubtful humility we all felt about our own part of the country; we reverenced our great dead, like Lincoln, but we couldn't easily believe that anything really epochal could come from living people among us. With all the world dreaming of flying, and all the centuries behind us believing it could never be done, you don't suppose that anybody in Ohio could have imagined that down in Montgomery County two sons of a Middle West minister were really flying! Such things were done by people called Christopher Columbus or Fernando Cortez or Galileo, names rare in Ohio and strikingly unlike Wilbur and Orville. Don't you see why we paid so little attention?"

"Yes, in part. But nevertheless——"

"Nevertheless," she said firmly, "most people over the country would have been just as unmoved as we were. It was our incredulity that made us seem apathetic. For my part, I actually saw a secret photograph of the Wright machine in flight and did not believe it. The photograph was made by someone who did investigate, you see—a man I happened to know who had his own reasons for investigating. He was a queer fellow, an anarchist who was himself trying to build a flying machine, and a farmer had told him that strange things were happening at dawn out in the country where there were some wide fields called the Prairies. The man went out there one morning and hid himself with a camera. He showed me confidentially the picture he had taken and in great excitement pointed out something I at first mistook for a butterfly, thirty or forty feet above the ground. He said no, it wasn't a butterfly; it was a machine and there was a man in it! Then, indistinctly, I saw the little figure of the man myself, but I didn't really believe it was a man in a flying machine. I couldn't believe that any more than we could believe now in ghosts, if we saw a photograph of a ghost. I thought the thing queer—that's all, and pretty soon almost forgot about it. The anarchist didn't talk; he was anxious to make his own machine fly before the Wrights let their secret be known. His machine did fly, too, eventually, and killed him in a fall, poor man; but by that time Dayton was organizing a great testimonial reception for the Wrights because the world was acclaiming them."

I had seen Santos-Dumont in one of his dirigible balloons and I had seen his machine that hopped; but it was a long time after the Wrights' first flights before most of us saw airplanes. We began presently to know them from reproduced photographs in the illustrated journals and magazines, and to gasp at the daring of the men who sat on flimsy strips of metal or wood in the opening between the wings and manoeuvred the machines in the air. It was impossible to believe that we should ever grow accustomed to seeing such things, or that some day human beings indoors would hear them overhead and not rush out to stare at them. For my part, I had no opportunity to see men flying until 1910; and even then I went many miles, to be still incredulous while I looked and looked and looked at that strange and exalting sight.

This was an excursion far outside the theatrical boundaries that had then become my customary limits of peregrination. The life of the theatre is an enclosure for those who lead it, like the walls of a mediaeval town. They are so encircled that the movement of the world outside seems relatively vague and unimportant; and for me the theatre was an encirclement whether I was engaged abroad in writing manuscripts to offer it, or, in the manner of a playwright, disturbing the stage directors in New York when they were trying to translate the manuscripts into acting and painted scenery.

At last, however, feeling too much pressure from the enclosing walls, though I was far from ungrateful to the theatre, I decided to stop writing plays and also to break off a habit that had become too clutching. This was the habit of thinking of Paris as my fixed habitation, though I knew all the time that only in the flat lands of the Ohio Valley was there a spot that could ever wholly mean "home" to me. The American, settled abroad, comes upon pathetic moments sometimes; no matter how charmed he is with European life, no matter how suavely he fits himself into it, and no matter how thoroughly weaned away he may be, he always has these moments when he feels that he is neither fish, flesh, fowl, nor good red herring.

I had been on an island in the Mediterranean where an old American painter, who had lived there thirty years, was finishing the building of a villa for himself and his family.[2] He took me to see it.

"Yes, it's beautiful," he said. "But I've always lived in rented houses, thinking that next year I'd go home to stay. Now I've built this place I realize that I never will. I know now that my old bones will be laid away over here, under a foreign flag. My bones won't mind that, but I do. I can joke about it, I suppose; but if you'll lift the flap of the joke from my breast you'll see a pretty deep scratch."

---

2. This was late 1903. The island was Capri, and the painter Elihu Vedder (1836–1923). Vedder had been enabled to build this villa by the illustrations he had done for Edward FitzGerald's English translation of *The Rubaiyat of Omar Khayyam*.

I remembered what he had said and I decided to go home to the Midland country to live. But first I went with some friends for a final summer of motoring over the Alpine passes.[3] We came down out of the mountains into Germany at the end of August, and one morning we rolled out of Strassburg, which was German then, to cross over into France on our way back to Paris. We rolled not alone, however; batteries of light artillery rolled beside us; uhlans were seen riding on all the roads; and infantry regiments moved in the direction—toward Nancy—that we were taking.

Of course this was no extraordinary sight in Germany; but, for the preceding two or three days, as we approached the frontier, we had been increasingly aware of troops and troops and more troops going our way, horse and foot and guns. "Army manoeuvres," we said wisely, and thought little more about it. But when we came to the barrier at the frontier itself— a gate across the road at the edge of a small town—we could see cavalry and artillery and infantry uniforms everywhere; they lined the frontier for miles in each direction apparently; and, as we sat, waiting for the gate to be opened, uhlans were all about us, expressionless men on splendid horses. It was odd to see an army so close against the frontier that separated Germany from France; and, indeed, these manoeuvres seemed to be so peculiar that we asked questions of the man who opened the gate for us, an amiable German in uniform.

"What's it all about?" we inquired. "Do the frontier gates need all this protection against smugglers?"

"Smugglers!" he exclaimed. "Don't you know? Haven't you read the papers?"

"No, we haven't. We've been travelling for pleasure. What's going on?"

"A crisis!" he said. "There is a great diplomatic crisis. There may be war."

"What?" We laughed heartily. "A war? We must cross between the lines, must we?"

"Yes, truly," he said, and, to show his friendliness, he laughed, too. "You will see the French just on the other side of the neutral ground, like us here. You will see them in a few moments—the French regiments called to face us in the crisis. They are very near us, the French."

But when we had crossed the strip of neutral ground between the two countries and came to the French frontier, there were only two men in sight in all the expanse of fields and woods before us. The two were customs officers, and we asked them where their army was.

---

3. The friends were his sister's husband Ovid Butler Jameson and Ovid's son John, who had just completed his junior year at Princeton.

"It is ten kilometres from the frontier. We are careful not to risk provocation or irritation in a crisis by bringing our men too close to the German soldiers. You will see no uniforms for ten kilometres more."

It was as he said; but when we had passed the ten kilometres we began to meet French infantry in numbers; and they looked serious, even anxious, we thought; but again we laughed. What if there was a crisis? We knew there would be no war. We were Americans, and we knew that the business of the world would never permit another war on the grand scale such as a war between France and Germany must be. Besides, neither of those countries would dare thus to shatter its prosperity; and I recalled what a young French engineer had said earlier that summer.

"The *Revanche*?" he said. "For Alsace-Lorraine? No, we do not want it. Yes, I know that one or two patriotic societies and some old people who remember 1870 now and then put mourning wreaths on the Strassburg statue; but those people are only a few, and all that feeling is really old-fashioned. For the great multitude of us, for the French nation, there is no longer a thought of the *Revanche*; we are too busy; we ask only to be let alone so that we can work and attend to our affairs. It is the same with most of the German people; they are busy and prospering; they are not so insane as to wish to ruin themselves and us with a war."

So we rolled merrily on, continuing our way to Paris and amused by the "crisis." That was 1911 and we knew there would be no war between France and Germany then or at any other time. To imagine such a thing was as absurd as to imagine that airplanes would be mad enough to fight one another in the sky.

XIV

"Coming back home to stay, are you?" a fellow traveller said, the night before we landed. "That isn't like the casual little runs 'back home' you make when you're living abroad. When you're settled down in London or Paris, or somewhere in Italy, and just slide over to 'the States' on business, or perhaps because of the illness of one of your relatives, your life is centred elsewhere; you're really a visitor and you get only a visitor's slight and preoccupied impressions of our native land; your observation of the changes that are going on is as casual as your visit, so you don't feel them deeply, because you know they aren't going to affect you for any length of time. But you'll feel the changes now. 'Coming back home to stay'—ah, that's different!"

"What change will I feel most sharply?" I asked.

"We've been growing," he said. "We've been growing and growing and growing, and I think you'll hear the sound of it. Yet, after a little while, probably you'll perceive that with all the growing and growing and growing we've done, we've just barely begun to grow!"

He was right about my hearing the sound of it. The sound of it was in our ears that September morning in 1911, as we sat in the hansom cab we had hired at the Hoboken dock and waited for our ferryboat to be made fast in its Manhattan slip. And although the noise of New York's growing had always been in ears not wholly deaf upon that island, since the Indians sold it to the first Knickerbockers, the sound did strike more significantly than ever before, as the man in the smoking room had said, upon ears that had "come back home to stay."

It seemed to be the sound of metal driven upon metal, of steel rattled violently and of metallic explosions muffled under concrete. The conglomerate street sound of Latin cities was softer and incomparably more agreeably easygoing, being characteristically the sound of voices, the talking and calling—even the singing, while at work or play—of a vocal people. But here in New York, where growth was prodigiously in action and nothing ever was finished, and the continuous building up always as continuously tore down, where the paving of a street was scarce laid before it became tremulous and cracked with undermining, and where the walls of vast and high buildings were crashed down to make room for walls even vaster and higher, there was no sound of voices. If a truck driver enraged himself with injustice done him at a crossing, his cursing was inaudible, smothered under the metallic uproar. His lips and jaw could be seen to move, his expression to contort, his neck to swell and inflame, his eyes to bulge with the love of murder; yet all his rage became a futile pantomime; and, if he could not endure life without making his curses heard by him he cursed, he must wreck his throat with hoarseness. In effect, the people were silent in the streets.

The uproarious discordance was racking to a traveller returned from long sojourning in less vehement parts of the world; and not much less disturbing were the discords in the proportions and in the architectural modes of buildings that neighboured one another. Up and down the great streets architects seemed to have fought and still to be fighting an immense and insane battle, every man madly for himself, and, without thought to his own horrible wounds, rearing up immeasurable weapons to destroy whatever was near him. And there was no arboreal palliation, as in the most intelligent foreign cities; the softening rows of trees along the boulevards, the verdurous charm of Paris, had no place in the hard and stark avenues of New York. And yet to an eye returned from foreign parts to stay, there was a solace in these streets, a sight to warm and inspire a patriotic heart. The old friend who travelled with me, a man seldom enthusiastic and never sentimental, spoke of it.

"You have to be away a long time to appreciate them," he said. "Coming back, you only need to see them moving briskly along these sidewalks to be glad you're a compatriot. I'm speaking of the American women, those alert, bright-eyed matrons and cheerful know-how-to-take-care-of-themselves girls we're seeing all about us now. After living awhile on the Continent, how grateful one is to look at such enheartening creatures as these! The Continental women have charm enough and their own kind of good looks, of course; and anyone admits that they're 'talented as women.' But these Americans—they aren't content to be 'talented as women'; they insist upon being intelligences without regard to their sex; they're intelligent persons, not merely intelligent women. And how delightful it is to see whole streetfuls of women all wearing their own good complexions, with not a trace of artificial colour on cheek or lip or eyelid! They're briskly going about their own affairs, not preoccupied in the slightest with the fact of their being women and our being men; you can see they know how to think without thinking of that; it's visible in their faces. Here in New York we see not only New York women—they're from all over the country, and how keen and fine and how independent they look! In fact they're splendid and they make a man prouder to be an American than anything else does."

No one could have failed to share his enthusiasm, which contained nothing detrimental to the ladies of Europe, but only a sparklingly deserved appreciation of those native to his own country. They wore skirts almost to the ground, long and narrow, those "know-how-to-take-care-of-themselves" girls who kindled his eyes with delight in their intelligence and their superiority to cosmetics and conscious allure. Invariably they had long hair—all the hair Nature had given them—and plainly they cherished it; but they seemed much less emphatically hourglasses than they had been of yore; and something about them—especially that look of independence my friend had mentioned—appeared to mean that they had more freedom than ever before. They had the air of having made this freedom for themselves, and of intending to make it complete, no matter who didn't happen to like their having it.

XV

New York, however, was not my destination, being but a way station on this decisive journey to the verdant plain that had for me the persistent claim of native soil calling always, however faintly, to its wandering sons, "Come home!" A stranger, looking forth from his sleeping-car after a night of curving among the hills, might wonder why anybody should come home to this level monotony of landscape and the reiterating shabby back ends of wood and brick country towns, all alike. Moreover, a native son might himself feel a qualm or two of that same wonder, especially if he had been living in Paris. The flat lands were bleaker than they had been aforetime; the ground was dark and fertile, but great stretches of forest were gone, leaving only clumps of woodland here and there. The old bosky "snake fences" had disappeared, replaced by unamiable wire; and sometimes there would be a glimpse of a country road whereon an efficient, ugly little automobile bounced viciously into sudden distance, leaving the farmers' buggies and wagons, as it passed, enveiled and strangled in its long thick tail of dust. And sometimes, too, racing with the train, a demon of an interurban trolley-car would tear shrieking across the landscape.

Something of what had been the wistful charm of the long and wide flatness seemed to have disappeared; something of its old-time sleepy peacefulness seemed to be gone with the deep woods and rail fences. Nevertheless, it still had a voice and still could seem to murmur in its old-fashioned way, "Yes, this is home. It always will be home for those who were born in it. You have come home." And when I actually had reached home again, "old Charlie," the trolley-car conductor, who always remembered anybody that had ever lived on his "line," was warm in his congratulations. To him it seemed that any absence from his town must be unwilling, a hardship enforced. "You are certainly mighty lucky to get back to God's country again!" he said.

At first it did not appear to me that the Midland city had changed a great deal. It had grown, of course, because it was alive; and it was obviously not so clean as it had been. Almost into the Twentieth Century, natural gas had made it speckless, except for the ordinary dustiness of summer; and when the gas failed, anthracite helped to keep the air clear. There were not many factories in what was essentially a market town, the capital of an agricultural state, and what smoke there had been came principally from the railroad engines. Now, however, one was conscious sometimes of soft-coal smoke in the air, particularly at nightfall; but the traces were comparatively faint, far from unendurable.

The same pleasant old "principal residence streets" stretched serenely northward; the same green arches of joining branches shaded them; and the same solid, big old houses stood among the sun-and-shade-flecked green lawns; the same people lived in those houses. Two or three new buildings downtown had replaced old ones for offices and business; but the new ones were not veritable skyscrapers—the tallest building in town was of twelve stories—and although the first apartment house was now more than ten years old, not more than half a dozen others had been built. One could stroll everywhere about the town, and, except for the automobiles, find only here and there a noticeable change.

Nearly all the old landmarks were still as they had been in the Nineteenth Century; everything was familiar. The same old liquor smell floated out over the sidewalks from the swinging doors of the saloons, and those doors themselves—now extinct, unless the antiquarians collect them—were the same. They swung easily, inviting but the slightest pressure, and their bases, being knee-high, revealed to the passer-by the feet and lower trousers legs of the convivial who dallied at the bar within. Quavering snatches of song, "barber-shop" chords, uncertain bits of ballad, often floated out with the liquorish fumes, adding zest to the sidewalk games of children; and not infrequently, too, hoarse strong language issued, increasing the information, in such matters, of the young.

Like the body of a man infected from scalp to toe, the body politic had the saloon running visibly and dangerously in every part; and, although many years were needed to prepare for the final operation of removal, it is hard to believe now that the infection could have been dissected out so quickly, leaving but such surreptitious and sporadic traces as the "speakeasy." For the saloon had a part in everybody's consciousness every day. The huge beer wagons, piled with symmetrical vastnesses of cold kegs, and drawn by grand Percherons or massive Flemish or Norman horses, sometimes three abreast, sometimes as a splendid four-in-hand, were a constant pageant, provocative to the thirsty. They were driven by mountainous barbarians, huge-girthed men with great fiery faces and huskily roaring voices. No one could have believed that all this Gothic powerfulness could be whisked away, made utterly to disappear, by a flutter of mere paper ballots. The brewers to whom the great wagons belonged seemed as potent as these symbols of their power. Breweries and distilleries infiltrated politics and business; every saloon keeper was a politician—indeed, he had to be one for his own protection—and the saloons copiously sent forth that now forgotten aroma of theirs in every quarter of the town.

There were no public bars upon the upper reaches of the "principal residence streets," nor within a short fixed distance from a church or a schoolhouse; yet nowhere, in all the broad area the city covered, did a thirsting citizen need to walk more than a block or so to solace a dry throat. Downtown, in clean alleys and convenient among the business houses and offices, there were quiet, well-behaved bars where the solid and prominent, even bankers, might refresh themselves under only a discreet observation; but in the poorest neighbourhoods the saloons and "barrel houses" were thickest. Indeed, their numbers increased in perfect proportion to the decrease in affluence of the quarter—a fact of somewhat too uncomfortably apparent significance. For the saloon, of course, was the "poor man's club."

Sunday was his holiday; he could not afford to keep a horse and drive out to the country with his family; the "church influence" did not allow him baseball or even a "nickel theatre" on that day, and the brewery in power with the police authorities had the profit: saloons buying beer of that brewery could sell liquor illegally but lavishly after eleven o'clock Saturday night and on Sunday—other saloons would be raided—and so the weekly wages were likely to evaporate into the purple mist of alcoholic gaiety.

This Sabbatical gaiety—painfully followed by "Blue Monday"—seemed to be the only alleviation in the lives of a great many working people, and there were theorists who said that if the "workingman's Saturday Night" and his illegal Sunday beer were taken from him, he would become a revolutionist out of sheer boredom. Perhaps these theorists were not wholly fantastic; perhaps they were not so far off what might have been the fact; the abolishing of the convenient saloon with its ready liquor might have made the one holiday, in conjunction with six days of drudgery, unendurably dull for a great many people. But sometimes the large processes of life appear to give us glimpses of a certain orderliness behind them, a symmetry that hints of undiscovered laws of progress, and in the apparent coincidence of the annihilation of the saloon almost simultaneously with the arrival of the automobile of small price there seems to be something more than mere haphazard luck. Already, in 1911, there were workingmen who had bought "used flivvers" and were spending their Sundays with their families in adventurous scourings of the countryside.

For, although most things "looked about the same" to the returned native, and the same old people and houses and trees and lawns and saloons appeared to be but slightly altered, principally by seeming a little older, there were tokens of a stirring, of something moving underneath, of unknown powers at work to produce a new kind of growing; but at first these hints were faint and not insistent. One felt that the town had somehow become more "citified"; it had become not only larger, that is to say, but more formal. Downtown there were traffic officers at several corners, and you couldn't drive just where and how you pleased, as in the easy-going old days of a little while before. In fact, one felt that the easy-going old days were gone forever. In this larger town young people wouldn't dance on a platform in somebody's yard by the light of paper lanterns; romantic gentlemen wouldn't pile an orchestra into "express wagons" and go midnight serenading; never again would a pretty young lady light the gas to show a bright window for the young Dons with fiddles, flutes, and a harp upon the lawn below.

There was a great deal more asphalt and there were a great many more automobiles. A few "family carriages" were still to be seen on the streets, with a victoria or two and one or two broughams and coupés; "hired hacks" were still to be had at livery stables and horse cabs at the station; but the red-wheeled runabout had disappeared forever; the town's *jeunesse dorée* (in the phrasing loved by the *fin de siècle*) now shot itself out to the country club with gas; the "fast trotter," that willing and faithful friend of youth, was gone with the red wheels, and so was the bicycle as the friend of pleasure. The little bells chimed no more above the darting lamps along the highways of a summer evening: there were too many automobiles.

Some of the streets had lengthened surprisingly and appeared to contemplate even more suprising extensions; asphalt and cement were stretching far into suburban territory, through what had been "picnic woods," not so very long before. In the boyhood days of my own generation, Tinker Street had been the northern border of the compact town; beyond it the houses were a scattering fringe and country roads led northward to the creek, a mile away, where we went to swim in the waters of "Sycamore Hole." No joyous bathers dived from the bank there now; Tinker Street had become Sixteenth Street; the old dirt roads that had wandered out from it were compact—much too compact with crowding houses—to the creek; and there had been a migration across the stream. A dozen new millionairish mansions, with lawns and gardens about them, prophesied a new quarter of fashion beyond it, and a concrete bridge replaced the old rumbling planks we had pattered over so blithely on our way to "Sycamore Hole." The millionairish houses were not alone; all up and down the creek, and deep into the meadows and woods beyond, the "bungalows" and "two-story frames" were built and building. East and west, too, ran the new boulevard-and-park system with a widening fringe of new houses on all its borders.

Downtown, there were obviously many more people than aforetime upon the streets, especially on Saturdays, when it seemed that the long inter-urban cars must fairly have drained a great countryside of life to pour it into the city. Moreover, the crowds of country folk were not easily distinguishable, as they once had been, from the city people. They had become of the urban pattern in clothes and manner; they spoke the same slang the city used and rusticity appeared to have vanished like the farmer's whiskers—for of hairy faces, old "Family Albums" and Civil War photographs offered now the only apparent supply. And there was a change, too, in the characteristic face—the composite face, so to speak—of the thronged streets downtown. There was something new and puzzling to me in that face. I could not be sure what the change was, but I felt it there, and one day I spoke of it to an old citizen and asked him if he shared my impression.

"Why, yes," he said. "You'd notice it more than I would, I suppose, because you've been away so long. This composite face you're talking about, that you see downtown—it isn't the face you see on the uptown streets, is it?"

"No. The uptown face seems to be the same as ever."

"Yes; but if the face downtown has changed, the change will reach uptown in time. Your composite face, made of blending all the faces into one, is swarthier than it used to be, isn't it?—swarthier and what you'd call more foreign-looking?"

"I think so—a little."

"Yes," he said, "it's just a shade mongrel. It's not so mongrel as the New York composite face, nor the Chicago one, for that matter. Compared to those places, this is still an 'all-pure American' town. You go to the theatre in New York and then come back and go to the theatre here; the difference'll make you gasp! In a New York theatre, between the acts, you'll hear everybody speaking our language, but you wonder why they do. Between the acts in a theatre here you aren't surprised when they talk American, because they still generally look that way. But you're right; they don't look that way as much as they used to. There's just enough difference for a person to be able to see it."

"It's immigration that's making the difference?"

"It's immigration that already has made it. These darker foreign-looking people among us talk just the same as anybody else and dress just the same as anybody else—maybe a little showier. They aren't hunting for hard jobs at low wages or a patch of land to raise market truck on. The bulk of 'em are second generation, born in this country, though a good many came when they were little, with their families. They're prospering more and more; they're in every profession and every line of business. They'll be uptown, too, in a little while—more of 'em already are uptown than you've noticed, and they have good houses. They're nice people, most of 'em, too; and their young folks go to school and college and are around with our own young folks. They've been raised with different ideas from ours, but they have a good deal the same manners. The smartest of the immigrant stock are 'thoroughly Americanized'—'snappy modern business men' and all that; but—well, you've had an ice-cream freezer get a little salt inside the can, haven't you? It's never quite the same ice cream again."

"But perhaps we old-stock Americans shouldn't set up to be the pure ice cream, Judge."

"No, maybe we shouldn't; but we're bound to seem like it to ourselves, at least; and anyhow we're getting salted. The immigrant has Americanized himself, but in the process he foreignizes us a little; he takes on our ideas, but he can't help spreading among us some of his. A few years ago the 'typical American'—or maybe what we called the 'average American'—was a lot more old-stock Anglo-Saxon, with German and Irish traces, than he is to-day. I expect the cartoonists ought to begin to draw Uncle Sam a little differently from the way they used to. Uncle Sam wouldn't talk with exactly his old twang, either, if you could listen to him. There's a change in his vocabulary and he's got another kind of twang. You'll hear just hints of it in the common speech of the streets, because the touch of salt has got into that, too. It's not so agreeable—at least not to the old native ear—as it used to be."

"Will my own old native ear detect any other differences, Judge?"

He frowned and sighed. "I think you'll find it will if you listen for 'em. You know the rest of the world was always accusing us, in the old days, of being 'money mad'; we were supposed to worship the Almighty Dollar more than other peoples did. Well, of course, that worshipped dollar was just what the immigrant came here to pursue. Our old-time spread-eagle orators used to brag about his coming here to enjoy the Liberty we offered the world, and how the poor oppressed slaves of foreign monarchies crossed the ocean in order to breathe the Air of Freedom. But everybody knows that they left home for economic reasons—that is, they came to make money. Well, they do make it—the more industrious and the smarter ones do—they make more and more. And since that was their great motive and what they were thinking about all the time, why, naturally it goes on being their great motive and they go on thinking about it all the time. All over the country you'll hear more talk about making money than you ever did before. Money's a greater god than it was."

"The ice cream's salted with gold dust?"

"With diamonds! That salt gets into our taste—especially into what we thought of as our 'good taste.' There are a great many more prosperous people than there used to be—a great many more who have 'come up from nothing' than there used to be. And a lot of them still have nothing—nothing but money. But money being the god, they become 'representative.' They infiltrate our social body. The salt in the ice cream begins to mean a certain amount of change in some of our representative ideals. That's dangerous to all our old fundamental principles, because a change in ideals is always dangerous to the whole body of what's been established. It may be just barely perceptible one year and the next year you suddenly find it's the fashion. It's a sort of snowball on a downhill grade; once it begins to roll, the faster it rolls and the bigger it gets."

He looked gloomy, but I ventured to laugh and say that I hoped our country wasn't going to the dogs. "A great many of the older people have always felt that, you know, Judge. To those who like things to stand still, progress nearly always seems to be a going to the dogs."

"No doubt," he said; but he shook his head. "I don't say we're going to the dogs; I only notice that we're changing in a way that makes an old-timer a little uncomfortable. I think that what we hoped was our refinement and our 'good taste' isn't so good as it was, and I'm afraid the salt in our ice cream is having its effect upon what we felt were our moral standards. I don't deny that we're making progress immensely, but I wonder where it's taking us except into materialism. For one thing, we have begun to love giantism with passion; everybody wants to have everything as big as possible. When any man mentions his city, the first thing he does is to lie about its size: that's the most universal lie in the United States. I suppose you've noticed that our own town is growing dirtier as it grows bigger. You haven't run across any business man who's worrying about that, have you?"

I had not. If the business men were worried about the increasing smoke—for there was visibly more of it almost from day to day—they worried for fear some other city should have even more of it than we did. Two new automobile factories had just been finished, and that made nine.

XVI

With winter, of course, the black grime in the air became even more noticeable—noticeable enough to be annoying. It came from every direction. The nine automobile factories were not the only new industries; and, for that matter, a great part of the smoke did not come from the industrial outskirts, but from the houses, the hotel, the office buildings, from the governmental edifices and the big brick schoolhouses. Indoors as well as out we often breathed a grimy air, and our throats and lungs were the worse for it. The business men said that "good clean smoke" wasn't really dirty; it meant money in the bank and was wholesome for everybody, including the babies. The city's health was excellent and the statisticians' tables proved it. "A little extra coughing isn't going to hurt anybody," they said. "It exercises the lungs and expands the chest. Besides, ours is good clean smoke; there isn't half so much coughing here as there is in other places."

On the street one day, I met an old friend who thought the business men were mistaken about this. He was an actor—a comedian in a "road company" playing that week in one of our theatres. "I always used to like making this town," he said. "It was a nice, appreciative place and I looked forward to playing here. It's not the same nowadays."

"You mean the movies are——"

"I wasn't thinking of our business," he said. "Of course that isn't quite what it used to be, either. The nickel theatres didn't affect it much. But now that they've begun to charge a dime, and even a quarter sometimes, and are fixing up their show houses and using orchestras, they are eating into us—especially into our gallery business—quite a little. But we can meet that, I guess, by raising our price downstairs. What I was thinking of, the thing that makes me less enthusiastic about coming here is the smoke."

"I see. Of course it's thicker downtown where the hotels are. I suppose it must be pretty disagreeable to visitors in the city."

"Dear me!" he said. "I don't mind a little soot on my collar! I mean what it does to my stuff in the theatre."

"But how——"

"It's the coughing," he explained. "A few years ago I could put over all my lines here without any trouble at all—I was sure of every laugh in the piece. But now, every night when the show's over, I'm shaking like a leaf from exhaustion and nervousness. You know how a laugh works—every laugh I've got in this show depends on a key word or phrase. If I don't get the key word over right, or if anything blurs it and they don't hear it all through the house, the laugh is killed. Well, nowadays I begin to tremble with every laugh-line I come to, because I know that some elephant out front is going to cough on the key word and kill me dead. I hear the cough starting, so I pause and hold the word back till the elephant gets through. But half the time it's no use, because just as I do finally spring the word some other elephant out front lets go a *blah-blocketty-brash* that coughs me as dead as a stepped-on potato bug. Every year I dread hitting this belt of soft-coal towns more than I did the year before. If the coughing gets much worse, it's going to wipe out the theatrical business entirely in this section, unless we can get audiences trained to hold their coughs till the show's over. People'll quit coming to shows where they can't hear the laughs; we'll have to play the anthracite towns exclusively."

But the increasing smoke, not yet so voluminously soiling as to make audible the long and futile outcry of the housewives, was not the only token of the stirring and change that moved under the surface; other prophetic signs were visible. Some of the houses nearest to downtown business were abandoned by families long associated with them in the memories of "old citizens"; two or three of them became boarding houses; a real estate and insurance agent moved into one of them and the elderly and friendly brick building had an air of pathetic mortification that it should have come to wear a violent black-and-gilt sign across its home-like front. Farther up the street, another of the old houses—a pleasant one, built in the Fifties, with a shady yard about it—was torn down the next spring and replaced by a huge oblong shell of concrete and glass, rearing a great flat façade where a well-remembered picket fence and gate had been. Some kindly old big trees, well-remembered, too, had perished here to make room for this incredible "automobile sales building."

That "sales building" was like the first fastening of the tentacle of an octopus upon a victim. The old happily livable "principal residence streets," with their solid houses, plate-glass windows, sunny lawns, and shady trees, were doomed; and the fashion of saying "I remember when" could henceforth belong to the comparatively young, for the doom worked swiftly. Moreover, the old houses had themselves done something to advance it. The value of the land had increased since they had first sat themselves down in the midst of their ample lawns, and many of them had parted with their "side yards," selling ground room for cheaper and narrower houses—neighbours that crowded closer and yet decreased the old prevailing neighbourliness. The new houses became shabby quickly; here and there one of them showed a placard with the word "Rooms" upon it.

After that first "sales building," the second came quickly—and a third and a fourth and a fifth, and then a great brick apartment house, and then another—all on the same "principal residence street," the most comfortable, the handsomest and richest and most spacious thoroughfare in all the town. It suddenly began to look queer. We recognized it, of course, but it began to have the unfamiliar-familiar look of a friend who has an attack of poison ivy. Downtown, the change began to move even faster; wreckers laid old office buildings flat and in their places we saw steel cobwebs rising against the sky.

Underneath the growth, one began to feel a powerful unrest, a movement of enterprise, of determined and adventurous optimism, a spirit iconoclastic toward whatever was old or delicate or lacked size—a spirit immensely set upon newness and bigness. "I will build a new city here upon this old one," it seemed to say. "I will build a noisy city upon this quiet one. I will build a dirty city upon this clean one. My new city may be as ugly as sin, as black as coal, as noisy as ten thousand boiler factories; but it will be beautiful to me, because it will be big—big—big!"

For the passion for giantism, an immemorial mark of races growing toward command of the world, or at least the struggle to command it, was now at work over all the forward-moving parts of the country; and, although some sleepy places in the South and in New England might for the time avoid it and continue on in their antique civilized content and comfort, yet it would move them too some day. And nowhere, not even in the turmoil of New York or Chicago, was it more evident than where our Midland town writhed in the throes of transformation, beginning to be that scene of endless change we call a "modern city."

A returned native, more and more disturbed to see what had called him home now thus engage itself in the act of disappearing forever, became subject to personal misgivings. The very house I lived in—the house I'd grown up in and had at last returned to, when I "came home to settle down for good"—that house, too, must be swept away before long. And so, by the time Europe was involving itself in the impossible war that never could be, I was transcribing this impression of what I saw before me:

"The growth was now visibly upon the pleasant and substantial town, where all had once appeared to be so settled and so finished; for, just as with some of man's disorders that develop slowly, at first merely hinting in mild prophetic symptoms, then becoming more sinister, and attacking one member after another until the whole body writhes and alters, so it is with this disorder that comes racking the Midland towns through distortions and turmoil into the vaster likenesses of cities; haphazard and insignificant destructions begin casually, but gradually grow more sweeping and more violent until the victim town becomes aware of great crashings—and then lies choking in a cloud of dust and smoke wherein huge new excrescences appear.

"Cameras of the new age sometimes record upon strips of moving film the slow life of a plant from the seed to the blossoming of its flower; and then there is thrown upon the screen a picture in which time is so quickened that the plant is seen in the very motions of its growth, twisting itself out of the ground and stretching and swelling to its maturity, all within a few minutes. So might a film record be made of the new growth bringing to full life a quiet and elderly Midland town; but the picture would be dumbfounding. Cyclone, earthquake, and miracle would seem to stalk hand in hand upon the screen; thunder and avalanche should play in the orchestra pit.

"In such a picture, block after block of heavy old mansions would be seen to topple; row on row of stout buildings would vanish almost simultaneously; families would be shown in flight, carrying away their goods with them from houses about to crumble; miles of tall trees would be uprooted; the earth would gape, opening great holes and chasms; the very streets would unskin themselves and twist in agony; every landmark would fly dispersed in powder upon the wind and all old-established things disappear.

"Such a picture would be but the truth with time condensed—that is to say, the truth made like a man's recollection of events—and yet it would not be like the truth as the truth appeared to the men who made the growth, nor like their subsequent memories. For these men saw, not the destruction, but only the city they were building; and they shouted their worship of that vision and were exultant in the uproar. They shouted as each new skyscraper rose swimming through the vast drifts of smoke, and shouted again as the plain, clean, old business streets collapsed and the magnificent and dirty new ones climbed above the ruins. They shouted when business went sweeping outward from its centre, tearing away the houses where people had lived contentedly for so long; and they shouted again as the new factory suburbs marched upon the countryside, far and wide, and the colossal black plumes of new chimneys went undulating off into a perpetual smoke mist, so that the distant level plain seemed to be a plain surrounding not a city, but an ever-fuming volcano.

"Once again, in the interminably cycling repetition of the new displacing of the old, then becoming the old and being displaced in turn, an old order was perishing. The 'New Materialism' that had begun to grow with the renewed growing of the country after the Civil War, and staggered under the panic of '73, but recovered and went on, growing egregiously, had become an old materialism now. It had done great things and little things. Among the latter, it had furnished Europe with a caricature type of the American—the successful American business man. On the shelf, beside the figure of the loud-tweeded boxing Briton with his 'side whiskers,' Europe set the lank and drawling, chin-bearded, palace-buying boaster of the Almighty Dollar, the 'Yankee' of the great boom period.

"That had been a great railroad-making and railroad-breaking period; the great steel period; the great oil period; the great electric-invention period; the great Barnum-and-Bunkum period; the period of 'corrupt senators,' of reform, and of the first skyscrapers. All this was old now, routed by a newer and more gorgeous materialism. The old had still its disciplines for the young and its general appearance of piety; bad children were still whipped sometimes, and the people of best reputation played no games on Sunday, but went to church and seemed to believe in God and the Bible with almost the faith of their fathers. But many of these people went down with their falling houses; a new society, swarming upward above the old surfaces, became dominant. It began to breed, among other things, a new critic who attacked every faith and offered, instead of mysteries, full knowledge of all creation as merely a bit of easily comprehended mechanics. And in addition to discovering the universe, the new society discovered golf, communism, and the movies; it spread the great American cocktail over the whole world, abolished horses, and produced buildings fifty stories high.

". . . In the din of all the tearing down and building up, most of the old family names were not heard, or were heard but obscurely, or perhaps in connection with misfortunes; for many of the old families were vanishing. They and their fathers and grandfathers had slowly made the town; they had always thought of it as their own, and they had expected to sit looking out upon it complacently forever from the plate-glass of their big houses. They had built thick walls round themselves, these 'old families,' not only when they built the walls of their houses but when they built the walls encircling their close associations with one another. The growth razed all these walls; the 'sets' had resisted the 'climbers,' but the defences fell now; and those who had sheltered behind them were dispersed, groping for one another in the smoke."

For, by the time Europe was horribly swamped in war, the growth had overwhelmed the "old citizen," and so had the manifestations that accompanied it and dumbfounded him. He was already sufficiently dazed: "Votes for Women" and Prohibition were near at hand. "Everybody" was beginning to own an automobile; "speed mania" spread massacre everywhere, especially on Sunday, and nothing whatever abated it; and then, in the midst of all the tearing down and building up, with all the whirling of dollars in the air and of rubber wheels on every street and road, when the turmoil seemed wildest and most deafening, all the country fell to dancing. Jazz and the "turkey trot" had arrived.

XVII

EVEN THE LATER HOURGLASS girls had danced the Cake Walk in philanthropic pageants. There had been "Kermesses" for charity, too, when girls over fifteen danced in costume, with skirts that exposed their ankles; and in the private dancing-schools gifted pupils were sometimes selected to learn "fancy dances" supposedly expressive of festal but decorous moments in exotic lives. The "Fishers' Hornpipe" and the "Highland Fling" (with no flinging) were the most prevalent of these; though there was a more flashing one, called with sweeping simplicity "Spanish Dance," in which rhythmic coquetry unfurled and snapped shut a wicked black fan. The Señorita sometimes went so far as to cover all of her face, except the eyes, with her fan, and then look over it roguishly at the audience, or even at her male partner in the dance, if she had one. Her boldness was more applauded than criticized, though conservative older people thought the Cake Walk not daring precisely, but perhaps a little coarse, even if danced with the utmost refinement of gesture. It depicted nothing worse than a supposedly negroid joviality; but some audiences were a little disturbed to see "well brought up young people" engaged in even that much depiction of low-lived emotional gaiety.

After the old "square" dances disappeared (except from a few bucolic "town hall" fiestas where they still may be seen, upon lively occasion, even to-day) the "two-step" and waltz prevailed monotonously until the "Boston" was devised, the last new dance before the débâcle. Until after the "Boston" our polite dancing expressed nothing more than gaiety and rhythm; it was a part of youth, and a part of youthful courtship, too, of course; but it was essentially the light heart moving the feet to lightness in harmony with it. The older clergy of the more rigorous sects had little approval of such harmonies; they put all dancing to the ban as they did the theatre, the circus, cards, dice, "low corsages," and Sunday fishing; they called it sensuous, and no doubt it was; but they didn't call it sensual, for that would have been a patent exaggeration. If it was sensuous it was no more so than is the love of flowers; and a room full of young dancers was a pretty sight, charming to the elderly onlooker who frequently became reminiscently sentimental upon beholding it.

No one became sentimental either reminiscently or otherwise, looking on at the Bal Bullier, in Paris, after the "machiche" began to prevail there, in the latter part of the first decade of the Twentieth Century. The "machiche" was said to have come from the Argentine and to have been known to fetid midnights in many cities, including San Francisco, before it ever dared to be danced publicly. It had been seen by tourist peep-hole parties in Paris, under the conduct of sleek "guides"; it became for a time one of the dreary obliquities of the old Jardin de Paris; but finally it openly ravaged the Bal Bullier, where it displaced the ancient can-can and was danced by hundreds of Boule' Miche' young couples without a blush anywhere visible. American tourists went there to see it as they had formerly gone there to see the can-can, and the "machiche" more embarrassingly startled them (or enthused them, according to their natures and alcoholic content) than ever the can-can did. Yet it was a dance apparently not intricate, the steps were of the simplest, for the dancers merely walked in time to the music, and sometimes, at rhythmic intervals, they paused at almost a standstill, so far as their feet were concerned. The dance appeared to be essentially Oriental, consisting of wriggles and wagglings, and in order that these gestures should be in concert the partners found it necessary to clasp each other more closely than in any other kind of dancing. Shocked travellers from our country, looking on at the "machiche," were heard to exclaim, "Thank God, we live in America!" Nothing was less possibly imaginable than that the "machiche" could ever be performed in open, public dance halls in a land morally conducted in all outwards by the New England conscience.

But the "machiche" dumbfoundingly came to America, where it had some joggling negroid modifications, being danced principally with the shoulders and hips, and became humorously known as the "turkey trot." The extremely tight clasp—somewhat convulsive in appearance—was no less necessary than with the original "machiche," and what the dancers did with their feet was as relatively unimportant. The "steps" could be learned by anyone in no time; they were merely a walking to music; no agility whatever was required; but, what distributed the contagion, youth itself, was not required.

This made the "turkey trot" revolutionary. Until then, dancing had been for the young; by the time the children were old enough to dance their fathers and mothers were too old; that field of diversion was abandoned to the exclusive use of the young, with here and there a quaint exception—an indomitably nimble old bachelor or a reviving widower. Of the previous generations, married people over thirty were supposedly—and nearly always really, for that matter—seriously engaged in business and housewifery, in bringing up their children, in domestic life generally, and in church work or charity work or the intellectual divertissements of literary clubs. They danced more and more rarely; and by the time they were forty-five they had usually forgotten how even to waltz, just as they had usually forgotten how to skate.

But domestic life was no longer what it had been. Greater and greater numbers of parents were rich enough to leave their children to the care of nurses and servants; while others, observing and emulating the leisure thus afforded, gave children the opportunity to learn self-reliance and other things by looking after themselves. Men and women of any age could dance the "turkey trot," since anybody who could walk and waggle a little could dance it; gray heads and white heads came forth from easy-chairs and the evening lamp; more heads became dyed heads; bald heads gleamed over all the dancing-floors, and the dancing-floors were everywhere; the hotels set tables merely as a border about waxed surfaces, for people could no longer bear to eat without dancing. They had soup and danced; they ate fish and danced; they danced from cocktails to coffee and went out to a movie and came back to dance. They danced to syncopations that humorously and inspiringly synchronized with the clasping and waggling and waddling. The syncopations employed, as punctuation marks, drums, brasses, saxophones, and whatever else could rip and scarify the ear; and to this hell-born punctuation added misplaced sliding wails of unbearable tinniness, incessant animal screeching, and hideous impendings of worse: jazz became triumphant. People who had never danced began to dance; people who had forgotten how to dance began to dance again; young and old danced; widowed grandmothers danced and grandmothers not widowed; the rich danced; the poor danced; invalids danced; even bankers danced. The "turkey trot" swept over the country.

"I'd never have believed it," one of the older citizenry said, one night, at the club. "I wouldn't have believed it if anyone had told me: I had to go and see it with my own eyes—and I certainly did! At first I could hardly believe I was seeing what I saw; but no, there it was—they were all at it, wagging their backs and flopping from one hip to the other, and clutched up to their partners in a way that would have got a Knights of Labour ball closed by the police not so many years ago. But there were our 'best people,' old and young; I never thought I'd live to see such a sight. Between the dances a crowd of the older ones, all of 'em middle-aged fathers and mothers, had highballs at a table and began to sing 'When good fellows get together'—men and women just screeching it out, something terrible! Then three or four of the girls were smoking in the terrace without caring who saw 'em doing it. Yes, sir, right young girls they were, daughters of friends of mine—smoking and not blinking an eyelash when they saw me looking at 'em! I guess female emancipation is pretty nearly here—these New Women are going to get the ballot as sure as you're born! They're going to do everything the boys do, I expect, and it looks as if it's too late to stop 'em. My heavens! What's the next generation going to be like with this one behaving the way it does? What's a child going to think of its parents when it sees 'em both drinking highballs and smoking and hears 'em singing and whooping the way they do? And if any child saw its mother and father wriggling around in this turkey trot dance, making themselves look as low-life and ridiculous as that, how in the name of goodness could they ever expect to have any authority over a child afterwards? What a queer time we're living in! This town's being torn to pieces and rebuilt right over our heads; our coloured laundress comes to work every Monday morning in her son's automobile; he's a barber, I give you my word! There isn't anything the way it used to be, and I tell you it's getting to be a mighty confusing world: it makes an old-timer's head spin!"

Then the world of the old-timer became more confusing than merely with the building up and tearing down of cities accompanied by Feminism, automobiles for working-people, and the "turkey trot." We went to war.

XVIII

ONE DAY IN MY boyhood I looked out from a window and saw standing on the shady corner, beyond our lawn, the broad-shouldered sturdy figure of a neighbour who was waiting for a street-car. He had been a soldier in the Civil War and had come home wearing a General's epaulettes; but he didn't wear them long. He took off his uniform and went quietly back to work in his law office. Now he was a Senator and would soon be going to Washington with a higher rank than that, for he had been elected to the Presidency of the United States.[1] Looking out at him from the window and seeing just the familiar figure of a neighbour, it seemed strange that he wore no new and glamorous aspect; the only visible token of the tremendous experience before him was that he seemed more thoughtful-looking than usual.

So, in April, 1917, I happened again to look from that same window and see another neighbour who approached a great experience. He was riding slowly by upon a bay horse, and he, too, was more thoughtful-looking than usual; his expression was that of a man who confronts a grave problem but is not afraid of it; and it seemed to me just the look I might most have wished him to wear. For, although he was not yet in uniform he was a Colonel in our forming army and was to lead a regiment of artillerymen across the sea and into battle in France. When one thought of these soldiers as a "regiment of artillerymen" they seemed warlike and suggested a destructive power like that of some great bristling engine for the crushing and rolling under of a foe's beleagured walls; but really, of course, they were only Midland boys, some of them the sons of my own friends and neighbours. They were just kindly and cheerful young fellows who liked the exercise of drilling in the National Guard; many of them had sweethearts they hoped to marry; some of them were already married and bringing up young families; and nearly all of them were heartily ambitious to succeed in businesses or professions now so sharply interrupted.

---

1. This, of course, was Benjamin Harrison (1833–1901), elected president in 1888.

They went away quietly—as quietly, it seemed, as their thoughtful-looking Colonel had ridden by my window—for the romantic glamour that in former wars made the departure of our troops a heroic pageantry was nowhere to be found.

Almost sixty years had passed since our regiment of Zouaves, on the way to war, marched down to the State House and knelt there, taking a solemn oath "to avenge Buena Vista" and a great soprano sang "The Star Spangled Banner" while their colours were presented to them, and the populace wept and cheered.[2] In 1917 and 1918, when war was not only "at the front" but danger reached under the sea for the soldier, departure was made silently and destinations were secret. Then training camps and schools and the draft took the younger men away, as quietly, one by one and yet in millions, while "war work" of one kind or another occupied other millions. Our "war work" at home was necessary; many fine lives were exhausted by it and given for it, and the work was done. We accomplished prodigies, but, being inexperienced and anxious and excited, we wasted prodigious energy and wealth. Also, we were officious; we got in one another's way and ordered everybody about ridiculously; we were so jumpy with strained nerves that now the memory of those two years is like the memory of a nightmare. For that time was indeed a nightmare, haunted every hour by the fear of what messages might reach us from a battlefield or from a hospital or from the sea.

In one sense, no doubt, war is an expression of "herd instinct"; it might even appear to be an expression of a herd mania. More speculatively, it may be thought one of the adolescent disorders of undeveloped mankind—mankind made up of herds not yet drawn into one herd as they might be if more enlightened or if attacked from other planets. Probably under compulsion of a law now obscurely glimpsed, the hugely growing herds have been brought closer into an interdependence that must ultimately make them one; but they are still ignorant of this vast process, and every herd is naturally determined, not only to maintain its own integrity but to increase its numbers and possess the grazing-ground essential for these increased numbers—no matter what other herd already grazes upon that ground. Thus they jostle and irritate one another, become warrantably suspicious of aggression, and breed warrantable suspicion. And when, through crowding, or suspicion, or the memory of wrongs, or ambition, or all four, adjacent herds set to sharpening horns, then other herds beyond must necessarily sharpen theirs or risk destruction. Formerly, when there were great spaces and time was slow,

---

2. Tarkington refers to the Mexican-American War. His memory of this event is obviously not personal, as he was born twenty-one years after it ended.

two or more herds could fight while the others continued a peaceful grazing in their distant roomy enclosures; but by 1914 the herds were too large and some of them were too encroaching; the earth was too small; distance had disappeared, and neither space of land nor space of water was a separating partition.

There was no choice; we could not be either arrogantly or desperately trampled under. It was hard for our young men; many of them wondered why they had to give up all that they were hoping and planning to do for themselves and go forth to fight in France; and there great numbers of them suffered and died—and of these not a few were still tragically puzzled even as they died. But the youthful sons of the Republic had made themselves into soldiers; they valiantly ended the ruinous war that had seemed endless; for it was visibly their fresh strength that brought the victory. More, that strength and valour of theirs, and all the limitless energy and resource of the immense war effort, made the nation better aware of its own power. America was to be self-confident henceforth with a firmer knowledge, and the long lines of our white crosses in France helped us to bear criticism quietly.

Not many of the soldiers who came back to the welcome at home returned wholly unchanged; but the prevalent change, after a first restlessness had passed, seemed clearly defined in a sharp and sturdy patriotism: what they have fought for men will not meekly allow to be tampered with, and as the Grand Army of the Republic and the Loyal Legion became the oaken heart of the nation's patriotism after the Civil War, so does this newer Legion become that after the Great War. But in numbers of the young men who had fought there were other changes; and for some of them the shock to their lives had shaken all the old fundamentals they had formerly accepted: they questioned everything and especially they questioned whatever seemed to them dogmatic. They questioned the historic conclusions upon which they had been brought up—particularly historic ironclad conclusions that certain things were right and certain other things were wrong and in this questioning and challenging they were not alone. All youth, everywhere, had begun to question and challenge; and many new prophets offered plausibly to lead them against the old.

This was a disturbed and questioning world, indeed, at the end of the Great War; it was like the sea covered with heaving wreckage and seething after the hurricane; fierce winds blew sporadically where the heaviest storm had passed and there were gulfs still in wild turmoil. After the Russian Revolution had made that enormous country a republic, the comparatively small but perfectly organic Bolshevik party had adroitly and violently disposed of the revolutionary leaders and had restored Absolutism with Lenin and themselves in place of the Czar. Their method of "appeal to the people" was essentially the immemorial appeal of any political party platform, or, for that matter, of any dictator's pronunciamento: "We're doing this all for you." And the Bolsheviks did promptly "pass a farmers' relief bill," vastly increasing the number of property owners in "communist Russia." Naturally, everywhere else, the poorest people, and those who were out of work or who had a hard time to make both ends meet on low wages, the troubled and discontented all over the world felt a great deal of sympathetic excitement.

In the defeated countries this excitement became a contagion; there were riots that became temporary revolutions, and even in America there was uneasiness; many substantial citizens were disquieted, not trusting the intelligence of the "masses." Agitators, orators, and pamphleteers did what they could to bring the populace to more or less radical socialist ways of thinking, and for a time they seemed to be having a rather dangerous amount of success. Most of them were foreign born or of foreign parentage; they were theorists who had contracted abroad the habit of being resentfully "against the government," or they had inherited that habit from their parents; and in some instances the habit had become actually a profession, the practitioners of which had no other means of livelihood. But almost every one of them was passionately sincere in the pathetic belief that his own socialistic prescription was the universally healing medicine for ailing humanity—even if the greater part of humanity had to die of the remedy.

They made converts, especially among the young of that disquieted and questioning time. For it is true that if a person is a socialist at twenty his heart is right and that if he is one at forty his head is wrong, even though his heart may still be right.[3] The academic kind of socialism, of course, is but a laudable Christian sentiment for universal brotherhood; it cannot be translated into a working system, however, until men universally are governed from within themselves by brotherly feeling; it is a feeling that cannot be imposed from without, either by legislation or revolution. Moreover, "state ownership," in this country particularly, proves to be in reality control by politicians, "smothering bureaucracy," not economical, and a loss of that individual liberty congenial to "the land of the free." The socialist's attack upon the "capitalistic system" is often only a generous and confused mind's indignation with nature itself for not making mankind angelic at the outset;

---

3. This quote, or something like it, is usually attributed to Winston Churchill. But it was French Premier Georges Clemenceau (1841–1929) who said "Not to be a socialist at twenty is proof of want of heart; to be one at thirty is proof of want of head," and this is probably where Tarkington gets the aphorism—although Clemenceau was himself adapting François Guizot (1787–1874): "Not to be a republican at twenty is proof of want of heart; to be one at thirty is proof of want of head."

though sometimes it hints of an origin in what lately our youth are so fond of calling the "biological"—an ancient urge still surviving many ages after bees and ants branched off as communists; something still appears to survive in man, sporadically exciting the wish to become only a cell in a single organism of uniform cells. The urge is impotent; socialism is communistic at its base, and communism as a reality actually attempted is the most mocking of all delusions, being merely a change in the names used to designate bosses. It does not really matter whether the man in the limousine is called "millionaire" or "commissar" if he has the same actual power under either title, and he necessarily has unless there is chaos. The Russian collapse, before it was realized that the word "capitalistic" really meant "human," approached chaos for a time and produced one small but reasonable party—the extreme leftward feather of the left wing, the party of chaos or Perpetual Revolution. Lenin recognized it when he told the "very poorest" to attack those who were somewhat less poor and seize their goods. After that, of course, there would again be some who were the "very poorest," and they in turn must attack and seize. Never could there be equilibrium, and the nearest approach to actual communism must be reached only by incessant revolts. And as the revolts would have to continue until everybody was killed, this party did indeed offer a consistent, logical programme; they were the only thoroughgoing realists among the whole body of communists.

Many of our American young people and others who were older in years, having been agitated and troubled in thought by the war, caught at socialistic straws for the world's salvation and turned hopeful faces toward Russia. Socialism, usually of a benevolent, rather vague kind, began to be a vehemence among groups not too humble minded to resist being defined as "young intellectuals"—a type as well as a definition seeming to spring in this country from that time. Not a few of them had their own idea (seldom derived from the dictionary and frequently not from Karl Marx) of what socialism meant, though they were nearly all familiar with such phrases as "everything for use and nothing for profit"; and they enjoyed a pleasant kind of superiority not unnatural to youth. Particularly this superiority is congenial to youthful socialism, which from a height characteristically pities the stupid and uncomprehending world far below. The complexities of life seem simple to the kind of thinking that perceives no great difficulty in the way of altering instinct by statute; it is, however, somewhat disturbing to imagine the size and necessary wisdom of a bureaucracy capable of putting into practice by force an ideal thus expressed: "From everyone as much work as, by the decision of a government official, he ought to do; and to everyone whatever the government official decides that everyone needs." And yet to those who believe that it is possible to eliminate nature by legislation no insurmountable obstacles appear to stand in the way of "from everyone according to his strength; to everyone according to his need." For this is the angelic will-o'-the-wisp they follow and offer to capture and fix as the desk light of millions of government clerks. Nevertheless, the youthful socialism that followed the war was born of sympathy for the under dog and of the effort to think how redemption could be brought to a troubled world; and as an emotion it was genuine and generous.

As thought, it was a symptom of change; it was a part of the new questioning, the new doubts of the value of all established things. The characteristic questionings of every new generation as it begins to think a little for itself were not quietly simmering as aforetime. The minds of this generation of young people had been startled and shocked by the most colossal and terrific war the world had known. No wonder they began to question the old order since, so far as they could see, it appeared to bear the responsibility for all that madness of destruction.

XIX

As our army disbanded and the tensity of the country relaxed, there seemed to be a period of uneasy anticlimax; the saloon was gone; Prohibition had come with the war; "equal suffrage" was certain, and presently women would vote; there was a pause during which men seemed to be asking in tired voices, yet anxiously, "Well—what now?" Then, slowly at first and after a trying depression, business attempted to be "resumed as usual"; the young soldiers, not often easily or with great immediate satisfaction to themselves, began to get back into their former occupations, or to find new ones, or to continue interrupted educations. Most of them suffered from restlessness; changed themselves, they came back into a changed world that was still confusedly changing.

Moreover, during service under arms military discipline had taken the place of the former accepted guides to conduct, and as on furlough "all rules were off" for the gayer or wilder spirits, so, when military discipline was permanently removed, those former rules it had supplanted were not immediately resumed in all their pristine force. That force, indeed, was shaken by doubts, not only in the minds of many of the returned young soldiers, but in those of the girls who had been kind to them when they went away to war and now welcomed them home. For girls were changed, too; thousands of them had crossed the dangerous seas and made themselves part of the war; other thousands had prepared themselves to follow; and all the rest had done "war work" of one kind or another. Some of the work girls had done was rough as well as perilous; some of it was heartbreaking; some of it was shocking. "Feminine delicacy" and chaperonage had become almost extinct ideas—temporarily almost extinct at least—and when revived later they were found to be greatly enfeebled.

That uneasy pause of depression and confused readjusting was a long one; it lasted longer than the time we had spent in war; but finally it began to pass, and the country entered upon a period that was like what the old spectacular drama programmes loved to call the "Grand Transformation

Scene." The blaze of glory, so to speak, in which this present epoch was to culminate sent forth preliminary showers of sparks.

During the war, babies had been born as usual, and, after the Peace, when ships were no longer needed for carrying soldiers and war supplies, immigration once more began to be multitudinous. In the meantime there had been no building; but all these new people needed housing, and the government having finally decided to become economical after its vast war spending, money lost its timidity. Building began again.

Once begun, it became almost overnight of a furious energy, and never before was seen such building up and tearing down. Our Midland city, after the pause in its heaving up and spreading out, now heaved and spread incredibly, as did all other strongly living cities. It began to pile itself higher and higher in the middle, and its boundaries moved like the boundaries of a rising spring flood. It overran its suburbs, leaving them compacted with the town, and then immediately reached out far beyond them. A new house would appear upon a country road; the country road would transform itself into an asphalt street with a brick drug store at the corner of a meadow; bungalows and theatrical-looking cottages would swiftly cover the open spaces of green; a farm would turn itself hastily into a suburb and then at once join solidly to the city. What was in spring a quiet lane through fields and woods was in autumn a constantly lengthening street with trolley-cars gonging and new house-owners hurriedly putting up wooden garages in their freshly sodded "side yards."

Deeper in the city, more old houses came down, until those that were left became pathetic and ridiculous among the buzzing automobile "sales buildings" and tall apartment houses. They were begrimed, crowded, deafened with city noises, and seemed to know that the day of demolition was already set, yet they struggled to maintain some appearance of dignity as they breathed their last among the fumes of the gasoline that had doomed them. And in the sooty "back yards" of some of them there still stood, as a final irony, the reproachful spacious shapes of brick stables long since empty.

To the old citizen, passing by, these expiring mansions spoke wistfully of ancient merry times within such solid walls as the frantic new and costlier buildings could not afford. There had been music at night on these cramped and dirty lawns, under trees that were gone long ago; there had been laughter and good cheer and dancing on the other side of those dingy, carved walnut front doors; white hands had waved, long ago, from friendly windows that were gaunt and hollow windows now; sleek young horses had trotted eagerly out of the white-painted iron driveway-gates long dusty in the junk shops; and even the ghosts of the happy little dogs that had barked so gaily at the horses must now be choked in the city smoke.

Some of the people who had spent their youth in these houses still survived and had part in the strong life of the new city; for now it was indeed a city built upon the ruins of the old. What had happened to New York and to Boston and to Chicago happened in its own way here. As Fifth Avenue disappeared to rise again, all changed, so did Euclid Avenue and so did Meridian Street; and as New York became "foreign," so did our own "old stock" become less typical. Of the grown people who called the Midland city home, less than a third had been born in it. Most of the newcomers were natives of smaller towns; but there was a German quarter; there was an Italian quarter; there were many Irish neighbourhoods; there were Jewish neighbourhoods; there were large groups of Poles, of Hungarians, of Rumanians, of Servians; and there was a negro quarter covering square miles. The old "typical Midlander" was visibly not what he had been; a new one—in fact, a new American—could be obscurely seen emerging.

"A new spirit of citizenship has sharply defined itself," I took note of it then. "This spirit is idealistic and its ideals are expressed by the new kind of business man downtown. They are optimists to the point of belligerence, and on their marching banner they inscribe the words, 'Boost! Don't Knock!' They are boosters, out to 'sell' their city to the world. They believe that boosting pays and their boosting advertisements are of a new phrasing believed to be both vigorous and seductive. The new type speaks, too, in a pretentious vocabulary apparently of the noblest altruism. Nevertheless, these men are sincere and they believe that honesty pays. The politicians dare not give them too much bad government because the new type of business man will not endure bad government when it is so bad that it depresses the value of 'real estate'; the politicians understand that they cannot go to this length. The idealists constantly shout that their city shall be a better city and what they principally mean when they use the word 'better' is 'bigger and more prosperous.' They seem to have one supreme theory: that the perfect happiness and beauty of cities and of human life are to be brought about by more factories. There is nothing they will not do to cajole a factory from another city and they are never more despondent than when another city gets one away from them. As the city grows and grows, it grows dirtier and dirtier. The idealists are putting up enormous business buildings that are repulsively begrimed before they are finished; but the idealists cannot see the dirt for the size, and boast grandly. They boast of their monuments and rain soot on them. Every year they boost a great 'Clean-Up-Week' when everybody is supposed to get rid of the empty cans in his back yard. Of course this new idealist, with his booming and boosting and hustling, with his pretentious vocabulary, his flawless self-confidence, and his perfect unconsciousness of all the little sophistications, is drawing the satire of the sophisticates. He can afford it; the Rotarian is the great man of this time. He is strong and devoted; he loves his country and humanity, and some day he will know more about beauty. Then he will make his city not only big but beautiful, for his city is his passion."

XX

Now, WITH THE NEW growth surpassing all former growing and such enormous building of everything as never had been before, and more people than ever before taking out money from every pocket to spend it, and with an agonizing war to be forgotten and left to historians and the past, there seemed to arrive, on wings of glittering gold and silver, a vast spirit of diversion.

Nothing could have been more natural than that such a spirit should prevail when an increasing prosperity began to succeed the wondering pause that followed the war. And the means for diversion were now what they had never been before, just as the people who diverted themselves might have seemed to the eye of a Rip van Winkle, waking then, what they had never been before. The outward change in people, indeed, had become so marked that I took note of it in a book, published at about that time; this note took the form of a slight allegory concerning such a Rip van Winkle, and the allegory seems to be in point here as an expression of that period; and of the change.[1]

... The nurses at the sanitarium were all fond of the gentlest patient in the place, and they spoke of him as "Uncle Charlie," though he was so sweetly dignified that usually they addressed him as "Mr. Blake," even when it was necessary to humour his delusion. The delusion was peculiar and of apparently interminable persistence; he had but the one during his sixteen years of incarceration—yet it was a misfortune painful only to himself (painful through the excessive embarrassment it cost him) and was never for an instant of the slightest distress to anyone else, except as a stimulant of sympathy. For all that, it closed him in, shutting out the moving world from him as completely as if he had been walled up in concrete. Moreover, he had been walled up overnight—one day he was a sane man, and the next he was in custody as a lunatic; yet nothing had happened in this little

---

1. This story, titled "Jeannette," was included in *The Fascinating Stranger and Other Stories* (Garden City, NY: Doubleday, Page & Company, 1923).

interval, or during any preceding interval in his life, to account for a seizure so instantaneous.

In 1904 no more commonplace young man could have been found in any of the great towns of our Eastern and near-Eastern levels. "Well brought up," as we used to say, he had inherited the quiet manner, the good health, and the moderate wealth of his parents; and, not engaging in any business or profession, he put forth the best that was in him when he planned a lunch for a pretty "visiting girl," or, again, when he bought a pair of iron candle snuffers for what he thought of as his "collection." This "collection," consisting of cheerless utensils and primitive furniture once used by woodsmen and farmers, and naturally discarded by their descendants, gave him his principal occupation, though he was sometimes called upon to lead a cotillion, being favourably regarded in the waltz and "two-step"; but he had no eccentricities, no habitual vices, and was never known to exhibit anything in the nature of an imagination.

It was in the autumn of the year just mentioned that he went for the first time to Europe, accompanying his sister, Mrs. Gordon Troup, an experienced traveller. She took him through the English cathedrals, then across the Channel; and they arrived unfatigued at her usual hotel in Paris after dark on a clear November evening—the fated young gentleman's last evening of sanity. Yet, as Mrs. Troup so often recalled later, never in his life had her brother been more "absolutely normal" than all that day: not even the Channel had disturbed him, for it was as still as syrup in a pantry jug; he slept on the French train, and when he awoke, played gently with Mrs. Troup's three-year-old daughter Jeannette who, with a nurse, completed the small party. His talk was not such as to cause anxiety, being in the main concerned with a tailor who had pleased him in London and a haberdasher he made sure would please him in Paris.

They dined in the salon of their apartment; and at about nine o'clock, as they finished their coffee, flavoured with a little burnt cognac, Mrs. Troup suggested the theatre—a pantomime or ballet for preference, since her brother's unfamiliarity with the French language rapidly spoken might give him a dull evening at a comedy. So, taking their leisure, they went to the Marigny, where they saw part of a potpourri called a "revue," which Mrs. Troup declared to be at once too feeble and too bold to detain them as spectators; and they left the Marigny for the Folies Bergères, where she had once seen a fine pantomime; but here they found another "revue," and fared no better. The "revue" at the Folies Bergères was even feebler, she observed to her brother, and much bolder than that at the Marigny: the feebleness was in the wit, the boldness in the anatomical exposures, which were somewhat discomfiting—"even for Paris!" she said.

She remembered afterward that he made no response to her remark but remained silent, frowning at the stage, where some figurantes just then appeared to be dressed in ball gowns, until they turned, when they appeared to be dressed almost not at all. "Mercy!" said Mrs. Troup; and presently, as the costume designer's ideas became less and less reassuring, she asked her brother if he would mind taking her back to the hotel; so much dullness and so much brazenness together fatigued her, she explained.

He assented briefly, though with some emphasis; and they left during the entr'acte, making their way through the outer room where a "Hungarian" band played stormily for a painted and dangerous-looking procession slowly circling like torpid skaters in a rink. The *bang-whang* of the music struck full in the face like an impulsive blow from a fist; so did the savage rouging of the promenaders; and young Mr. Blake seemed to be startled: he paused for a moment, looking confused. But Mrs. Troup pressed his arm. "Let's go out to the air," she said. "Did you ever see anything like it?"

He replied that he never did, went on quickly; they stepped into a cab at the door; and on the way to the hotel Mrs. Troup expressed contrition as a courier. "I shouldn't have given you this for your first impression of Paris," she said. "We ought to have waited until morning and then gone to the Sainte-Chapelle. I'll try to make up for to-night by taking you there the first thing to-morrow."

He murmured something to the effect that he would be glad to see whatever she chose to show him, and afterward she could not remember that they had any further conversation until they reached their apartment in the hotel. There she again expressed her regret, not with particular emphasis, of course, but rather lightly; for, to her mind, at least, the evening's experience was the slightest of episodes; and her brother told her not to "bother," but to "forget it." He spoke casually, even negligently, but she was able to recall that as he went into his own room and closed the door, his forehead still showed the same frown, perhaps of disapproval, that she had observed in the theatre.

The outer door of the apartment, giving entrance to the their little hallway, opened upon a main corridor of the hotel; she locked this door and took the key with her into her bedchamber, having some vague idea that her jewels were thus made safer; and this precaution of hers later made it certain that her brother had not gone out again, but without doubt passed the night in his own room—in his own room and asleep, so far as might be guessed.

Her little girl's nurse woke her the next morning; and the woman's expression showed such distress, even to eyes just drowsily opening, that Mrs. Troup jumped up at once. "Is something wrong with Jeannette?"

"No, ma'am. It is Mr. Blake."

"Is he ill?"

"I think so. That is, I don't know, ma'am. A *valet de chambre* went into his room half an hour ago, and Mr. Blake hid himself under the bed."

"What?"

"Perhaps you'd better come and see, ma'am. The *valet de chambre* is very frightened of him."

But it was poor young Mr. Blake who was afraid of the *valet de chambre*, and of everybody else, for that matter, as Mrs. Troup discovered. He declined to come out from under the bed so long as she and the nurse and the valet were present, and, in response to his sister's entreaties, he earnestly insisted that she should leave the room at once and take the servants with her.

"But what's the matter, Charlie dear?" she asked, greatly disturbed. "*Why* are you under the bed?"

In his voice, as he replied, a pathetic indignation was audible: "Because I haven't got any clothes on!"

At this her relief was manifest, and she began to laugh. "Good heavens——"

"But no, madame!" the valet explained. "He has his clothes on. He is dressed all entirely. If you will stoop and look——"

She did as he suggested, and saw that her brother was fully dressed and making gestures as eloquently plaintive as the limited space permitted. "Can't you take these people away?" he cried pettishly. "Do you think it's nice to stand around looking at a person that's got nothing on?"

He said the same thing an hour later to the doctor Mrs. Troup summoned, though by that time he had left his shelter under the bed and had locked himself in a wardrobe. And thus, out of a clear sky and with no premonitory vagaries, began his delusion—his long, long delusion, which knew no variation in the sixteen years it possessed him. From first to last he was generally regarded as a "strange case"; yet his state of mind may easily be realized by anybody who dreams; for in dreams everybody has undergone, however briefly, experiences similar to those in which Mr. Blake fancied himself so continuously involved.

He was taken from the hotel to a private asylum near Paris, where he remained until the following year, when Mrs. Troup had him quietly brought home to a suburban sanitarium convenient for her to visit at intervals; and here he remained, his condition changing neither for the better nor for the worse. He was violent only once or twice in the whole period, and, though he was sometimes a little peevish, he was the most tractable patient in the institution, so long as his delusion was discreetly humoured; yet it is probable that the complete records of kleptomania would not disclose a more expert thief.

This was not a new form of his disease, but a natural by-product and outgrowth of it, which within a year or two had developed to the point of fine legerdemain; and at the end of ten years Doctor Cowrie, the chief at the sanitarium, declared that his patient, Uncle Charlie Blake, could "steal the trousers off a man's legs without the man's knowing it." The alienist may have exaggerated; but it is certain that "Uncle Charlie" could steal the most carefully fastened and safety-pinned apron from a nurse, without the nurse's being aware of it. Indeed, attendants, nurses, and servants who wore aprons learned to remove them before entering his room; for the most watchful could seldom prevent what seemed a miraculous exchange, and "Uncle Charlie" would be wearing the apron that had seemed, but a moment before, to be secure upon the intruder. It may be said that he spent most of his time purloining and collecting aprons; for quantities of them were frequently discovered hidden in his room, and taken away, though he always wore several, by permission. Nor were other garments safe from him: it was found that he could not be allowed to take his outdoor exercise except in those portions of the grounds remotest from the laundry yard; and even then, as he was remarkably deft in concealing himself behind trees and among shrubberies, he was sometimes able to strip a whole length of clothesline, to don many of the damp garments, and to hide the others, before being detected.

He read nothing, had no diversions, and was immersed in the sole preoccupation of devising means to obtain garments, which, immediately after he put them on, were dissolved into nothingness so far as his consciousness was concerned. Mrs. Troup could not always resist the impulse to argue with him as if he were a rational man; and she made efforts to interest him in "books and the outside world," kindly efforts that only irritated him. "How can I read books and newspapers?" he inquired peevishly from under the bed, where he always remained when he received her. "Don't you know any better than to talk about intellectual pursuits to a man that hasn't got a stitch of clothes to his name? Try it yourself if you want to know how it feels. Find yourself totally undressed, with all sorts of people likely to drop in on you at any minute, and then sit down and read a newspaper! Please use your *reason* a little, Frances!"

Mrs. Troup sighed and rose to depart—but found that her fur cloak had disappeared under the bed.

In fact, though Mrs. Troup failed to comprehend this, he had explained his condition to her quite perfectly: it was merely an excessive protraction of the nervous anxiety experienced by a rational person whose entire wardrobe is missing. No sensitive gentleman, under such circumstances, has attention to spare from his effort to clothe himself; and all information not bearing upon that effort will fail of important effect upon his mind. You may bring him the news that the Brooklyn Bridge has fallen with a great splash, but the gravity of the event will be lost upon him until he has obtained his trousers.

Thus, year after year, while Uncle Charlie Blake became more and more dexterous at stealing aprons, history paced on outside the high iron fence inclosing the grounds of the sanitarium, and all the time he was so concerned with his embarrassment, and with his plans and campaigns to relieve it, that there was no room left in his mind for the plans and campaigns of Joffre and Hindenburg and Haig and Foch. Armistice Day, as celebrated by Uncle Charlie, was the day when, owing to some cheerful preoccupation on the part of doctors and attendants, he stole nine aprons, three overcoats, a waistcoat, and seventeen pillowslips.

Rip van Winkle beat Uncle Charlie by four years. The likeness between the two experiences is pathetically striking, and the difference between them more apparent than actual; for though Rip van Winkle's body lay upon the hill like a stone, the while his slumber was vaguely decorated with thousands of dreams, and although Uncle Charlie Blake had the full use of his body, and was all the time lost in one particular and definite dream, still, if Rip van Winkle could wake, so could Uncle Charlie. At least, this was the view of the younger alienist, Doctor Morphy, who succeeded Doctor Cowrie in 1919.

In the course of some long and sympathetic talks with his patient, Doctor Morphy slightly emphasized a suggestion that of late tin had come to be considered the most desirable clothing material: the stiffness and glitter of tin, as well as the sound of it, enabled a person to be pretty sure he had something over him, so long as he wore one of the new tin suits, the Doctor explained. Then he took an engraving of Don Quixote in armour to a tinsmith, had him make a suit of armour in tin, and left it in Uncle Charlie's corridor to be stolen.

The awakening, or cure, began there; for the patient accepted the tin armour as substance, even when it was upon him, the first apparel he had believed to be tangible and opaque enough for modesty since the night his sister had taken him to the Folies Bergères in 1904. The patient's satisfaction when he had put on this Don Quixote armour was instant, but so profound that at first he could express it only in long sighs, like those of a swimmer who has attained the land with difficulty and lies upon the bank flaccid with both his struggle and his relief. That morning, for the first time, he made no dive under his bed at the sound of a knock upon the door, and when he went out for his exercise, he broke his long habit of darting from the shelter of one tree to another. He was even so confident as to walk up to a woman nurse and remark that it was a pleasant day.

Thence onward, the measures to be taken for his restoration to society were obvious. The tin greaves pinched him at the joints when he moved, and Doctor Morphy pointed out that silver cloth, with rows of tiny bells sewed upon it here and there, would glitter and sound even better than tin. Then, when the patient had worn a suit of this silver cloth, instead of tin, for a few weeks, the bells were gradually removed, a row at a time, until finally they were all gone, and Uncle Charlie was convinced by only the glitter that he went apparelled. After that, the silver was secretly tarnished, yet the patient remained satisfied. Next a woollen suit of vivid green and red plaid was substituted; and others followed, each milder than its predecessor, until at last Uncle Charlie grew accustomed to the daily thought that he was clothed, and, relieved of his long anxiety, began to play solitaire in his room. His delusion had been gradually worn away, but not to make room for another; moreover, as it lost actuality to him, he began to forget it. His intelligence cleared, in fact, until upon Thanksgiving Day, 1920, when Mrs. Troup came to take him away, he was in everything—except a body forty-six years old—the same young man who had arrived in Paris on a November evening in 1904. His information, his point of view, and his convictions were those of a commonplace, well-brought-up, conventional young American of that period; he had merely to bridge the gap.

Doctor Morphy advised Mrs. Troup that the bridging must be done with as little strain as possible upon the convalescent's mind—a mind never too hardily robust—and therefore the devoted lady took her brother to a mountain health resort, where for a month they lived in a detached cottage, walked footpaths in the woods, went to bed at nine, and made no acquaintances. Mrs. Troup dispensed with newspapers for the time (her charge did not appear to be aware of their absence) but she had brought such books as she thought might be useful; and every day she talked to him, as instructively as she could, of the terrific culminations history had seen during the latter part of his incarceration.

Of Bolshevism he appeared unable to make anything at all, though Mrs. Troup's explanations struck out a single spark from his memory. "Oh, yes," he said, "I remember a rather talky chap—he was one of the guests at that queer place where I used to live, you know—well, he used to make speeches the whole day long. He said the doctors got all the money and it was *our* money. If it wasn't for us, the doctors wouldn't have a cent, he said; and since we produced all the wealth, we ought to organize, and lock the doctors up in the cellar, and get the money ourselves. I remember some of the other guests seemed to think there was a good deal in the talky chap's speeches, and I suppose it must be something of this sort that's happened in Russia. It's very confusing, though."

And when her lessons, as mild as she could make them, had proceeded somewhat further, he passed his hand over his brow, professing himself more confused than ever.

"I declare!" he said. "No sensible person could make head or tail of it, if I may use such an expression. I never dreamed anything could actually come of all these eccentricities—women's rights, socialism, blue Sundays, prohibition, and what not. I've heard of such people—heard jokes about 'em—but never in life met a person that went in seriously for any of 'em, except that speechifying chap I told you about. How on earth did it all *happen*?"

Upon this she was able to enlighten him but feebly, and he rubbed his forehead again.

"It's no use," he told her. "There's no *reason* behind these things: the only thing to do is to realize that the world's gone crazy. We used to think that civilization was something made of parts working together as they do in an engine; but, from what you tell me, it must have been trying to split itself up, all the time. The nations split up and began to fight one another; and as soon as they'd all got so crippled and in debt that they couldn't fight any more, the other splits began. Everybody had to be on the side of the women or on the side of the men, and the women won. Now everybody has to be either a capitalist or a labourer, it seems, no matter what *else* he is; and even if he doesn't know which he is, he'll have to fight, because somebody's sure to hit him. And besides *that*, the people have gone and split themselves into those that drink and the others that won't let 'em. How many *more* splits are there going to be, with the people on each side just bound to run the world their way? There are plenty of other *kinds* of splits that could be made, and I suppose we might as well expect 'em; for instance, we can have all the married people on one side in a 'class-conscious class,' as you were explaining, and all the unmarried ones on the other. Or all the parents on one side and all the children on the other." He paused, and laughed, adding: "However, I don't suppose it's gone quite so far as children versus parents yet, has it?"

Mrs. Troup looked thoughtful. "I suppose it always *has* been 'children versus parents,' at least in a sense," she said. "I've been thinking lately, though, that since all revolts are more apt to take place against feeble governments than against strong ones, if the children *are* in revolt, it must be because the parents are showing greater laxity than they used to."

Mr. Blake went to his afternoon nap, shaking his head, but in silence. Naturally he was confused by what he heard from her, and once or twice he was confused by some things he saw, though in their seclusion he saw little. One mistake he made, however, amazed his sister.

From their pleasant veranda a rounded green slope descended slowly to the level lawn surrounding the Georgian upheavings of an endless hotel; and at a porte-cochère of this hotel a dozen young women, come from a ride on the hills, were getting down from their saddles. Mr. Blake, upon the veranda of the cottage a hundred yards distant, observed them thoughtfully.

"It may be only the difference in fashions," he remarked; "but people's figures look very queer to me. The actual shapes seem to have changed as much as the clothes. You're used to them, I suppose, and so they don't surprise you, but down there at that porte-cochère, for instance, the figures all look odd and—well, sort of bunchy. To me, every single one of those boys seems to be either knock-kneed or bow-legged."

"Boys!" Mrs. Troup cried.

He stared at her. "What are they?"

"Good gracious! Don't you see? They're women!"

He still stared at her, while his incredulous expression slowly changed to one of troubled perplexity. But he said nothing at all, and after a moment more turned away and went to his room, where he remained until dinner time. When he appeared at the table, he made no reference to his mistake, but reverted to the topic of which he had been speaking that afternoon before his attention wandered to the horsewomen at the porte-cochère.

"Prohibition must have altered a great many people's lives quite violently," he said. "I suppose it was quite a shock for people who'd always had wine or Scotch at dinner—giving it up so suddenly."

"I suppose so—I don't know——" A little colour showed below Mrs. Troup's eyes. "Of course, quite a number of people had supplies on hand when the day came."

"But most of that must be gone by this time."

"Quite a good deal of it is gone, yes; you don't see wine very often any more. People who have any left are getting very piggish about it, I believe."

"It must be odd," he said contemplatively, "the whole country's being absolutely sober and dry, like this."

"Well——" she began; then, after a pause, went on" "It isn't like that—exactly. You see——"

"Oh, of course, there would be a few moonshine stills and low dives," he interrupted. "But people of our circle——"

"Aren't exactly 'dry,' Charles."

"But if they have no wine or——"

"It's my impression," said Mrs. Troup, "that certain queer kinds of whiskey and gin——"

"But we were speaking of 'our circle'—the kind of people *we*——"

"Yes, I know," she said. "They carry these liquids about with them in the most exquisite flasks. Jeannette has one—a boy friend gave it to her—and it must have been made by a silversmith who is a real artist. It must have been fearfully expensive."

Mr. Blake's open mouth remained distended for a moment. "Your Jeannette!" he exlaimed. "Why, she's only——"

"Oh, she's nineteen," his sister informed him soothingly.

"But was it exactly nice for her to receive such a gift from a young man?"

"Oh, he's one of the nicest boys we know," Mrs. Troup explained. "They swim together every day."

"Swim together?" her brother inquired feebly.

"Yes," said Mrs. Troup. "His aunt has a tank."

"'His aunt has a tank,'" the convalescent repeated in a low voice, as if he wished to get the sentence by heart. "'His aunt has a tank.'"

Mrs. Troup coughed placatively. "It may be a little difficult for you to understand," she said. "Of course, even I feel obliged to have something in the house at home—a certain amount of whiskey. I don't approve of such things, naturally, but Jeannette feel it's necessary on account of the young men and the other girls. She doesn't like whiskey and never touches it herself."

Jeannette's uncle uttered a sigh of relief. "I should think not! I was afraid, from what you told me of her flask——"

"Oh, in that," said Mrs. Troup, "she keeps gin."

"Gin?" he said in a whisper. "Gin?"

"She's rather fond of gin," Mrs. Troup informed him. "She makes it herself from a recipe; it's quite simple, I believe."

"And she *carries* this flask——"

"Oh, not all the time!" Mrs. Troup protested, laughing. "Only to dances and girls' lunches." And, observing her brother's expression, she added: "Of course, she never takes too *much*; you musn't get a wrong idea of Jeannette. She and all the girls of her set don't believe in *that*, at all—I'm positive none of them has ever been intoxicated. They have the very highest principles."

"They have?"

"Yes; you see, Jeannette has read Wells and Shaw since she was twelve. When we go home and you meet Jeannette, you must try to understand that she belongs to a different generation, Charles. You see, Jeannette has had so *many* influences that didn't affect your own youth at all. For instance, she always insisted on going to the movies even when she was a little girl, and I rather enjoy them myself, when I'm tired; and then there's the new stage—and the new novel—you know, we have everything on the stage and in books that we used to think could only be in books and on the stage in France, because here the police——"

"But in France," he interrupted, "—in France they didn't let the *jeune fille* read the books or go to the theatre."

"No," she agreed. "But of course over here we've had feminism——"

"What's that?"

"I don't know exactly, but I think it's something to do with the emancipation of women." She paused, then added thoughtfully: "Of course, Jeannette smokes."

"What!"

"Oh, that's nothing at all," she said hastily. "They've had to permit it in nearly all the restaurants."

He rose, leaning heavily upon his chair, as if for support, and looking rather more pallid than usual. In fact, his brow was damp from the exertion its interior workings had undergone in the effort to comprehend his sister's conversation. "I think, if you don't mind," he murmured, "I'll go directly to bed and rest."

"Do," she said sympathetically. "We'll talk some more about Jeannette to-morrow. She's the most lovably pretty thing in the world, and you'll be cra——" She changed the phrase hastily. "You'll be delighted to have such a niece."

But, as it happened, when she began to speak of Jeannette the next day, he gently protested, asking her to choose another topic. "I'm sure I couldn't understand," he said, "and the effort rather upsets me. It would be better to wait and let me form my own impressions when I see her."

His sister assented without debate; and nothing more was said about Jeannette until a week later when they were on the train and half the way home. A telegram was handed to Mrs. Troup by the porter, and after reading it she glanced rather apprehensively toward her brother, who, in the opposite seat, was so deeply attentive to a book that he had not noticed the delivery of the telegram; in fact, he did not observe it, still in her hand, when he looked up vaguely, after a time, to speak a thought suggested by his reading.

"So many of these books about the war and the after-effects of the war say that there is to be a 'new world.' All the young people have made up their minds that the old world was a failure and they're going to have something different. I don't know just what they mean by this 'new world' the writers talk so much about, because they never go into the details of the great change. It's clear, though, that the young people intend the new world to be much more spiritual than the old one. Well, I'm anxious to see it, and, of course, it's a great advantage to me, because I stayed so long at that queer place—where the doctors were—it will be easier to start in with a new world than it would be, maybe, to get used to the changes in the old one. I'm mighty anxious to see these new young people who——"

His sister interrupted him. "You'll see some of them soon enough, it appears. I really think Jeannette shouldn't have done this." And she handed him the telegram to read.

> thought i better let you know in case you prefer taking uncle charles to hotel for first night at home as am throwing toddle about forty couples at house sausage breakfast at four gm to finish the show and blackamaloo band might disturb uncle charles.

Uncle Charles was somewhat disturbed, in fact, by the telegram itself. "'Am throwing toddle'——" he murmured.

"She means she's giving a dance," his sister explained, frowning. "It's really not very considerate of her, our first evening at home; but Jeannette is just made of impulses. She's given I don't know how many dances since I went away with you, and she might have let this one drop. I'm afraid it may be very upsetting for you, Charles."

"You could send her a telegram from the next station," he suggested. "You could ask her to telephone her friends and postpone the——"

"Not Jeannette!" Mrs. Troup laughed. "I could wire, but she wouldn't pay any attention. I have no influence with her."

"You haven't?"

"No." And upon this Mrs. Troup became graver. "I don't think her father would have had any either, if he had lived; he was so easy-going and used to sing so loudly after dinner. Jeannette always seemed to think he was just a joke, even when she was a child. The truth is, she's like a great many of her friends: they seem to lack the quality of respect. When we were young, Charles, we had that, at least; our parents taught us to have that quality."

"But haven't you taught Jeannette to have it?"

"Indeed I have," Mrs. Troup sighed. "I've told her every day for years that she hadn't any. I noticed it first when she was thirteen years old. It seemed to break out on her, as it were, that year."

"How did it happen?"

"Why, we were staying at a summer hotel, a rather gay place, and I'm afraid I left her too much to her governess—I was feeling pretty blue that summer and I wanted distraction. I liked tangoing——"

"Tangoing?" he said inquiringly. "Was it a game?"

"No; a dance. They called it 'the tango'; I don't know why. And there was 'turkey trotting,' too——"

"'Turkey trotting'?" he said huskily.

"Well, that," she explained, "was really the 'machiche' that tourists used to see in Paris at the Bal Bullier. In fact, you saw it yourself, Charles. A couple danced the 'machiche' that night at the Folies Ber——" She checked herself hastily, bit her lip, and then, recovering, she said: "I got quite fond of all those dances after we imported them."

"You mean you got used to looking at them?" he asked slowly. "You went to see them at places where they were allowed?"

At this she laughed. "No, of course not! I danced them myself."

"*What!*"

"Why, of course!"

"No one——" He faltered. "No one ever *saw* you do it?"

"Why, of course. It's a little difficult to explain this to you, Charles, but all those dances that used to seem so shocking to us when we went to look on at them in foreign places—well, it turned out that they were *perfectly* all right and proper when you danced them yourself. Of course I danced them, and enjoyed them very much; and besides, it's a wholesome exercise and good for the health. *Everybody* danced them. People who'd given up dancing for years—the oldest *kind* of people—danced them. It began the greatest revival of dancing the world's ever seen, Charles, and the——"

He interrupted her. "Go a little slower, please," he said, and applied a handkerchief to his forehead. "About your seeming to lose your authority with Jeannette——"

"Yes; I was trying to tell you. She used to sit up watching us dancing in the hotel ballroom that summer, and I just couldn't make her go to bed! That was the first time she deliberately disobeyed me, but it was a radical change in her; and I've never since then seemed to have any weight with her—none at all; she's just done exactly what she pleased. I've often thought perhaps that governess had a bad influence on her."

He wiped his forehead again, and inquired: "You say she's given dances while you've been away with me?"

"Oh, she asks plenty of married people, of course."

"And it wouldn't be any use to telegraph her to postpone this one?"

"No. She'd just go ahead, and when we got home, she'd be rather annoyed with me for thinking a dance *could* be postponed at the last minute. We must make the best of it."

"I suppose so."

"We won't reach the house till almost ten, and you can go straight to bed, Charles. I'm afraid the music may disturb you; that's all. Dance music is rather loudish, nowadays."

"I was thinking," he said slowly, "—I was thinking maybe I'd dress and look on for a while; I do want to see these new young people. It might be a good thing for me to begin to get accustomed——"

"So it might," she agreed, brightening. "I was only bothered on your account, and if you take it that way, it will be all right," she laughed. "The truth is, I enjoy Jeannette's dances myself. I like to enter into things with her and be more like a sisterly companion than a mother in the old-fashioned strict sense. That's the modern spirit, Charles—to be a hail-fellow of your children, more a wise comrade than a parent. So, if you feel that you would be interested in looking on, and won't be disturbed—well, that's just too lovely! And you'll adore Jeannette!"

He was sure of that, he said: and added that as he was Jeannette's uncle he supposed it would be proper to kiss her when she met them at the station.

"Oh, she won't be at the station," said his sister. "In fact, I'll be surprised if she remembers to send the car for us."

But as it happened, Mrs. Troup was surprised: Jeannette sent the car, and they were comfortably taken homeward through a city that presented nothing familiar to Charles Blake, though he had spent his youth in it. The first thing he found recognizable was the exterior of his sister's big house, for she had lived in it ever since her marriage; but indoors she had remodelled it, and he was as lost as he had been under the great flares of light downtown. Mrs. Troup led him up to his room and left him there. "Jeannette's dressing, they tell me," she said. "Hurry and dress, yourself, so as to see her a minute before she gets too busy dancing."

In spite of her instruction, he was too nervous to dress quickly, and several times decided to get into bed instead of proceeding with his toilet; but an ardent curiosity prevailed over his timidity, and he continued to prepare himself for a state appearance, until a strange event upset him.

There were a few thin squeaks and low blats of warning—small noises incomprehensible to him, and seemingly distant—when suddenly burst forth the most outrageous uproar he had ever heard, and he thought it just outside his door. When it happened, he was standing with his right foot elevated to penetrate the orifice of that leg of his trousers, but the shock of sound overturned him; his foot became entangled, and he fell upon the floor.

Lying there, helpless, he heard a voice sweet as silver bells, even when it screamed, as it had to scream now to make itself heard. "No, *no!* I don't want 'The Maiden's Dream'! *Stop; damn it!*" And the outrage became silence, murmurously broken by only the silvery voice which was itself now indistinguishable, except as ineffable sound; he could not make out the words.

Fingers tapped on his door. "Do hurry, Charles dear," Mrs. Troup said. "Jeannette's arguing with the musicians, but she might have a moment or two to see you now. People are just beginning to come."

"With whom?" he asked hoarsely, not attempting to move.

"'With whom' what? I don't understand," his sister inquired, shouting through the closed door."

"You said she's arguing. With whom?"

"With the musicians."

"With whom?"

"The musicians. They began to play 'The Maiden's Dream,' but she doesn't like it; she wants something livelier."

"Livelier?"

"I must run," Mrs. Troup shouted. "Do hurry, Charles."

In spite of this departing urgency, Charles remained inert for some time, his cheek upon a rug, his upper eye contemplating the baseboard of the wall, and his right foot shackled in the trousers. Meanwhile, voices began to rise without in an increasing strident babble, until finally they roused him. He rose, completed his toilet, and stepped outside his door.

He found himself upon a gallery which looked down upon a broad hall floored in wood now darkly lustrous with wax. He had a confused impression of strewn and drifting great tropical flowers in haphazard clusters and flaring again, in their unfamiliar colours, from the reflecting darkness of the polished floor; such dresses as he had never seen; and flesh-tints, too, of ivory and rose so emphasized and in such profusion as likewise he had never seen. And from these clusters and from the short-coated men among them, the shouting voices rose to him in such uproarious garbling chorus that, though he had heard choruses not very different, long ago, it increased his timidity; and a little longing floated into his emotion—a homesickness for the old asylum, where everything had been so orderly and reasonable.

Suddenly he jumped: his hands were clutched upon the railing of the gallery, and they remained there; but his feet leaped inches into the air with the shock; for the crash that so startled him came from directly beneath the part of the gallery where he stood. In his nervousness, he seemed about to vault over the railing, but as his feet descended, he recognized the sound: it was of a nature similar to that which had overcome him in his room, and was produced by those whom his sister had defined as "the musicians"; they had just launched the dance music. The clusters of tropical flowers were agitated, broke up. The short black coats seized upon them, and they seized upon the short black coats; something indescribable began.

The dance music did not throb—the nervous gentleman in the gallery remembered dance music that throbbed, dance music that tinkled merrily, dance music that swam, dance music that sang, and sometimes sang sadly and perhaps too sweetly of romantic love—but this was incredible: it beat upon his brain with bludgeons and black-jacks, rose in hideous upheavals of sound, fell into chaos, squawked in convulsions, seemed about to die, so that eighty pairs of shoes and slippers were heard in husky whispers against the waxed floor; then this music leaped to life again more ferociously than ever.

The thumping and howling of it brought to the gallery listener a dim recollection: once, in his boyhood, he had been taken through a slaughterhouse and this was what came back to him now. Pigs have imaginations, and, as they are forced, crowding against one another, through the chute, their feet pounding the thunderous floor, the terrible steams they smell warn them of the murderers' wet knives ahead: the pigs scream horror with their utmost lungs; and the dumbfounded gentleman recalled these mortal squealings now, though there was more to this music. There should be added, among other noises, all the agony three poisoned cats can feel in their entrails, the belabourings of hollow-log tomtoms by Aruwimi witch doctors, and incessant cries of passion from the depths of negroes ecstasized with toddy.

A plump hand touched Mr. Blake's shoulder, and lifting his pale glance from below he found that his sister had ascended the gallery stairs to speak to him.

"What are they doing down there?" he shouted.

"Toddling."

"You mean *dancing*?"

"Yes, toddling. It's dancing—great fun, too!"

He was still incredulous, and turned to look again. To his perturbed mind everybody seemed bent upon the imitation of an old coloured woman he had once seen swaying on the banks of a creek, at a baptism. She jiggled the upper portions of her, he remembered, as if she were at once afflicted and uplifted by her emotions; and at the same time she shuffled slowly about, her very wide-apart feet keeping well to the ground. All of these couples appeared to have studied some such ancient religious and coloured person anxiously; but this was not all that interested the returned Mr. Blake. Partners in the performance below him clung to each other with a devotion he had never seen except once or twice, and then under chance circumstances which had cost him a hurried apology. Some, indeed, had set their cheeks together for better harmony; moreover, the performers, who, in this exhibition of comedy abandoned forever all hope of ever being taken seriously by any spectator, were by no means all of the youthfulness with which any such recklessness of dignity had heretofore been associated in Mr. Blake's mind:

heads white as clouds moved here and there among the toddlers; so did dyed heads; and so did portly figures.

"I came up to point Jeannette out to you," Mrs. Troup explained, shouting in her brother's ear. "I wanted you to see her dancing: she looks so beautiful. There she is! See! *Doesn't* she look pretty?"

His eyes aimed along her extended forefinger and found Jeannette.

Jeannette did "look pretty" indeed, even when she toddled—there could be no test more cruel. She was a glowing, dark-eyed, dark-haired, exquisite young thing shimmering with innocent happiness. One of her childish shoulders bore a jewelled string; the other nothing. Most of her back and a part of each of her sides were untrammelled; and her skirt came several inches below the knee, unless she sat. Nothing her uncle had ever seen had been so pretty as Jeannette.

To her four grandparents, Jeannette would have been merely unbelievable. Her eight great-grandparents, pioneers and imaginative, might have believed her and her clothes possible, but they would have believed with horror. In fact, to find ancestors who would not be shocked at Jeannette, one would have to go back to the Restoration of Charles Stuart. At that time she had five hundred and twelve great- great- great- great- great- great-grandparents, and probably some of them were familiar with the court. They would have misunderstood Jeannette, and they would not have been shocked.

"I just wanted you to see her," Mrs. Troup shouted. "I must run back to my partner and finish this. Come down when this number is over and meet some people."

He did not attempt to reply, but stared at her blankly. As she turned away, more of her was seen than when she stood beside him; and a sculptor would have been interested. "Don't forget to come down," she called back, as she descended the stairway.

But he did not appear at the end of the dance; nor could she find him in the gallery or in his room; so, a little anxious, she sent a maid to look for him; and presently the maid came back and said that she had found him standing alone in the dining room, but that when she told him Mrs. Troup was looking for him, he said nothing; he had walked away in the direction of the kitchen.

"How strange!" Mrs. Troup murmured; but as her troubled eyes happened to glance downward, both of her hands rose in a gesture of alarm. "Jennie where's your *apron*?" she cried.

"It's on me, ma'am," said Jennie; then she discovered that it wasn't. "Why, how in the world——"

But Mrs. Troup was already fluttering to the kitchen. She found trouble there between the caterer's people and her own: the caterer's chef was accusing Mrs. Troup's cook of having stolen a valuable apron.

Uncle Charles was discovered in the coal cellar. He had upon him both of the missing aprons, several others, a fur overcoat belonging to one of the guests, and most of the coal.

XXI

That vast spirit of diversion, seizing upon the country, was, however, less and less a spirit meaning diversion at home. More and more people seemed to feel the longings of unrest, the necessity for more and more movement at faster and faster speeds. Cabarets and night clubs succeeded the old roof gardens, and in these and in the road-houses that sprang up along the new automobile highways, crowding and noisy people "toddled" and paid Arabian Night prices for slightly poisoned alcohol, until dawn. The young people began to use an old word in a new and mystifying sense: it was the word "petting." The era of the obscurely "parked car" had begun.

New "movie theatres" were built and opened in all quarters of the cities and in every smallest town; negroes who lived in woodsheds bought phonographs that cost two hundred and fifty dollars; high-school boys, deprived of automobiles by stern fathers, easily stole others; the new profession of bootlegging, thriving so mightily that lawyers left their desks to join it, revived piracy, and merrily called the revival "hi-jacking." The automobile also revived a jovial form of banditry out of the Eighteenth Century. The earlier highwayman depended on the speed of his horse; the new one depended on the speed of his stolen automobile; he murdered a shopkeeper, robbed a till, disappeared at seventy miles an hour, and drank and danced the rest of the night with his girl at a road-house.

Among the less adventurous, the automobile was not content with mere revivals. In company with the phonograph and that compact culinary device called the "kitchenette" (to which the radio set now began to be added) it projected and created a substitute for the household of earlier times. Multitudes of apartment houses and apartment hotels supplied the demand of a new type of family—one that required no sand pile under a shade tree, for it consisted only of a husband and wife, with perhaps a tiny dog to interest the latter at odd times. Characteristically they lived in one room with a kitchenette and a bed that folded into the wall; they paid an exorbitant rent for this room, and their possessions were their clothes, a little jewellery, the phonograph, and an automobile (in which they seemed to live about as much as they did in the apartment) and as they had no other taxable property they were usually not greatly interested in good government; if election day was a holiday it meant longer automobile excursions. They danced, kept bootleg alcohol in the kitchenette, followed the murder trials in the newspapers, went tirelessly to movies; some of them played golf; some of them played bridge; and if they were bored they moved to other kitchenette apartments or got divorces. Some of them did none of these things and were strict sectarians; some of them devoted their time to charities, hospitals, or local mission work; but, whatever they did, their numbers continually increased and so did the buildings that sheltered them. When the weather was warm and the windows were open, the air in the neighbourhood of one of these buildings vibrated day and night with the warring of tinny jazzes.

Bootleg alcohol was also kept, and more copiously, in more ambitious forms of residence than the "kitchenette apartment." Except in isolated and old-fashioned drawing rooms, "afternoon tea" became the great modern cocktail party. With similar exceptions, dinner parties devoted a preliminary hour or so to chilled alcohol, virulent and emetic in orange juice; the food was served later and later, becoming merely an adjunct—an entirely superfluous one when the cocktailing was long protracted. Theatre curtains rose at a later hour to please the cocktail diners, and, after rising, showed more and more boldly what was perfectly to the taste of somewhat drugged audiences.

. . . It used to be said, along the coasts of Bohemia in New York, "To the pure all things are impure," a shot at the Puritan. But even a Bohemian of that day must have begun to feel some misgivings when he went to the theatre in this new period of "frankness," or read what was called the "modern novel" and some of the livelier journals, for apparently he had become purified and was in danger of being penetrated by the arrow he himself had aimed at the late Mr. Comstock.[1]

In this new age of "frankness in art" the old-fashioned liberal discovered that he was now become a puzzled conservative protesting against what appeared to him a prevailing tainted ugliness, anything but frank. The moment he did protest, however, he encountered hot defenders of the new frankness: they assailed him in the sacred name of "realism," and were loftily scornful of him. "You belong to the age of half-truths and the old hypocrisies," they informed him. "You called legs 'limbs.'"

---

1. Anthony Comstock (1844–1915), the moralist and U.S. Postal Inspector who persuaded Congress to pass the Comstock Act (1873), which banned from the mails materials considered obscene.

"No," he replied. "As a matter of record, I didn't, unless I spoke of arms and legs together. But it is a curious thing that I hear you repeatedly charging old-fashioned people with this crime. Whenever we ask you to tell us precisely what are the old hypocrisies that you have so usefully swept away, you almost always fall back upon 'limb.' It seems to make you very bitter with us to believe that we said 'limb' for 'leg.' You repeat and reiterate the accusation, evidently regarding it as serious. You are not historians and fail to understand that 'limb,' instead of 'leg,' was a euphuism of the feebler spirits practising the art of being genteel—an art that disappeared in our youth, when we ourselves assisted it to disappear. But, just to please you, let us imagine that we did say 'limb' when 'leg' would have been more definite. You are not indignant with us when we sometimes say 'seat' for 'chair,' or 'building' for 'warehouse,' perhaps, or 'pets' for 'dogs' and 'cats,' or 'bird' for 'parrot.' In fact, I think you may say such things, upon occasion, yourselves, without any subsequent great amount of moral anguish or remorse. How does it happen that you concentrate your attack upon 'limb'? Why is 'leg' of such overpowering importance to you?"

"Because you felt that 'leg' had some connection with sex," they replied, "and you declined to speak frankly of sex."

Here the liberal of a former age had again to make an inquiry: "What do you mean by 'frankly'?"

"The way we are speaking now is art—our honest realism in art. You charge us with offering as art a 'tainted ugliness.' Well, life has uglinesses. We are frank enough to represent in art the uglinesses as well as the beauties of life, as they are in reality. How do you justify the use of the word 'tainted' that you apply to our honest realism?"

"I have been to your serious theatre," the old liberal answered. "I have read your novels and, also, I have listened to your frank comedies. You say truly there are uglinesses and beauties in life, but the uglinesses I find you concerned with are mainly those of what you call sex; and, in this euphuism of yours, 'sex' for 'sensualism' and 'sexuality' and 'animalism,' you yourselves are far more genteel than the poetess who spoke of 'limbs' in Eighteen-seventy. Out of all the uglinesses of life you select but the one for your great subject; and when you consider it a beauty of life, not an ugliness, you make it hideous by your 'frankness'—a maiden upon a hilltop is something in anatomy for you. You are interested in her dreams only as they may reveal something about her 'sex life,' and, when you speak of her heart, you love the jargon of sex-specialist psychologists better than English. You appear to found your claim to a universal honesty upon your own predilection for the sexual, which is your topic."

"We are compelled to make it our topic because you denied its existence by ignoring it."

"Ignore?" the veteran returned. "If I write of a man eating his dinner, do I ignore his digesting it? If I say that he stood without a raincoat or umbrella for hours in a heavy rain, must you be informed that he got wet? And, without ignoring, if I omit from detailed description the inevitable results, common to all men under such circumstances, leaving descriptive details to the imagination of a reader, or an audience, may I not also, without ignoring, omit descriptive details of universal intimate and private sexual experiences when those details may possibly stimulate imaginations unhealthily?"

"No," the new champions retorted with ardour, "you may not. Unless you report such details faithfully, you are not honest and give us nothing of life."

"While you, on the contrary," the veteran responded, "are busy giving us nothing of art."

This seemed to be, so far as a spectator could make out, something like the inimical dialogue between the old and the new in "realism." The new charged the old with lack of frankness and the old charged the new with dirt, and in this latter charge there was matter of concern to the bystander. He had no need to be concerned with the former; the charge of lack of frankness in the old was negligible. It was merely a form of saying that certain artists did not choose the sexual, or the digestive, or the obvious for their subjects.

Of course any artist may choose whatever subject he pleases: the Nike of Samothrace is not a dishonest work because she is draped; and although the undraped Venus of Syracuse lacks the "frankness" believed necessary by the "new realists" of Pompeii, and by those of to-day, yet it is evident that the Venus of Syracuse is a very great work of art. Lack of realistic frankness, or merely imitative literalness, is therefore no impediment in the way of truth and beauty: there is no more sex or sexuality in Gray's Elegy than there is in the Sainte-Chapelle; the old has already proved itself, that it is honest art. Hence, in the dispute between the older "realists" and the newer, the only question that concerned us, as bystanders thinking of art, was whether or not there was dirt in the "new realism." That is to say: When is "art" art and when is it dirt? With this problem in mind, I went to New York and attended the theatre, for, if I could discover the essential truth of the matter there, the same truth would apply to any other art anywhere.

It was necessary to go to New York because New York had apparently become the United States, at least so far as the commercial theatre was concerned. The Little Theater movement was independent of the metropolis; so were several excellent stock companies. Moreover, a few special enterprises in classic drama, revivals of Sheridan's or Goldsmith's comedies, or of Shakespearean plays, and a few theatrical stars, personally admired for their talents and for themselves, might successfully ignore New York; but these were exceptions. Chicago or Philadelphia or Los Angeles might exhibit symptoms of theatrical independence, as regional dramatic capitals; but, for the purpose of general practical consideration everything outside of New York, theatrically speaking, had become "the provinces." This was not the most agreeable view for the rest of us, who were the provincials; but more and more we had been forced to accept it.

"If there's anybody who doubts it," said a New York manager who would have liked to doubt it himself, "he has only to produce a play in New York and take it out on tour. After he's read the New York opinion of his play, rehashed in the newspapers of one-night stands in the Midlands, New England, the South, and the Far West for a couple of years, he'll begin to see what he's up against."

However, to say that New York was the United States theatrically was not to say that New York opinion could make audiences out of Minneapolis or Kansas City people who had stopped going to the theatre. The provincial theatre had become so often discouraging to managers that they found themselves more and more stressingly forced to depend, for any success at all, upon a New York run. Since the provincial audiences wouldn't go to see a play unless it had secured a New York run, and, since they wouldn't go often enough, even then, the New York run might, indeed, become the manager's whole means of support. Therefore he must please the New York audience; he must either give New York what it wanted or perish—and even theatrical managers cling to life, though I have known them to wonder why they do.

It may not well be doubted that a Rip van Winkle of a playgoer who went to sleep theatrically in 1906 and woke twenty years later to visit the New York theatre would have been amazed and delighted by many things. It is true that he would have found a little of the old artificiality here and there, and some of the old and cheap stencils of pathos and of humour; but Rip van Winkle would have discovered that most of the old offences against theatrical plausibility had been swept away. Improvements in the technique of the drama and in stage direction would have astounded him, while in naturalism of character building and in the writing of dramatic dialogue there was such an advance as he could hardly have dared to hope.

He might have wished to strike medals in honour of the people responsible for so much improvement; the distribution of such medals should have included the first-nighters, and especially the dramatic critics, who are apparently the first-nighters made articulate. For it is, in most cases, the enthusiasm of the first-nighter that gives a play its chance of life. A not ill-founded opinion is that the critics and first-nighters who opened the way for the success of that fine "Harlem-flat" play, *Paid in Full*, by Mr. Eugene Walter, would be entitled to special recognition for their encouragement of what was the beginning of a new epoch in naturalism. No one can doubt that the best dramatic criticism in the New York newspapers has been not only the expression of the first-nighter but his education; and we must not deny the critic his medal, for it is the better critic who gives the better playwright, better actor, better director, and better manager the chance to exist.

A new generation of critics found that a gay mockery was a keener weapon than any other; and, mocking the old-school balderdash and clumsiness, they pretty well cleared the stage of a great clutter of nonsense and pinchbeck monstrosity. At least the old-school clumsiness and balderdash have gone; and, if there is a new balderdash come in with the moderns, a newer school of critics may, in turn, clear it away. Something must always be left for critics to do, and we may thank the present ones for depositing upon the trash heap stage villains, perfect heroes and heroines, stencilled maternal pathos, stencilled patriotism, stencilled virtue, valour, and a great deal of stencilled humour.

They laughed, too, at the stencilled coincidences that made the success of many of our old melodramas and comedies; they laughed at anomalies in stage settings, furnishings, and lighting; they laughed effectively at so many false and cumbersome things that elaborate research would need to be undertaken to make a fair list of what they have laughed to death. One thing above all others the true audience of a play asks of those who put plays upon the stage: it asks to be allowed to believe what it sees and hears; and the New York best critics of these recent years have done more to allow an intelligent playgoer to believe what he sees on the stage than was accomplished by all the previous forces for naturalism since Sheridan. In a word, the theatre was prepared, by intelligent criticism, to be more intelligent than it had ever been.

We had seen the advance in naturalism, for which we have just been thanking the newer criticism; and it was certainly true that naturalism had come to prevail. But it may be that in this new naturalism there was something done halfway—a naturalism that was not yet natural—and also something that was distasteful to us, though acceptable to the New York first-nighter.

Going over the plays of recent seasons in New York, we seemed to find among all sorts of plays a type that prevails over the other types; and the prevalent play appeared to be what we provincials in our unsophisticated way called a "sex play"; or, when we were still more unsophisticated, a "realistic play," thus bringing two inoffensive words into rather wide and wholly undeserved disrepute through misuse. For, although there may be some modernist opinion to the contrary, it is fairly safe to assume that a love theme in any expression of art depends for its interest upon the principals being of opposite sexes. Hence, any play constructed about a love story is a "sex play," and *Hazel Kirke, The Lady of Lyons, Fanchon, The Banker's Daughter,* and *The Little Minister* are "sex plays," while *Damaged Goods* and *Mrs. Warren's Profession* are not—the former being instructive propaganda against disease and the latter a moral allegory.

Realism in any art means only lifelikeness, and since likeness to life cannot be complete in art—for even the best waxworks have no digestions—realism in a play or novel can mean no more than that an apparently natural effect is presented, which, of course, may be done in plays wholly lacking a love theme and not depending on a relation between the sexes. Both terms, "sex play" and "realistic play," are misnomers, therefore, though they have attained a kind of acceptance as jargon. What we mean when we thus slangily speak of a "sex play" or a "realistic play" is rather definitely a play in which there are represented or discussed more details of animal sexualism than police authorities used to permit as part of public exhibition in this country. A "sex play," more accurately speaking, would concern love, while what is generally called a "sex play" dwells upon and emphasizes man as merely an animal, though not broadly or realistically, since it represents him as primarily concerned with—and generally consisting entirely of—only one animal function, and that one not the most important; whereas, even when considered entirely as an animal mechanism, he has several.

Now, retaining the jargon form "sex play" to avoid confusion, and, in spite of its inaccuracy and the fact that other definitions much more to the point suggest themselves, we may pertinently inquire how and why the "sex play" has become prevalent and for what reasons the first-nighter has applauded it into its prevalence. Also we might plausibly ask how even the first-nighter could give it prevalence, since it is so obviously a fragmentary statement, no more than a half-truth, naïvely unrealistic and quaintly old-fashioned in theme. Of course, the theme is more than old-fashioned; but the English public and police heartily sanctioned its theatrical use no longer ago than the Stuart Restoration. People are likely to speak of it as modern, because its treatment and present excellent manner of presentation are modern.

A clue to why the first-nighter himself likes it might be delved out of the fact that the "sex play" was so long in disuse because it was forbidden by fashion more effectively than by the police. True, there have been sporadic appearances, and elderly theatrical people will easily recall one such appearance that was contrary to the will of the first-nighter; for the first-nighter of twenty-five years ago characteristically did not permit the "sex play" to exist. This one was attempted on Broadway, and the first-nighters laughed contemptuously at it; but the newspaper reviewers, instead of pointing out its stupidities, put emphasis upon its sensuality; they called it "filthy" and said that it was a failure because decent people would not listen to indecencies. The critics, in all sincerity, meant to kill that play, and, until they heard the news from Broadway, believed it dead after the one night. But their reviews had reached the public and the theatre was already "selling out" for a long run.

The production of this play, however, was only a bit of commercial audacity on the part of a manager; the first-nighter himself was against when he then called "indecency" and what he now calls "frankness." The two facts—the two things—of which we are roughly speaking when we use these two words in this connotation are much the same. But when you call a thing "indecent" you need an excuse if you look at it; while, if you call it "frankness," it seems all right to bring Grandmother and the children to enjoy it with you. The old-time first-nighter called the "sex play" an indecency; the present first-nighter calls it an expression of honesty. Evidently there has been an alteration in vocabulary; but the alteration goes deeper than that.

To understand the intelligent first-nighter—for, of course, there are some first-nighters who are not intelligent—we must first have an idea of the conditions under which he thinks. To form this idea sympathetically we might aid ourselves by eating a partridge a day for ten or twelve months. After a few weeks anybody who could cook a partridge for us in a new way, or devise a sauce that would disguise the partridge flavour, would be our true benefactor. We could not easily moderate our enthusiasm for him or call him less than a genius, and, for a while, we should eat our partridges only in the new manner. Of course it would be a matter of time before the new flavour would cause our gorge to rise and we should pine for a new genius. Now suppose that there were a flavouring matter that culinary fashion among chefs declared unwholesome for the system and held as taboo; and suppose that we had tried all other possible flavours until we could never rid ourselves of their dreary taste, and that somebody daringly cooked us a partridge with the tabooed sauce upon it. We should be grateful, and, however wholesome or unwholesome in fact the forbidden sauce might be, it would seem wholesome to us—it would seem a sauce from heaven.

Thus we might obtain a hint of one reason, at least, for the first-nighter's indorsement of the "sex play." His calling is horrifyingly like the partridge eater's, and as distorting to the natural functions of the palate; the wonder is that he has any capacity for taste left at all. Yet this fantasy explains the "sex play" only in part, and comes far from being all the story. If "sex plays" were the only "sex" in fashion, the partridge fantasy might serve completely; but simultaneously with "sex plays" we had "sex novels," "sex magazines," "sex music," "sex painting," and "sex sculpture," so that the arts and literature appeared to be assaulted by squads of practitioners and apprentices bent upon indecency, or frankness, as you may choose to call it. Only structural architecture has seemed to be a little difficult to render with sex motives; though no doubt sex architects may someday emerge from Europe and be imitated here in some of our more liberal railway stations.

Moreover, science and philosophy, as well as art, had been invaded by sex. We possessed an already voluminous sex psychology, for instance, and the invasion was so enthusiastic and general that it appeared but a question of time until mathematics should be perceived as essentially a sex problem and algebraists, in examining their students, would require them to set forth not the binomial but the bisexual theorem.

This is to say, all in all, that although the American theatre is the expression of the New York first-nighter, the first-nighter himself is only a mechanism, being in fact no more than the expression of a fashion. He produces nothing in the sense that artistic creation is production; he declares what artistic creation of one kind may have an existence, and he is not responsible for "sex music" or "sex sculpture," of course, nor for the other "sex arts." Obviously, his present judgment in favour of "sex plays" is not a judgment at all, any more than twenty-five or thirty years ago it was a judgment in favour of the rapiers, gadzooks, and Zenda kingdoms he so warmly indorsed. He is fashion's automaton, creaky with dried partridge; and the better automaton he is, the more instantly he is lubricated by the oil can of a new fashion to enact the vehement gestures of enthusiasm. If there was to be indictment, then, on account of the "sex play," the true writ must be brought not against the first-nighter but against the general fashion of which he, in his own specialty, was but the mirror and the beau.

In other words, though the first-nighters are arbiters, they are but arbiters within the machine, being merely at the top of the fashion, not above it. They go cycling round and round with it; they do not spin it; and so are not blamed or praised for it. Individually, of course, they are not here considered at all; though it might well be added that individually the more significant of them are generous, witty, patient, and kind—one might honestly say that they are touchingly kind. They go hopefully to the new play and their state of mind is one of entreaty; they humbly beg the play to let them like it, to give them the slightest chance to like it, or to afford them any justification for saying pleasant things of it; and, if they can possibly bring themselves to like even a part of it, they will lay stress on that part of it, and, when it is at all possible, minimize the rest. They are not vultures, but highly gifted and intelligent men and women whose greatest anxiety is to find something they may honestly like and befriend.

Yet manager, actor, playwright, and director dread them and speak of them as the Death Watch. For manager and actor and playwright and director know but all too guiltily well that they are about to offer the surfeited partridge eater another partridge. How anxiously, then, must the poor cooks study the newest flavour that has seemed least intolerable to him!

"That last sauce he liked," they say, "contained three curses, six blasphemies, and nine franknesses concerning illicit love. Ours shall consist altogether of these. We will give him thirty-six curses, seventy-two blasphemies, and one hundred and eight franknesses about illicit love. This is undoubtedly the surest present means to stuff a partridge into him and not get killed for it. Heaven helping us, we shall make our partridge so spicy that he may almost believe it a new dish altogether, and even remain unconscious that he is eating partridge until he has finished the meal." Thus the cooks are compelled by the fashion that compels the partridge eater to compel them.

The fashion appears to be mainly interested in hints of sexual detail offered for its inspection—and getting more and more interested and asking for stronger and stronger hints. For one of the oddest things about all this frankness is that frank is the one thing it certainly is not. The toughest and most illicit lovers on the whole sex stage speak of their sins like rather literary people playing a game of synonyms; though of course now and then one of them will use a good, strong, fashionable, literary bad word to show how frank the author is being.

Our digestions are more important to us than our sex, as we should easily discover if we had a food shortage. Our sex, historically speaking, was an incident in our existence, developing long after we had digestions. There is more realism to our digestions than to our sex. Our lives are more vitally dependent upon our digestions than upon our sex. Digestion therefore offers a more vital subject to the realist; and can any impartial person deny that true frankness requires a digestion play before it does a sex play? But, on all the stage to-day, there is not yet even a frank and open food play. It will come some day—from Russia, of course; and, unfortunately, there are parts of Russia where people would attend such a play with interest. But as yet there are no signs in either western Europe or America of anything at all serious and frank about either nourishment or digestion in plays or novels.

The "sex plays" and "sex novels" seem to take all the details of those things—so much more important—for granted, which is so inconsistent it makes one's head swim to think about it. They leave those details absolutely to the imagination of their audiences. Pompeiian art was much deeper and more rotund; it at least went so far sometimes as to portray indigestion.

Only a little while ago the prevailing theatrical and rather literary fashion was irony. The popular prevalence of irony got to be a little dreary to provincial readers and audiences, and yet it was pleasantly humorous to see so many earnest writers determined to be ironical about everything, or be nothing. There were as many, immediately afterward, even more earnestly convinced that they must get "sex" into everything or be ruined as true artists.

For fashion is a terrible thing; but of course it isn't permanent, since, if it were, it wouldn't be fashion. Yet the sex fashion may last a long time, though the Puritan might kill it if it does. For the characteristic of the Puritan in action is massacre. Because some people play cards for money, he destroys all cards. Because some people get tipsy, he destroys all the liquor he can get his hands on. Because some people dance wickedly, he bans all dancing. And, when art has been insulted by fleshliness, he destroys even the statue of the Madonna. He makes a painful world of it, indeed, for the innocent bystander.

Perhaps that is what we provincials who used to like to go to the theatre really are—innocent bystanders—and we couldn't very well keep on going to the theatre and remain innocent.

XXII

Yet even in New York there are unfashionably taintless plays upon the stage—some of them warmly approved by the first-nighters—and they hold their own bravely and handsomely against the fashion. Upon my experimental journey to the metropolis I went to see only two plays and the first of these, a comedy, which had been warmly praised for its realism, was of this taintless type.[1] In it I found no glint of light upon the question that had sent me forth: When is "art" art and when is it dirt?

Yet the play was realistic and could not well have been more frankly honest. The portraits were of kinds of people familiar to any American; the action shown was the action of commonplace natural selfishness in commonplace lives. If I could have been made invisible and had inhabited for a time the living-room of an ordinary American house, I might have seen just what I saw upon this stage. The playwright did not take me upstairs to the bedrooms or even to the bathrooms, but I understood without difficulty that there was a second story where the people slept and bathed. There was no smell of cooking, yet I understood that there was a kitchen, and, indeed, I believe I saw a housemaid come in from there once or twice. Perhaps she had a lover; perhaps he had a low nature; I got no information about that. The people all appeared to have sex, though it is true that they didn't seem to have just excitedly made the discovery, as the curtain went up, that they were not neuter. They had the air of being accustomed to take their sex for granted and of supposing that other people took it for granted without needing any explanation at all.

Evidently I could have sat in that theatre night after night without learning anything useful about "dirt"; my quest would never be advanced

---

1. Tarkington wrote on this topic for *Collier's* in response to the February 9, 1927, arrest of Mae West, Helen Menken, Basil Rathbone, and others by New York City police. Menken (who was then Humphrey Bogart's wife) and Rathbone were arrested for their roles in *The Captive*, which had lesbianism as its theme. West and the cast of *Sex* were arrested as a warning and to prevent the opening of *The Drag*, which was written by West and dealt with male homosexuality.

there. So I tried the other play that I'd heard praised as a "fine modern realistic thing" in its way—it was extremely in favour with the public, but was not known as a "sex play." Nowhere had I heard a hint that it was unclean, though it had been authoritatively spoken of as "frank" and as "original," too. It was definitely of the "new realism." To my surprise, the story told in this drama was not strikingly unfamiliar. There was a virtuous young girl, the heroine, and she had an honest, hardworking, smooth-shaven young lover, the hero, who meant marriage and had fathomed the villain's intentions. (In spite of the fact that villains had supposedly been erased from the stage, there was undeniably a villain.) He was unscrupulous and handsome; he had a dark moustache and smoked cigarettes. He had dishonourable designs upon the heroine; he did not mean marriage. He was well dressed, rich, and powerful, and he had detestable myrmidons (one of them comic) who aided him in his continuous plots to get the innocent girl into his power. There was an honest detective with a good heart, and he had suspicions of the villain.

At the climax of the play the honest young hero defied the villain and was cast into prison by the lying machinations of the scoundrel and his wicked myrmidons. Thus the pure young girl was at last in the villain's power, but the honest detective with a good heart secured the hero's release from prison, and a happy ending was brought about by the rightful slaying of the villain. The girl never for a moment would have been safe from his plots as long as he lived, so he was put out of the way by the sweetheart of a man whom he had foully assassinated; and, that nothing might be lacking to the audience's pleasure, the meritorious lady who performed this sympathetic execution was protected and released by the honest detective with a good heart.

None of these people analyzed himself at the audience in the author-now-speaking manner of new realistic "characters"; none of them mentioned that he found himself caught in the inexplicable mechanistic formlessnesses of life; no one sat down to face the inevitable meaningless tragedy produced by his having a sex. No one swept away the veil of false conventionality that covers the hideousness of life; no one even defied the old hypocrisies and went out into the sunlight. No; this play had at least to be granted these special merits of novelty.

It had also other novelties, some of them amazing to a Midland visitor in search of light upon art and dirt. The pretty heroine and her girl-friends were a great part of the time more undressed than they were dressed; they were seen in a principally bare condition, and, possibly to save them from embarrassment, the honest young lover, in approaching the climax of his anxiety for his dear's honour, bravely appeared before the audience in no more than his underwear. Moreover, all of the people, except the kind-hearted detective, used language startling to a provincial of somewhat reclusive habits.

From the stage one heard strong profanity and also what the old-fashioned might define as indecency, and, during the depiction of a felonious orgy, there was an unmistakably honest pantomimic representation of the frankest obscenity. Beyond question, one saw lewdness and heard foulness, but I was not sure that this lewdness and this foulness must inevitably be labelled "dirt."

In the first place, of course, no actual obscenity was before the audience: we were seeing only the representation of it by excellent and conscientious actors who were doing their best to interpret it to us in the frank manner of the "new realism." The characters they enacted were low forms of human life; and the whole representation and portraiture appeared so plausibly to be of a complete truthfulness as to convince the auditor that, although he himself might never have seen such people, nevertheless, creatures almost identical could easily be found if he chose to look for them.

There was also, in the selection of these low forms of life as the topic of the play, a plausible, realistic reason for the barenesses exhibited and for the profanity, and for the obscenity, and even for the honest young hero's underwear. Thus, as the evening wore on, although I was sometimes embarrassed and hoped that there were no very young people in the audience, I inclined to the opinion that what I beheld might not necessarily be defined as "dirt." From my own point of view, I did not like it; but that, of course, was a personal matter, and I was present neither as a moralist nor as a protector of morals: I was only seeking light upon a question about art.

There were times, it is true, when I was startled into thinking, "No, this is dirt: this is meant to interest me by the cheap and urchin means of shocks; they want me to pay money for the enjoyment they think I take in being shocked. Or perhaps they charged me six dollars for this seat because it gives me a chance to exhibit my sophistication in not being shocked by what is either pleasurably exciting dirt or repulsive dirt to the unsophisticated. They are selling dirt to every taste."

Thus wavering, I sat unenlightened almost to the final curtain, when suddenly from the stage there came a "line" that cleared the air for me. It was a "laugh line," and, if what we saw and heard had been actual, the words would not and could not have been spoken. They were out of character, false, and whatever questionableness had preceded them there was no question about this lugging in of a sly and leering double meaning, borrowed from the old garbage of the smoking-car. It was a "line" directed at the most vulgar risibilities of an audience led by degrees to the proper point for receiving it; as if someone on the stage had said to us, "Well, I guess after that last you can stand this one!"

The calculation was just: the audience of well-dressed people had descended to the expected level and shouted their hilarious delight in what was, beyond all question, sheer dirt. Immediately the hovering of art that I had felt was revealed to me as a temporary charitable illusion of mine, and I seemed to perceive instead the dexterous hand of a cunning salesman. For an artist will not suffer dirt, nor, though he may need and hope for reward, will he make anything with the mere motive of selling it.

So in this play I had before me a thing very adroit, shrewdly made, and craftsmanlike, designed to be sold, and the pinch of unmistakable dirt that had been added, to give it greater value to buyers fond of dirt, seemed to warrant a suspicion that the whole had been calculated merely to be salable. Apparently, in this suspicion of what I had heard was one of the better and cleaner plays on exhibition before the matinée-going children and adolescents and theatre-loving adults of our country, I had come upon a clue to the answer to my question. I perceived that a thing is not art if a pinch of dirt is deliberately added to it to make it sell. That is to say, a thing may not be partly a work of art and partly dirt, though dirt may be cunningly and skillfully used to look like a work of art.

Art is expressed to the cool intellect and to the emotions that are not animal; and herein lies the difficulty of expressing an animal sexual subject by means of a work of art, for, in order to express this subject, men must be represented in their animal aspect. Moreover, the honest artist, attempting the animal sexual subject, must find himself in the inevitable company of two competitors who make use of the same subject, and with these he may be but too readily confused. One is the outright pander who sells "shock" or stimulation to the animal part of man, whether on the stage, or in books, or in surreptitious photographs and drawings. The other competitor is the revolutionary moralist, evangelistic in his use of shock to destroy "Victorian reserve"; he is so ardent that if he possesses any art he will use it as an adjunct to his propaganda, and a revolutionary preacher is infectious company for an artist: the artist will presently be using arguments out of theology to justify his art. Thus he too becomes an evangelist and not an artist.

Art is the language of a heart that knows how to speak, and a work of art is a beautiful interpretation of a truth. However ugly the truth, its interpretation must be informed with beauty. A realistic or literal and photographic imitation of the physical aspect of a truth is not a work of art; mere imitation is never art, and a pretended work of art that stimulates the animal part of a spectator is dirt. If its creator makes money by the sale of this stimulation, he comes under the suspicion of consenting to the rôle of pander.

Now, having felt that these uncomfortable conclusions might be thought just and inevitable, I submitted them to a "new realist."

"What?" he cried. "By such a rule, if I modelled the Venus of Milo itself you might call me a salesman of dirt because some moron looked upon the Venus as a half-naked woman!"

But I had taken the precaution to have an older realist present, and now he stepped forward. "No," he said. "But if what you make is a half-naked woman and you get rich by exhibiting her, we must believe you to be in that kind of business and not in art. When you can model a Venus of Milo we will forgive you the moron!"

Art knows no limit to its subject; it has never suppressed sex. But when it touches sex, as when it touches anything, it touches with neither a hot nor a heavy hand, nor yet an itching palm. The struggle with the Puritan was won long ago. We could dance; we could sing love songs; we could write realism; and now the "sex play" and "sex novel" arrive upon the field to commit excesses after the battle. Henry James wrote of some subjects that the most audacious of the sex writers may hardly dare to hint, even when they use no punctuation and omit all capital letters; they are too heavy-handed and would perhaps get into jail, in spite of the fashion. For they cannot do what Henry James and Alphonse Daudet and Thomas Hardy and Bernard Shaw have done; they cannot talk without grossness of anything no matter how gross.

XXIII

But the change in the kind of theatrical entertainment in which popular enjoyment was most conspicuously found was only a blown leaf on the storm of change; yet no doubt it showed as well as anything else did the direction of the wind. After all, the commercial theatre itself was no longer universally popular. It was a diversion for the opulent because of the prodigious increase in the price of tickets. The "masses" got their drama from the movies which had begun by taking the "gallery gods" from the theatre and had remained in taste what the "gallery gods" had always liked. And, studying the tastes of new generations of "gallery gods" who were now become millions and millions and thus brought millions and millions of dollars to the movies, the movie magnates provided huge palaces, or at least what they judged "gallery gods" might think were palaces; and, in company with the pictures, tabloid revues and tabloid vaudeville were offered; for, as part of the speed of life, there had come a necessity for instantaneous and tabloid things, so that even newspapers were administered as tabloids. The challenging and questioning spirit of the age of speed was itself often tabloid and expressed in the paragraphs of columnists.

Challenging and questioning had begun, of course, long before the Great War; it really began in the most ancient times and had always gone on among small groups of constitutional critics and objectors. But, after the war, the old men who had headed these groups began to find themselves the chieftains of large and fashionable coteries. Hordes of young followers imitated them, learned their manner of speech, and proclaimed faith in an old god they thought was a new one because he had a horrible new name, Debunking: on this altar, they said, everything old must be burned as incense; all believers in anything old were either fools or hypocrites and must be jeered to death. The new questioning, believing Science to be new, could therefore have faith in it—at least so long as it could be interpreted as maintaining the ancient theological theory of predestination now masquerading in the new phrase, "mechanistic universe." For, like the automobile and all the new machines men had invented for greater speed and for ease to labour, the fast-whirling universe itself must be, these new questioners argued, a machine—and they insisted, a little inconsistently, that it was a machine of its own invention. Hence all of its parts, including themselves, could never be anything but machinery moving to the inevitable. Wherefore, "Eat, drink, and be merry," materialism's prehistoric motto, not precisely new.

And meanwhile, as the dancing and new theorizing went on, with automobiles swarming over the earth and airplanes darting across the skies, with the ether shaking to broadcast jazz, with giantism becoming colossalism, so that Atlas would have reeled at the sight of New York, and with Tennessee legislating against evolution, the women were cutting off their hair.

That was what most upset my neighbour Judge Olds.[1] He has always been what is called a prominent and public citizen; he was a captain in the war with Spain and by virtue of his ancestry belongs to several patriotic societies; he is a church member, though not an inveterate attendant at services; moreover, he has never been thought narrow or bigoted in any of his views—at least not until recently, his daughter being the first to bring such a charge against him. It was just after she brought it that I happened to drop in on him, in his library, and his face was still pink.

"I've been going to the same barber shop for fourteen years," he said harshly, as I sat down. "I went to it for the last time to-day. I took off my coat and necktie the way I always do, and then I noticed there were three women sitting there in the waiting chairs and looking at me as if I'd committed a crime. *Mad* at me for taking off my coat and collar in a place where they had no right to be, themselves! I thought probably they were there to solicit for a charity or something; but just then old George called 'Next!' and my soul! if one of those women didn't get right up and march to the chair and sit down in it! That wasn't the worst of it. The person that had just got out of the chair was wearing boots and breeches; but it wasn't a man. It was a girl—one that had been a nice-looking girl, too, until she sat down in that chair and had three feet of beautiful, thick, brown hair cut off. She was my

---

1. Judge Walter Olds (1846–1925) was a prominent Indiana lawyer and Republican who served on the Indiana Supreme Court from 1889 to 1893 before going to practice law in Chicago and ultimately Fort Wayne, Indiana. Tarkington is probably using the deceased judge as a prototype here—and perhaps also playing on his name. Walter Olds was a veteran of the Civil War but does not seem to have served in the Spanish-American War; he does not seem to have lived in Indianapolis after 1893; and it's not clear that he had a daughter, as a 1916 biographical capsule mentions only a son.

own daughter, Julie, nineteen years old. I didn't say a word to her—not then; I just looked at her. Then I told old George I guessed his shop was getting to be too coeducational for me and I put on my things and went out. I'll never set foot in the place again."

"Where will you get your hair cut, Judge?"

"I guess we'd better learn to cut our own hair, we men," he said bitterly. "There really isn't any place left nowadays where we can go to get by ourselves. Coming home from Washington the other day, I was in the Pullman smoker—what they call the club-car—and I'll eat my shirt if four women didn't come in there and light cigarettes and sit down to play bridge! Never turned a hair—didn't have any hair long enough to turn, for that matter. They won't let us keep a club-car or any kind of club to ourselves nowadays; they got to have anyway half of it. I said when we let 'em into the polling-booth they'd never be contented with that, and I was right. Remember all the fuss they made about their right to vote? Well, they've proved they didn't care about that at all, because more than half of the very women that made the fuss don't bother to vote now they know they *can*. They just wanted to show us we couldn't have anything on earth to ourselves. They haven't left us one single refuge. It used to be, a man could at least go hang around a livery stable when he felt lonesome for his kind; but now there aren't any more livery stables. He can't go to a saloon; there aren't any more saloons. Once he could go sit in a hotel lobby because that was a he-place; nowadays hotel lobbies are full of women sitting there all day. When I studied law there weren't three women in all the offices downtown; now you can't find an office without a bob-haired stenographer in it, and there are dozens of women got their own offices—every kind of offices. That's another thing I've been having it out with Julie about. She's not only cut off her hair; she wants to go into business as soon as she finds out what kind she'd enjoy most. She's like the rest: the one thing that gives her the horrors is the idea of staying home. What's become of the old home life in this country, anyhow? Everybody seems to have to be going somewhere every minute: there's the car in the garage; it'll take us anywhere—let's go! If there is such a thing, nowadays, as a National Motto it's certainly, 'Let's Go!' 'Let's Go' is the unceasing cry. I understand they do a great deal of what they've now invented a horrible word for—'necking'—while they're on the road between parties and movies and end-of-the-night breakfasts. But it's always, 'Let's Go—let's go anywhere except home!'"

He paused for a moment while his bushy gray eyebrows were contorted in a frown of distressed perplexity; then he looked at me almost with pathos and, speaking slowly, asked a question evidently sincere: 'Does it ever seem to you, nowadays, that maybe we're all—all of us, young people and old people both—that maybe we're all *crazy*?"

"No—I hadn't thought of it that way. Why?"

"Well, for one thing, a while ago I was remembering back to when I was a young fellow about Julie's age or a little older, perhaps, and what I'd have thought then if somebody'd told me I was some day going to have a daughter like her. We used to talk about the 'eternal feminine,' you remember. Think of that and then think of walking into a barber shop—a barber shop!—and seeing a creature sitting in the chair with its legs crossed—legs in boots and breeches—getting its hair cut, reading the paper, and smoking a cigarette in a holder six inches long. Then think of this creature getting up and sticking its hand in its breeches pocket and handing out a fifteen-cent tip and saying, 'Don't let all this money make you snooty, George!' Then think of recognizing the creature as your daughter! Think of seeing your own 'eternal feminine' swaggering around a barber shop, smoking, getting its hair cut, and wearing breeches!"

"But they've been wearing that kind of riding-clothes for twenty years, or more."

"Yes; but not just casually anywhere. At first they'd change back to skirts as soon as they came in from riding; then, at a resort hotel, maybe, they'd lounge around and have tea before they changed; but now it's all off—like their hair. They wear breeches into your own barber shop and drive you out of it. Breeches! Why, the other afternoon one of Julie's young men had been riding with her, and she came home laughing her head off over how funny he looked because she said his brother had taken his riding-breeches and he'd had to borrow Shorty's. Shorty isn't a boy; Shorty's a girl; she lives next door to the young man that borrowed her breeches. And when I told Julie it was horrible to me that she could laugh over such a performance, she said I was crazy, and it seemed to me that either I was or she was. It seems more so to me to-day, when she's deliberately destroyed what was the prettiest thing she had. She says she feels better without her hair and that she looks better, too. You could see she was in earnest about that; she honestly and serenely thinks that amputation a great success. Of course that's because it's the fashion—anything that makes them look more in the fashion makes them prettier, they think. If it were the fashion now to wear a big hump on their backs they'd all think a humpless girl lacked beauty."

I agreed with him there. "Yes, we saw that in our own boyhood. We can easily remember when a woman without a bustle seemed to be of a strangely meagre appearance."

"Yes, but a woman's hair is a natural ornament. Julie was a lovely girl this morning, and this evening she looks like a debilitated kind of scrawny boy. Either somebody's crazy or the devil's got into what we used to think of as our 'best' people, especially into our 'best' young people. It strikes me as an important question, because a good deal of what happens at the top is likely to filter all the way down through the whole body of a society. But just now it often looks to me as though what used to happen at the bottom of society when we were young had filtered up, so to speak, till at last it's contaminated the top. Every ideal we had when we were young—every one of our old rules of conduct, of good manners, of womanhood, of modesty, and of morals—is shattered. You can't find the remnants of any of 'em among these young people of to-day—not a remnant!"

"All because Julie had her hair cut?" I asked.

At that he looked at me fiercely. "My goodness!" he said. "Do you mean to say you find any *excuse* for the way they're behaving?"

XXIV

THE JUDGE DID MOST of the arguing, so to call it; he leaned forward and spoke with emphasis and severity. "Look here; you surely aren't going to sit there and tell me this younger generation to-day is anything like what our generation was in its twenties, or the generation of our fathers and mothers when they were that age. You know better than that, don't you?"

"Yes—I suppose so."

"When we were the younger generation," he said, "most of us went to church with our fathers and mothers pretty regularly. What proportion of these young people do you suppose do that now?"

"I don't know. I don't know the proportion of the fathers and mothers that go to church nowadays, Judge. The young people can't go to church with their parents if the parents don't go, can they?"

"That doesn't bear on the point I'm making," he said. "What I say is that in our day we maintained a conformity with the behaviour of the older generation. I admit that youth always is and must be a little wilder and more indiscreet than middle-age. I don't deny that when we were young men we were too lively sometimes—when we were out of sight of the girls we knew. Of course a good many did things they shouldn't have done. But when we were young, no matter how lively we were sometimes, we didn't just tear loose and raise Cain all over the place, girls and boys together, drinking poisonous, illegal liquor, gambling, dancing entwined to sensual and savage music, reading disgusting books, going to outrageous shows, chattering indiscriminately about unmentionable things, and, in our conduct as well as our talk, really scoffing at the ideals of our parents. Our generation didn't do any of those things."

"Whereas a great many of the generation now middle-aged do all those things, don't they, Judge?"

"They do indeed," he said, and his frowning brow grew darker. "It's dumbfounding and disheartening to see how they've broken away from the ideals of our youth."

"Then these present young people are really doing what you've just said we ourselves did: they're maintaining a conformity with the behaviour of the older generation. In that, then, they're doing not only what we did but what all younger generations do. This present one shocks us with its reflection of our own conduct, though, as you say, the reflection is livelier and more indiscreet than the original. If we are to place the blame it must be upon the originals, mustn't it?"

"I don't care where you place the blame," he returned irascibly, and with some inconsistency, I thought. "It's the spirit of the age and that spirit is either a crazy one or a bad one. There's never been such gross materialism let loose on earth. Nobody cares about anything but money and pleasure. What proportion of our people ever talk about anything except dollars and pleasure? Everything's been speeded up and has to go on being speeded up. Making money has to be speeded up; having fun has to be speeded up; life has to be speeded up to keep pace with the automobile and all it brought with it. A bricklayer, or even a college professor, can have luxuries now that a multi-millionaire of the Nineteenth Century couldn't have, and can move faster. People lived at seven miles an hour thirty years ago, now they live at forty and seventy. Nobody has time to do anything except rush; and the women rush worse than the men. Girls haven't time to learn to play the piano any more, or to study singing, or to acquire any of what we used to call the accomplishments. They buy all those things canned, just as all the cooking they can do is out of cans. They don't even spend any time over their clothes; they used to put in hours and hours at the dressmaker's, and more hours at the milliner's, having their hats trimmed becomingly on their heads. Nowadays, they see a wax figure in a window wearing a sack they call a dress, and they dash in and get a duplicate of it ready-made. For hats they buy little ready-made cloth buckets without any trimming. They haven't got any more time to put in on what's becoming than they have to cook and sew and play the piano. No wonder their music has to be fast and noisy! All you've got to do to understand this age is to listen to a jazz band doing what they call 'pepping it up.' Only people made of metal could stand it; and human beings actually are more metallic than they used to be; they're harder and brassier; but they still have nervous systems—that's why you hear of so many more 'nervous breakdowns' than you used to. Even ordinary talk has been speeded up; nobody listens unless you talk fast and yell; and I suggest you might notice some of the language our most prosperous classes are pleased, nowadays, not only to listen to from the stage and to read in books, but to use, themselves. You haven't anything to say for this age's attitude toward what we used to speak of as 'refinement of speech,' have you?

I suppose you know that's what the bulk of the younger generation seems to hate most, of all the old things they've cast aside, don't you?"

"It seems so, sometimes; yes. Their 'intelligentsia' got to distrusting refinement, I believe, because it appeared to them a way of 'covering up facts.'"

He took me up quickly. "What facts did our former refinement of speech cover up?"

"None, of course, but the young revolutionists didn't realize that it's a question of manner not of matter. Refinement of speech appears to consist mainly in avoiding, not at the cost of necessary accuracy, details that may have any physical effect, except laughter or tears, upon a reasonably sensitive listener. Refinement may find it useful to mention a garbage barrel, but will not detail its contents except of necessity. The contents are sufficiently sketched in the imagination of the listener by the mention of the barrel; to detail them would perhaps sicken him a little. But the young generation and the new age, overturning the old in everything, clamoured that the contents must be 'brought into the open' and spoken of 'frankly.' This is partly because it was the habit of many of the older generation, once, to shirk some uncomfortable subjects almost entirely. The young people and some of their elderly leaders confused this shirking with refinement; they also confused refinement with hypocrisy."

"No matter how it happened, you can't deny that their speech is coarse, can you?"

"No; and that's a loss; yet along with this loss there is some gain: the attack on refinement was an attack on the inoffensive bystander, the wrong party; but in the general mêlée the shirked subjects did get pulled out to where they can't very well go on being shirked."

"Yes! 'Pulled into the open,' Julie calls it!" he said indignantly. "They could always be spoken of with decent reserve and caution; but now this pulling them out into the open means pulling them into the foreground where they don't belong."

"But that always happens at first to subjects that have been kept in the dark."

"I don't care," he said. "It isn't wholesome. You don't argue that this present craze for sex stories and sex shows and sex discussion—yes, and sex jokes—you don't argue that it's wholesome, do you?"

"No, not while it's a craze or fashion. When the new age has got accustomed to what it still rather defiantly feels is this new privilege of 'open discussion,' the subject will take its proper proportion."

"It's not possible to make that subject a wholesome one for general discussion," he said. "That's what shocks and depresses me about this new age—its unwholesomeness. You can't go out on the street without seeing it."

"No?" I said. "It seems to me that I can."

"You can't!" he returned sharply. "If you pass a movie theatre you'll see the titles on the bill boards in front, won't you? Among others you'll see *Red Hot Stockings, Harem Love, Passions of the Night, Oriental Lulu, Fires of Innocence——*"

"Don't go on, Judge; the list is long; but I understand that most of the titles of that kind are misleading, and the films themselves have passed the censors."

"Nevertheless, you'd hardly say that the fact of its being profitable to use such titles as a lure is a token of wholesomeness, would you? You said you could go out on the street without seeing any signs that there's unwholesomeness in the new age; well, I'll ask you to take note only of the clothes but of the complexions of the women on any of the crowded blocks downtown. What about it? Suppose you'd seen as many painted faces twenty years ago, what would you have thought?"

"I suppose I'd have been startled."

"Startled!" he cried. "You'd have thought it was Babylon! What would you have thought, a few years ago, if you'd seen a woman in a street-car or a restaurant take out a little box with a mirror in it and powder her nose when she knew a lot of men were looking at her? You'd have thought she was either pretty unpleasantly common or pretty ludicrously vulgar, and she would have been. And if, in addition to powdering her nose, she went on to smear red on her lips or her cheeks, you'd have thought she was bad, and again she would have been. But nowadays half the older women and nearly all the younger ones are at it. They smear themselves with cosmetics and they do it right in your face. You can't tell which of 'em are good and which bad, because, according to the old standards, some look worse than others but they pretty nearly all look bad. They seem to *want* to look that way. Julie got me to go with her to a movie the other night and during the intermission she got out her 'vanity case' and began to redecorate her lips. I said to her, 'You put that box away or I'll take you home and do my best to whip you, no matter if you *are* nineteen years old!'

"She just laughed and went on with her art work. 'My heavens!' I said. 'Can't you see the craziness of what you're doing?'

"'How's that, Pops?' she asked me, and went right on using her lip-stick all the time I was talking.

"'You're trying to make people think that red smear is the natural colour of your lips,' I told her. 'In the name of conscience, if you can't see in the first place that it's cheap and deceitful, and if you can't see in the second place that besides being cheap and deceitful, it's an intimate detail of your toilet and therefore hasn't any business to be performed in public, then, anyhow, in the third place, can't you see that doing it in public defeats its own object?'

"How's it defeat its object, Pops?' she asked me.

"'My heavens!' I told her. 'The object is to make people think the smear is your own colour, and here you're deliberately proving to 'em that it *isn't*!'

"She never stopped looking in her little mirror; she just went on smearing; but she gave a little absent-minded laugh, as if an unimportant and rather imbecile person had said something a little amusing. 'Yes,' she told me, 'we're all aboveboard with it nowadays. Our generation is so much franker and honester than yours was, Pops!'

"That's the way she is. That's the way they all are. And what can parents do about it? We can't whip 'em; they'd probably have the law on us if we did. When we try to reason with 'em they talk the way Julie did to me that I've just been telling you about. If we threaten to cut off their allowances they laugh. 'All right, I've been wanting to get a job, anyhow!' There's no discipline left and no obedience. If you quote the Bible to them, the way our parents did to us when we were a little refractory, they tell you that ancient tribal ideas don't apply! The rule of the churches over the general people has almost disappeared, and, except with a small proportion of religious-minded young people, means nothing to the new generation. I remember how my father talked once to my younger sister when she'd let an out-of-town beau of hers call her after nine o'clock and stay until half-past eleven. 'What would our pastor say if he knew?' my father asked her, and Mary began to cry. I tried it with Julie. 'What would Dr. Halloway think of you?' I said. 'I wish you'd get him to tell me,' was what she answered. 'I think he's a cutie!' You can't reach their minds; you can't do anything; you're helpless. And yet Julie's as considerate and sweet and thoughtful in many things as any child could be. She'd be a lovely thing, except for the times we live in and the crazy ideas she's caught like a contagion. Lord knows where it all came from! New-rich people with no background or training; immigrants getting rich and sending their children to school with ours, and ours taking up with 'em; socialist writers upsetting the old morals in the minds of the young; the automobile getting young people miles out of reach in five minutes—natural youthful smartaleckism and native cussedness—anyhow, it's happened and we're in for it! Julie doesn't lip-stick and rouge as much as some of her friends do, but she does more than others. A few of them don't use cosmetics at all, and when I hold them up as examples she only says, 'Oh, that's their affair; it's the age of freedom.' Freedom! I should say so! Even the girls that don't use lip-stick wear the brazen clothes they're all so pleased with."

"'Brazen clothes,' Judge?"

He stared at me. "Good heavens! Modern indecency in dress is so glaring that I shouldn't have thought it need ever be mentioned."

"But what are your views upon dress, Judge? You've been upset by Julie's getting her hair cut, and I suppose, as that involves her appearance and the question of headdressing, it's a part of the general question of dress. You don't think it was indecent of her to shed her hair, do you?"

"As a relinquishment of her womanhood, I believe it to be bordering on that. Certainly you don't think it makes her appear more feminine, do you?"

"No. Much less so."

"You see that it's ruined her looks?"

"It's certainly detracted from them."

"Well, it's a woman's business to look as pretty and feminine as she can, isn't it? She's supposed to make herself attractive in those ways, isn't she? And not only that, but a good woman's supposed to look like a good woman, isn't she? If she doesn't, how are we to know which kind of woman she is? If she doesn't make us respect her, in the belief that she has a higher nature than we have, and if we lose our chivalry for her, how is she to protect herself and get along with us at all? Because, of course, mentally as well as physically, we're incomparably more powerful than she can ever be."

"Are we?" I inquired. "I'm afraid so long as we think we are they'll take an unmanly advantage of us: they'll fall back upon their heritage of an instinctive and superior wiliness that would prevent us from using our strength. But there seem to be symptoms among them just now indicating a willingness to forego that kind of advantage."

"Is that so? Then why are they so determined to show their legs? That's what I've tried to shame Julie with. 'You've cut off your skirt at the knee,' I said, 'and you've cut off your hair pretty near at the roots. Your hair was so lovely and you could use it to frame your face so charmingly that while you had it people naturally looked at you above the shoulders. You must have been afraid they wouldn't pay enough attention to the way you've exposed your legs!' I thought it would shrivel her up. In fact, I was ashamed to be saying such a thing to her, even though it seemed to be the wicked truth. If my father had ever said that to my sister, Mary would have died, I think; I truly don't believe she could have lived after such a thing had been said to her. Julie didn't even blush; she wasn't even *angry*! 'My legs?' she said. 'What do I care whether anybody pays attention to my legs—or my face, or my arms, or my hands? It's their affair, not mine.'"

"That seems fairly reasonable, doesn't it, Judge?"

"Reasonable?" he repeated angrily. "Do you remember when any respectable woman would have been sick with shame at the thought anyone could call her 'bold'? Along in the earlier days of the active period of the Equal Rights movement, I remember seeing two apostles of that creed wearing what were then called 'short skirts'—almost to the tops of their buttoned shoes and probably five inches from the ground. Women wore three or four petticoats under their overskirts in those days, and that made the two suffragettes look like two self-important little hens; but they were self-conscious, too, because everybody on the street was bursting with laughter at them, and I don't believe they ever publicly tried that form of feminism again. It wasn't immodest—there wasn't the slightest glimpse of their stockings—it was merely ridiculous; and, not until years afterward, about Nineteen-twelve or Nineteen-thirteen, I think it was, did the first symptoms of this wholesale modern immodesty appear. Women had got their skirts so tight, to be in the fashion of that time, that they'd begun to leave off petticoats and underskirts altogether. Finally they got 'em so tight, especially as the skirts tapered down to bind the ankles, they could hardly walk. Then some French hussy got the idea of splitting the tight skirt almost up to the knee. People said it wasn't an uncommon sight in Paris; and one day, downtown, in my own city, I saw a flashy looking girl wearing one of those split skirts. She had on black stockings and a black skirt; but the whole ankle and calf of her leg was exposed in the opening and I could scarcely believe my eyes."

"Why not, Judge?"

"Good heavens! he said. "You know as well as I do that self-respecting women never did such things! Managers made fortunes out of leg-shows; they didn't need to have any plot or any acting, or any music except jingle; even the dancing didn't amount to anything. Look at the *Black Crook* and the 'Extravaganzas' that followed it. All they had to have were some plumpish girls that were willing to wear tights for a salary; and some of the shows didn't need to go so far as tights—knee dresses were considered show enough for the gate-money. An old-fashioned leg-show couldn't do much business on that basis now—not in competition with any block downtown in the shopping district!"

"But for that matter," I suggested, "there were always the seashore beaches. Even in our youth knee-length skirts were thought proper there."

"They aren't now!" he returned grimly. "I must be getting really old, because I can remember when Ouida's *Moths* was considered a wicked book. One of the reasons was the description of a woman in a bare-legged bathing-suit. There's a new swimming pool at the country club I belong to, and one afternoon last summer I happened to drive out there. Some young people were diving from a board, and when I first looked I thought they were all boys. Then I recognized Julie. If my father had lived to see a granddaughter of his not wearing all she wasn't wearing, and with young men present, I think he'd have gone right down there to her and first prayed for her and then drowned her! But I suppose you'll be reminding me of the old platitude that other times have other customs."

"It seems to be true," I said. "You were proving to me that I couldn't go outdoors without perceiving the unwholesomeness of these times."

"I'm going back to that," he returned. "The split skirt didn't stay long, and not many dared to wear it—in some places women who wore it got arrested, and I think, myself, they should have been—it wasn't a fashion this country would stand for until the new jazz age got really under weigh. The split skirt disappeared; but the ice was broken, and it wasn't long before dresses got shorter and stockings began to be shown above the instep; the old 'windy corner' joke was already obsolete by then. Girls began to leave off their corsets, too, especially for dancing; and if the mothers found it out the daughters explained that they couldn't dance the new dances with all that encasing interference and, besides, they weren't 'popular' unless they left if off. Then, after the war, the skirts, instead of splitting up and down, began to split crossways, and the lower half dropped off altogether. That's how they've got 'em now, just about at the knee, and when they sit down the exposure is whatever it happens to be. I said you couldn't step outdoors without seeing the unwholesomeness of these times—painted women and full-grown girls in dresses we wouldn't have allowed a child of thirteen to be seen in when we were still a respectable people—but, my goodness! you don't have to go outdoors! I tell you when Julie's girl-friends sit around here in the house sometimes, when I'm home, I'm embarrassed!"

"Why are you embarrassed, Judge?"

"Why? My soul! They don't care how they sit; they cross their legs and wag their feet; they slide down on the small of their backs till their knees are as high as their heads; a passel of five-year-old children would show as much dignity and as much self-respect about exposure. Exposure! That's what they like! They flaunt it in your face!"

"No," I said. "No more than do the five-year-old children you mentioned. Exposure isn't exposure to the children, and it isn't to Julie and her friends, either. Exposure is an idea not in Julie's friends minds unless someone else puts it there, and Julie and her friends are determined not to be hampered by having it put there."

"Hampered!" he exclaimed angrily. "They're determined not to be hampered by any womanly shame."

"No," I returned. "No more than your great-great-grandfather was hampered by manly shame when he stopped wearing a wig and lace ruffles."

"What on earth are you talking about?"

"You'll have to get used to short skirts and to short hair, Judge. The skirts will be longer sometimes and shorter sometimes, in passing fashions; and so will the hair; but the skirt to the ground will never prevail again as a necessity of morals. You've got to change your whole conception of what you think is immodesty."

"Why will I?"

"Because women have changed theirs—and, as Julie intimated to you, it's really their affair."

"What!" he cried. "Don't their fathers and their brothers and their husbands——"

"No," I said. "The ladies don't belong to us any more, and they don't all live for us and to 'manage' us—not quite in the sense they used to. They've decided to live more for themselves. They're not abiding as they did by the rules we made for them as part of our possessions; they don't placidly accept our various kinds of 'double standards,' Judge. In fact, they seem about to lay aside something of both their guile and their meekness; they're doing a great deal of laying aside these days. Those stays you spoke of, the stays of the hourglass girl, and the long impeding skirts won't do for the new outdoor life that the automobile brought when it made open country a convenient playground for everybody. The hourglass stays and the long skirt had another reason, too, for disappearing just at the time when the new athletic life required their removal. For they were really, in spirit, the bindings that warped the tiny feet of the Chinese women."

"How were they?" he asked sharply. "The old-fashioned stays of whalebone and steel might offer you some ground to stand on there; but the long skirt——"

"Wearing a long skirt was originally a woman's way of keeping warm, Judge; but in time it gradually became the means of making her legs an interesting secret. That is to say, the long skirt became one of her weapons of coquetry, or her diplomacy, if you like, just as her hair was; and, like the crippled Chinese feet so beautiful to the eyes of Chinese gentlemen, the stays, the long hair and long skirt were flattering signs of the dependence and inferiority of what was valuable—to be protected by us and partly displayed, partly kept secret—because it could be possessed. The relinquishment of the long skirt and of long hair is startling, not because of any moral question's being involved, as you think, but because it means that women are beginning to feel independent of us. They can afford to abandon some of their means of 'managing' us, they begin to believe—because they can get what they want, not by making us get it for them, but by going after it themselves, in spite of us—that is, in competition with us. If they should ever go back, generally and permanently, to long skirts and long hair, it would mean that they were defeated and had given up their hope of doing anything better than first competing with one another to get hold of men to 'manage,' and then keeping—and of course, too, helping and cherishing—what they thus secure. So far they show no signs of apprehending any such defeat."

"No," Judge Olds said drily. "So far as I can see they're worse every day. I think you mentioned something irrelevant about my great-great-grandfather's wig and lace ruffles—or did it actually bear upon what you seem to feel is the significance of your discourse?"

"I think it's relevant," I ventured to reply. "I don't mean to say that Julie and her friends are conscious of all the obscure things underlying the great difference between them and the girls of our youth, Judge. Probably Julie just feels young, independent, and in the fashion, and instinctively objects to your ideas as tyrannical, rather low-minded and hypocritical nonsense."

"Yes. That describes her daughterly attitude quite accurately. What about my great-great-grandfather's wig?"

"Marshal Bassompierre paid what would be in money of today more than ten thousand dollars," I said, "for a coat to wear at a party. Pepys paid fifty pounds, I think I recall, for a periwig. We men used to be greater peacocks than the women; and, though we were cocks o' the walk and did not need to use the trickish weapons necessary to the weaker, we bedizened ourselves from head to foot in finery. When we wore our own long hair we sat for hours while a perruquier dressed it. We wore diamonds, pearls, rubies, emeralds—we covered our hands with rings, wore jewelled chains about our necks, wore earrings, covered our hats with ostrich feathers, hid our throats and hands and sometimes our meagre calves under showers of lace; we drenched ourselves with scent, and stuck decorative black patches upon our faces; rouge was not wholly unknown to us. Until the *fin de siècle* that brought the French Revolution the women never surpassed us in the expense and exquisite care we spent upon our persons. A new period in dress began for us then."

"Indeed?" the Judge said ominously. "We began exposing ourselves then, I suppose?"

"Yes, we did. We began to dispense with our plumage and all of our coquettish aids to the conquest of ladies. In our wars with one another weapons had been improved and the science of war had changed: our plumage had become more and more inconvenient. Taxes reduced our luxury at the same time that republican ideas of simplicity began to prevail. But what really ended our splendid peacockery was the beginning of the 'mechanical age,' after the close of the Napoleonic wars. We'd cut our long hair and given up the wigs that imitated it; then we cut off our ruffles. Lace isn't useful about machinery, and it's inappropriate on a cindery railroad train. The women didn't adopt the utilitarian costume when we did: they weren't in as close contact with the 'mechanical age' as we were. They waited almost a hundred years, and it's only now they're doing what we did so long ahead of them."

"You mean that just because girls can't hop in and out of automobiles in long skirts they're merely following our utilitarian example a hundred years later? You mean that's all they're doing?"

"It's certainly one of the things they're doing; but it's very far from being all that they're doing. It might even be possible, Judge, that obscurely behind all that they're doing now there's at least a hint of an end to the immemorial 'war between the sexes.' But if, with equality obtained, they add to the power to compete against us their ancient custom of cajoling us you see how dangerous that will be for us, don't you, Judge? Our great hope must be that they will play fair and not both compete and cajole. The 'woman of the new age' is as changed as everything else; it's of the most vital importance that we don't fight her; we certainly can't win if we do, and nobody knows what would happen."

"I fail to follow you," he said. "You don't seem very explicit."

"The topic of our discourse," I returned apologetically, "has always been one causing men to speak more or less gropingly. If you could endure it, Judge, I have at home upon my desk a highly unauthentic paper just finished that seems to bear upon the subject; and it might prove to the point if I should read it to you."

"All right," he said, "but I tell you beforehand it won't convince me."

"It isn't intended to be convincing," I explained; and, thereupon, making use of his telephone, I communicated with my own house and had the paper brought to me.

XXV

"I called this venture 'The Veiled Feminists of Atlantis,' Judge," I said; and, upon his expression's becoming even a little more repellent than it had been, I began the reading, with some timidity.

... Among certain occultists of the esoteric Buddhist group there was once this tradition concerned with the sinking of Atlantis. The continent disappeared as the climax of a conflict between the practitioners of White Magic and those who were experts in Black Magic. Magic, which was, of course, only science kept secret, had gone far in Atlantis, and the magicians ruled the continent. The general populace was morally unfit to be trusted with knowledge of the discoveries made by initiated chemists, psychologists, electricians, and biologists, just as a portion of our people today are unfit to be trusted with automobiles and gunpowder; and therefore the Atlantean scientists were an organized secret society, keeping their knowledge strictly to themselves and using it for the general good. Of course they easily became the ruling class, and the government was naturally a dictatorship, probably a hidden one, so that the populace believed itself to be a governing democracy.

Apprentices to the magicians were carefully selected; only young men of promising intelligence combined with the highest sense of honour and the most humanitarian impulses could be permitted to acquire knowledge dangerously potential, but mistakes were made in selection; ambitious and prying outsiders obtained copies of some of the sacred books, deciphering them and possessing their meanings; there arose factions, too; and, moreover, some of the greatest among the magicians, or scientists, could not control their own human impulses, and used their knowledge for selfish ends. Thus the opposing camps were formed. On one side were the benevolent White Magicians, who wished to use the secrets of nature for the benefit of the world at large; and on the other were the Black Magicians, whose purpose was to secure power to fulfill their own desires.

In the conflict, forces so terrific were employed by both parties that at last the very continent was riven and sunk beneath the waters of the ocean; the White Magicians, in their gigantic despair, thus destroying not only themselves but all their world as well, in order to annihilate their enemies of the dark cohorts and to prevent the further dissemination of knowledge which man was not yet fitted to receive. This is to say, they perceived that civilization was a failure with them; that man was better dead than left in possession of knowledge (meaning power) ungenerously employed; that evolution had produced civilization too rapidly upon Atlantis and must begin the work anew elsewhere.

Such, roughly, was the tradition, as I learned it from curious books years ago—so many years ago, indeed, that it had passed almost altogether out of my mind when a chance meeting last winter with a French archaeologist in the Djur Djurra mountains of the Atlas range recalled and freshened it. This was at Michelet, that surprisingly Alpine appearance among the Algerian clouds where the traveller expects to see Swiss chamois hunters descending the snowy peaks rather than robed and tattooed Arabs, and one must continually doubt that one is in Africa. Professor Paul Lanjuinais, of the Institute, was staying at the inn, and, beside the rather inadequate fire in the small smoking-room, we fell into talk of the Kabyle people, or "White Arabs," among whom our own party had been motoring. M. Lanjuinais was in the Djur Djurra region for the purpose of research among the Kabyles, he informed us, and presently he mentioned the Atlantean theory of their heavily disputed origin.

"No single theory wholly accounts for the presence of a 'White Arab' here," he said. "Blue-eyed fair people in Africa are spoken of by Egyptian hieroglyphs and rather definitely assigned to this region; my own conclusion is that the Kabyles have been here a very long time. No one can say authoritatively that they may not have sprung from a flight migration from Atlantis. It is a possible thing, even a rather plausible one; but the same speculation—for it is a speculation rather than a theory—has been made concerning the Basques, though the language roots of Kabyle dialects and Basque appear to have no relation. However, since if Atlantis existed it was of continental proportions, the peoples upon it were probably of widely different types, even if they were united under a common government." Here M. Lanjuinais paused to laugh. "Occult science, which formerly had an eccentric European prevalence, probably never touched American life, and so you are probably unaware of the occult tales of Atlantis, and do not know that some of the occultists believe themselves to be in possession of the true history of the sinking of the continent. You have never heard anything of that, have you?"

"It happens that I have," I said; and, as he spoke, my memory began to turn the legend up from the obscure stratum of recollections it had come to occupy in my mind. "I think it was this." And I repeated what I recalled of the tradition.

"Yes," he said, laughing again. "That was the substance of the occult vapourizing, if indeed substance may be attributed to what is so extremely tenuous a vapour. I think the occultists put their own rather forced interpretation upon a Berber story someone must have picked up hereabouts years ago and carried either to Europe or to India, perhaps to both."

"Hereabouts?" I asked. "Then there is some trace of a legend of Atlantis among the Kabyle people?"

"Not if one speaks carefully," he replied. "There is a story, yes; but one cannot say that it refers to Atlantis. It speaks of a Great Land to the West in the Waters. That might as well be America, except for the use of the phrase I translate as 'in the Waters,' which seems to mean '*within* the Waters.'"

"You find this story among the Kabyles?"

"Yes. I came upon traces and variations of it here and there; but its best and most complete form appears among them in some of the hilltop villages nearer Bougie, toward the coast."

"How does it differ from the occultist form?"

"In several curious details," M. Lanjuinais replied; and he smiled as a man smiles over something that is between the whimsical and the ridiculous. "Most strikingly of all, it differs in ending with a question that no Kabyle has ever solved and is not to be solved by anyone else, I think."

"But what a strange thing!" I exclaimed. "For a legend to end with a question seems extraordinary."

"But not unique. I believe, however, that there are not many traditions leading to questions as their main point. This one does that. There may be some connection, too, with the fact that the Kabyles do not veil their women; though that is only another speculation, and the story doesn't directly touch upon it."

"What is the story?" I asked. "Would you mind telling us?"

"Not at all," Professor Lanjuinais replied. "It is not too long. In a general way it follows the contour of the occultist legend, especially in representing that governmental control of Atlantis gradually came into the hands of a secret society, or sect, to which admission was most difficult and involved years of trial, or neophytism. Of course the Kabyles speak of this governing organization as a tribe—they call it the tribe of Wise People, which may well enough be taken to mean a society of educated persons, initiation taking place upon the completion of education. The Kabyle legend describes them as all-powerful and, until the great dispute arose between the two factions, wholly benevolent. Under their rule, everybody was contented in the whole land. There was no war; public opinion consisted of a general sense of brotherhood; and disease was conquered, for the Wise People could remedy all bodily defects. Also, they could direct the minds and inclinations of the populace, so that there was no such thing as sin. In a word, the 'Great Land in the West' was heaven as a *fait accompli* except for the lack of one item: the people lived to be very old, but they were not immortal. Death was the only fact the Wise People had not conquered; but, save for that, you had a most excellent heaven conducted perfectly by a band of angels, the Wise People; for even heaven itself must be conducted by somebody, one is led to suppose. The invariable circumstance about any organization is that it has officers."

I interposed. "But aren't there some religious organizations?"

"They must have at least a janitor," M. Lanjuinais returned. "And almost always a treasurer. At all events, the Wise People, who of course lived on mountain tops, presumably in fastnesses of learning, ruled this legendary paradise. I think the occultist tradition follows its own purposes in tracing the cause of the dispute to a selfish use of science; but I prefer the Kabyle story, which gives a radically different reason for the war."

"The Kabyle version doesn't give the factions as White and Black, benevolent and malevolent?"

"It gives the factions as White and Black," he answered, "but not as benevolent and malevolent. White and Black have no moral symbolic significance in the Kabyle legend; they are simply colour designations, as were the Blue and the Gray in your own Civil War. In that war there was a geographical difference between the two parties; in the White and Black war there was no such line of cleavage; and one of the curious things about it was that every family of the Wise People was divided against itself. In every family there was at least one White member and one Black member, which naturally made the war a bitter one."

"But what caused the war, M. Lanjuinais?"

"I am approaching that," he responded amiably. "Allow me to reach it by degrees. I told you there appeared to be a possible relation between the legend and the fact that the Kabyle women go unveiled; but this I wish merely to suggest, not to emphasize. You have seen these women on the mountain sides, some of them quite handsome in spite of the tattooing upon their faces; and you have observed a few of them in the villages of the valley—apparent anachronisms among the veiled Mohammedan women. You have caught the glance of these Kabyle girls and women—a glance a little hard, a little hostile, and within it a glint of something wild and driven. A very ancient look, one might call it; a look possibly beset by some historical fear against which there is still rebellion. One might say that a Kabyle woman's eyes are the eyes of a woman who has seen her grandmother beaten to death, but has not been tamed by the spectacle. There is still an antique horror in this glance, and an old, old heritage of defiance. Where did they get such a look? Well, of course, one does not need to go back to Atlantis for it; but if one were in a whimsical mood he might trace it to the war between the Whites and the Blacks in the 'Great Land to the West within the Waters.' You see, the curious thing about this was that all the women were upon one side and all the men upon the other. The women were the Whites and the men were the Blacks."

"Dear me!" I said. "So ancient as that! But what was the point at issue?"

"Whether or not the women should wear veils."

"I see. The women insisted upon casting the veils away, and the men——"

"It is not so simple," he interrupted. "In the earlier days, when the Great Land was entirely peaceful, the initiates in knowledge, the Wise People, were all men. At that time the women were merely of the populace, governed benevolently like the rest; but little by little the wives and daughters of the initiates began to steal glimpses of the sacred books and to penetrate the mysteries. In other words, they began to seek education; and of course many of the initiates themselves taught a little magic—or imparted scientific information—to their wives and daughters. In those days all the women wore veils; or, as one might express it, they were 'thoroughly feminine.' Gradually, as they acquired more education, and felt more equal to occasions, more able to stand on their own feet, they did not wish to be or seem quite so feminine: some of the bolder among them laid aside their veils and showed their faces openly. Naturally, this caused a little grumbling among the men; but more and more women grew bold, until finally it was thought old-fashioned to wear a veil. Then the women demanded complete initiation into the mysteries of the Wise People. 'We know all about it anyhow,' they said to the men. 'We are your equals in fact, so why deny us the mere acknowledgment of our equality?' There was more grumbling, of course; but the women were initiated, and after that none of them wore a veil. They divested themselves, as it were, of all femininity, and made good their equal footing. Of course some of the men still grumbled: their vanity was not soothed when the women sometimes surpassed them in certain branches of learning and even in special feats of reasoning; but in a general way the men were just, and after a time they accustomed themselves to the new equality. They perceived that it was a necessity if they were to be fair—although it cannot be said that they ever really liked it—and within a generation the Wise People consisted of as many women as men. The daughters of the members of the organization were taught as well as the sons, and were initiated with an equal standing. Then, when everything seemed to be settled upon an apparently permanent basis, a strange and unfortunate thing happened. Fashions forever move in cycles; some of the women returned to the fashion of wearing veils. Immediately those who adopted the veil began to be a powerful party within the organization of the Wise People where all were supposed to be equal. They elected all the officers and controlled the organization itself; whereupon, seeing their success, all the other women at once resumed the veil and joined them."

I interrupted the narrative of M. Lanjuinais at this point. "Did the men then adopt veils for themselves? Does the Kabyle story mention such a point?"

"No," he replied. "Men are not adapted to veils and are not screened by them. The men among the Wise People could not have helped themselves by wearing veils. But of course they could not endure what the women were doing to them. The men had accepted equality; they could not accept the new inequality, though at first they tried by peaceful means to remedy the disadvantage at which they had been placed. They held a great meeting to discuss the matter. 'You cannot be our equals,' they said to the women, 'and at the same time wear your feminine veils. That is worse than being unfair; it is treachery.'

"But the women laughed. 'When we formerly wore veils,' they said, 'we possessed something that we abandoned when we went unveiled. At the time, we did not perceive our loss, and it has taken us more than a generation to discover it. Now, in again veiling ourselves, we are merely reclaiming our rights—resuming our natural possession.'

"'No,' the men returned. 'You cannot justly retain this so-called possession of yours, because it is an advantage. Equality means that no one seizes an advantage, and for you to seize this one destroys the equality we have given you and leaves us your inferiors. Our ideal is equality, and to maintain it we will either take the veils away from you or cease to initiate you into the mysteries of our magic and reduce you to your former state of mere usefulness to us.'

"At that the women laughed louder. 'We do not need initiation from you. We possess the mysteries and can do our own initiating. The feminine veil, so alluring and exhaling such charm, is natural to us; it is a part of our long inheritance, and we could not permanently give it up even if we wished to do so, since it is our very instinct to wear it. If it is your destiny that our attainments and our veiling are to make you our inferiors, you might as well accept it. We accepted our destiny for a long, long time.'

"But the men were unable to be so philosophic as their opponents suggested; in fact, it is related that by this time they were in a condition of the deepest resentment. 'You shall not wear veils,' they said. 'You have abused our sense of justice and insulted our generosity. You shall not wear veils. We have got to know what you are thinking about!'

"Now when the men said they had to take away the veils so they would understand what the women thought, the women raised such a shout of mocking and indignant laughter that the fighting began then and there. Toward morning the survivors withdrew to opposing fastnesses and began their war with sand storms, which they sent against each other. The Kabyles say the Whites and Blacks used mountain ranges and thunder and lightning as familiar weapons; that they hurled earthquake and tornado upon each other; and that in their last battle they shook the sun so that it rocked in the sky; and the moon, which until then whirled noisily in the heavens like a spinning top, was struck dumb and still, so that it never turned again, and we have only the one face of it always toward us. Then, as the ocean came over the land in waves thousands of feet tall, all the Wise People perished; for the men were determined to the last not to be made inferior by an injustice, and the women, even though they would have made peace at any time, still protested that, even if they were willing, they could not give up the veil for it was their very nature itself. That is almost the end of the legend, but not the very end. As I told you, the end is a question; and, when the story is told in the evening, in one of the Kabyle huts of stone on a mountain top, the narrator always concludes with the great question. After that everybody goes to sleep."

"Is there ever any answer to the question?" I asked.

"The Kabyle people think not, and probably they are right. I have suggested that there is an apparent bearing upon it in the fact that the Kabyle women are unveiled and have that ancient driven yet hostile look in their eyes. You see, the tradition implies that the Kabyles escaped from the Great Land. They left at the beginning of the war, before the final cataclysm; but they were only a part of the uninitiated populace of the continent and not members of the Wise People. You perceive how easily it might be misleading to follow such a clue for an answer to the question."

"But what is the question?"

"I supposed of course it was obvious," M. Lanjuinais returned. "'Who won?'"

"Well," Judge Olds said, somewhat discouragingly, as I concluded the reading, "go on. Come to something."

"But that's all, Judge."

"Good heavens!" he cried. "Do you call that an argument?"

"No, I only thought——"

"You're absolutely wrong," he said. "In the first place, I don't know what you've been trying to express, and, in the second, whatever it is, it's nonsense. And what in the name of common sense do you think it's got to do with Julie?"

"She belongs to an age that has discarded your ideas, Judge, and she'll never adjust herself to them. She couldn't even if she wanted to! And I've been trying to suggest that it'll be a great deal better for us if she doesn't."

"You're all mixed up and you're all wrong, I tell you. I'll certainly never adjust myself to her ideas," he said grimly. "They're the ideas of a new age that won't last. The pendulum will swing back."

"What's to swing it back?"

He was unable to supply me with information upon this detail, and, after I had left him, I thought that his figure of the pendulum was not an accurate one. There are actions and reactions in the life of mankind, but a pendulum swings from a fixed point. In nature all is change, and so there is no such thing as a fixed point, which can be only an abstract conception. Looking forth upon the examples apparently set by the rest of the universe, we are encouraged to surmise that the world moves, not as a pendulum, but in an ascending spiral.

XXVI

Lately, in 1928, I motored home from New York to the Midland city. There was no need to take a ferry across the Hudson; automobiles beyond counting were humming incessantly, speeding east, speeding west, beneath those deep, broad waters: we had no sight of the new Titans' skyline growing mistier behind us. Little more than an hour later we looked down upon the Delaware from a high bridge, and one of us said: "Down there, not far, Washington forced his way across this river through the ice. What a strange sight that would be if we could see it now!"

"How much stranger a sight we'd be to Washington!" the other exclaimed. "The bridge alone would dumbfound him; but he could understand it. The automobile shooting across it would stagger him; and most of his half-frozen Revolutionary soldiers would take it to be either illusion or witchcraft." Then, as an airplane rose buzzing in the nearer skies, "But the plane," he went on, "I think they could hardly have borne. They'd have thought they were getting too much of the supernatural to be endured. I think there'd have been desertions when they reached the other shore: poor souls hurrying home to meet the Judgment Day with their families about them. Yet it's only a century and a half ago that the Father of our Country crossed here, and what would *we* think if we could see now what we should see from this spot a century and a half in the future? Would we, too, scurry home to prepare for the Last Trump?"

Probably not, we thought. We should be able to endure at least a glimpse of full-blown prodigies not even to be in bud during our lifetime. For we were "children of the mechanical age," inured to miracles; we had seen men doing almost everything that in previous ages they had been able to imagine themselves as doing. To do more they would need to imagine more; but already they had imagined interplanetary communication, the prolongation of human life, the end of war, and even the end of poverty. Some day, perhaps, they would imagine the end of ignorance—even the end of our ignorance of the meaning of life, and when that meaning is known we shall no longer be tragically ignorant of the meaning of death. For a hundred and fifty years is not long in the life of the Delaware River, and men will still be imagining when the river is gone.

But now our silent, hurrying slave, the automobile, had borne us far from the bridge; the great, hard, smooth highways built for that slave stretched before us in their thousands of miles, west, south, north, as we chose to go. There was company, too, in all directions; overland traffic of freight in thunderous motor trucks; motor vans, moving all the furniture and household goods of families from one town to another; automobiles built like cottages and with families living in them ever itinerant; long, swift omnibuses running on schedules and growing weeds in the interurban trolley-tracks; bootleggers' cars with mud-caked license plates and dusty windows; youthful speed cars, pedlars' coupés, workmen's cars, farmers' cars, rich men's cars, poor men's cars, beggarmen's cars, and thieves' cars. Tractors ploughed the fields beside the road; love letters, business letters, letters from anxious mothers shot through the sky over our heads; and, on all our journey, in the remotest mountain and woodland spot we reached, messages, news items, lectures, readings, recitations, weather prognostications and incessant music continually passed through the ether about us and through our very bodies. A racing car on the way to some track contest swept perilously by us at seventy miles an hour; we saw a monoplane "stunt flying" at a faster speed than that, and thus were made aware of the presence of the new athlete, the Twentieth Century's realization of the centaur fantasy, half-man, half-machine, and at his topmost far greater hero to the people than any Marathon runner, discus thrower, charioteer, or home-run batter has ever been.

We ourselves were no new centaurs, yet we moved at a speed for which nobody is arrested nowadays, and came home in only a few more hours of running than we should have spent on the express train. But we had been away from the Midland city for seven months, and so we came into it sooner than we expected, because it was still growing. Far, far ahead of us, when we entered the ever-extending streets, new colossi loomed in the smoke: more skyscrapers were building.

I walked at twilight through a street of new houses where long, long ago—yet how short a time ago it seemed, too!—I had driven a red-wheeled runabout, and a startled farm hand told me of lightning that came shattering out of a clear, sunny sky. The houses, all built within little more than a year, were of the newest fashions, yet not many were of the same fashion. They were of shapes and colours we once should have thought fanciful; indeed, many of them suggested stage settings and their picturesqueness was so extreme as to give them almost the unsubstantial air of "picture-book houses." They were adaptations of such themes as the Normandy farmhouse, the Italian villa, the Spanish cottage, the Tudor house, the Georgian manor, the Southern Colonial house, the New England Colonial house, and even the Donjon Keep. It was obvious that every architect, or every owner, had planned without thought to what would neighbour the new house; we were going ahead with our building in our old, naïve, individual way, and so this new street looked like a masquerade party wearing the costumes of all nations and all periods. Yet no doubt every house was beautiful to the family that lived in it. Probably when they looked at it they saw nothing else, being happily able to exclude from their consciousness all that they had not proudly built themselves.

Some of the new houses had been put up by builders to sell—probably on the new instalment financing plan that enables anybody to buy anything. Painted signs suggested alluring merit: "This Artistic Modern Home," "This Superbly Equipped Home, "This Beautiful New Modern Home"—for, of course, these empty houses were all "homes"; an apprentice in the new commercial publicity would probably be reprimanded if he were ever so indiscreet as to speak or write of even an unfinished house or cottage as anything except a "home." But what I wondered, as I walked along in the twilight, staring at these whimsical houses, was whether or not they were really an improvement upon the other kinds of houses that had preceded them in the Midland town; and, of course, the people who lived in the new houses and the architects who designed them and the decorators concerned with the interiors would all have thought this an absurd thing to be wondering.

Twilight having deepened as I walked, lights began to appear, and before one of the brightened windows I paused for a moment. The shade was up, no curtains impeded the view, and there was revealed a living-room interior in the "modernist" manner. A "modernist" painting hung upon the wall over a severe oblong hole, the fireplace, and the furniture was of a shaping unfamiliar to chairs, table, stools, and bookcases, and usually associated with engineering works of one kind and another. The painting was of a woman with a green head and no spinal column to hold it in place. She seemed about to enter a building smaller than she was and she carried in one hand, at the end of her shorter arm, a pottery bowl that must have surprised the potter, when he took it from the kiln, and made him resolve to live thenceforth more temperately.

Then, looking at this picture and at the furniture, I was reminded of earlier manifestations of "modernism" upon the banks of the Seine in the first years of the century; and I remembered how tactful visitors to the Salon des Indépendants forbore to laugh because the artists might be standing near the works of art. They had not all perished of neglect, those early modernists; some of them had lived to see their pictures hung on the walls of dwelling houses by people able to bear that daily association. Those who thus survived were the few who "knew how to put paint on canvas"; at least they were craftsmen; but whether or not their effort to "get back to the primitive" had brought any new beauty into the world was still a question. They were consciously primitive, which is certainly never a way to be primitive; and if they had indeed brought new beauty into the world they had certainly brought with it a lot of other things, including the pretentiousness of their apologists and the nightmares of their imitators. Upon the point of pretentiousness I remember a comparison made by a good painter I knew.

"All this modernist art," he said, "was founded upon a shrewd knowledge of the hypnotic power of a vacuum. To understand that we must recall the old story of the three weavers and the king's coronation robes. The thievish weavers kept all the money they were supposed to spend for materials, and said the robes they were making for the king were beyond compare the richest and most beautiful ever woven, and also had a magic quality: whoever was not virtuous and good could not seem them at all; they were visible to virtuous people only. So, when the courtiers came to look at the robes, no one dared to say he did not see them; and the king, himself, when the weavers went through the motions of putting them upon him, expressed the greatest admiration and delight. Then he rode forth to the coronation, naked, and all the people, afraid of giving it away that they couldn't see his beautiful robes, began to shout: 'What splendour! How superb! What wonderfulness in weaving!' Well, that's the wonderfulness of most of modernist art. The people who praise it are afraid of letting anyone find out that they don't see it."

Yet, whether they see it or not, some of those who praise it think they see it; for the "hypnotic power of a vacuum" is that strong if vacuums become a fashion. Fashion is the true hypnotic master of the eye; for fashion is mob vision, difficult to resist. The owner of the modernist painting that I saw through the lighted window surely thought his picture beautiful and was pleased to possess it and the new shapes of furniture, and to be, himself, as he would doubtless believe, a forefront slave of a lovely fashion.

So, before him, had the followers of all the dead fashions felt. In the latter part of the Nineteenth Century, before the *fin de siècle*, we had gone through what the fashion, with one of its inexplicable sophistications, called a "Queen Anne" period in building, accompanied by the "aesthetic movement" indoors. Wooden houses were built with little turrets and weather-boarded towers boiling out all over them; jigsaw work enriched gables, and at least one oval window of coloured glass seemed to be necessary somewhere. Within, there was Eastlake furniture, and pure decoration offered effects from the aesthetic revolution: cat-tails, sumach, sunflowers, formerly plain old chairs newly gilded, peacock feathers, fans tacked upon the walls, embroidered owls, wooden bread-rollers painted in floral designs, pansies painted on tambourines, and marble-topped rococo tables. Nowadays, everybody thought all of that bad enough to be funny; but it had seemed charming when it was the fashion—at least, it was charming to the people who built the "Queen Anne" houses and did the aesthetic decorating.

So I wondered, as I walked on, if some day, not far in the future, these fanciful new houses, so charming now to the owners, the architects, the builders, and the decorators, and undeniably excellent in pictorial composition, wouldn't in their turn appear to be as funny and as "bad taste" as the preposterous "Queen Anne" cottages and jigsaw work and cat-tails seem to all of us now. Nevertheless, the happiness in the world must be greatly enriched by the belief of every period that in matters of taste, at least, it alone has come to perfection and is the final authority.

In this, the new age was like the age before it, like the *fin de siècle* and all other ages; but it was not like the *fin de siècle* in many things.

Nature itself does not recognize a revolution; it works through evolution only, we are told; yet since the *fin de siècle* there had been an overturning thorough enough to bear the aspect of revolution to middle-aged and elderly people. They had seen their youthful conceptions of such vital things as time and distance disappear into nothing, and what was mystifying and painful to many who were of Judge Olds's way of thinking, they had also seen, at the same time and as if through some dire synchronism, their most rigid conceptions of morals and of proprieties and of manners first questioned, then challenged, then apparently tossed aside. Fetters had been broken; a great deal that was useless, impeding, and even evil had been swept away; startling new tolerances were beginning to prevail, and, contradictorily enough, there were new intolerances like the intolerance of refinement, for instance. But this was, of all, probably the special intolerance most characteristic of the new age, for refinement, in large part, seems to be a quality of leisure. And, in this swiftest moving and most restless time the world has known, leisure is for the dead, though not immediately—even the hearses are automobiles now.

. . . I walked on deeper into the town with the sky overhead growing darker and the city avenues brighter as the white globes of the street lamps became luminous with the movement of an engineer's hand, miles away. So I came at last to where the old, destroyed town had stood, and I paused again, looking up at the sparkling front of a tall apartment house. There had been an iron gateway here once, which I had often entered long ago, and beyond a fountain had tinkled in the midst of a green lawn. In the ample house lived an hourglass girl with a charming voice and a piano kept in tune, and about her, at that piano, boys and girls in their early twenties and late 'teens were wont to gather, of an evening, and sing with her, while older people listened amiably from the library beyond. And, by a coincidence, as I stopped there now a song was coming from the window of a first-floor apartment of the building that stood where the green lawn and the fountain and the ample house had been.

But this song came out of a box. The words were distinguishable:

> "He's my boy friend, I'm his sweety.
> When we dance my heart gets leapy.
> He's so amorous
> He gets me glamorous!
> Oh, my!
> I
> Wanta die
> With my
> Boy friend,
> Right then!"

There was, of course, an accompaniment of wirestrung banjos, saxophones, and drums; also there was another—the vehement jingling of a cocktail shaker. The sound of the ice in the shaker, however, caused me no uneasiness, although the shrieking laughter of women and deeper bellowings in male voices indicated that the liquor in the shaker was not a first filling. A friend of mine, informed upon the matter, had lately told me that nobody need drink poison now. "Of course," he said, "until some of the Canadian provinces adopted a more liberal policy, there was always a little danger. Naturally, prohibition couldn't be enforced. You can enforce a law hundreds or even thousands don't like, but not one that millions don't like. You've either got to get 'em to like it or you can't enforce it—at least, not until there are more eighteen-hundred-a-year men who won't take ten thousand dollars for looking the other way a minute or so. But for a long while any kind of liquor was expensive, most of it was bad, some of it was dangerous, and some of it was fatal. It isn't so now. With the new wetness in Canada, anybody can buy any quality he wants and all he wants, and for my part I regard this development as the settling of the whole prohibition question. Nobody wants the saloon back, and the millions that are determined to drink can drink almost without any risk. The only thing left to bother about is the effect on people, especially young people, of seeing a law so generally disregarded. It makes a young fellow say to himself, 'In their hearts, people believe it's all right to break any law they don't like if they can get away with it.' But, before long, the prohibition law will be like a lot of old Blue Laws, still on the statute books but forgotten, and then its last evil will have disappeared. Everything's satisfactory."

With this reassuring thought in mind, I passed on, going still deeper into the town; and presently stood before a vast and solemn shape that rose into the highest reaches of the electric light from the streets. It was the new War Memorial, a monumental shrine, unfinished and still building. It was of white stone and would have had a better appearance if it could have remained clean; but of course that wasn't to be hoped—not now; even our homage to the men who fought for us in the Great War must be soiled with the grime that was the mark of our prosperity. Nevertheless, the day would yet come when the great edifice would be cleaned and kept clean, to rise in the clear whiteness that would make it as beautiful as it should be. Some day, I thought, the Chamber of Commerce and the Rotarians and the Kiwanis Club and the Lions Club and the Junior Rotarians would do that work—for if they didn't, nobody else would; and some day they would understand the importance of doing it.

The monument was of modern design; something original and powerful had been added to a majestic old thought that at its base was Greek; and here, I felt, the design had done what an enlightened new age might do. For every new age has at its disposal everything that was fine in all past ages, and its greatness depends upon how well it recognizes and preserves and brings to the aid of its own enlightenment whatever worthy and true things the dead have left on earth behind them. And it seemed to me that the unfinished Memorial, for all its smoke stains and the incongruous huddle of buildings about it, was already magnificent.

www.ingramcontent.com/pod-product-compliance
Lightning Source LLC
Chambersburg PA
CBHW022001220426
43663CB00007B/913